Two Fish and the Tree

Two Fish and the Tree

Prioritizing Strengths, Embracing Differences,
and Transforming Role Alignment in Today's Workplace

Brice E. Jaggars

Two Fish and the Tree

Copyright © Brice E. Jaggars (2024)

All rights reserved. No part of this publication may be reproduced, stored in a retrieval system, or transmitted, in any form or by any means, without the prior written permission of the publisher.

Published by:

For my wonderful daughter Ashleigh, whose passion and perseverance are truly infectious. For my son Justin, whose transition to fatherhood has been inspiring. For my sister Traci, who never stops believing in me, even when I fall short. And finally for my amazing wife Kim, whose unwavering love and support have been the driving force behind everything I've accomplished.

Table of Contents

Introduction 1

The Critical Role of Soft Skills in the Workplace 9

The Role of Social Styles in Developing Soft Skills 15

The Harsh Reality 23

Cockeyed Optimist 25

The Challenge of Changing Poor Soft Skills at Work 31

The Diet Analogy 43

The Neuroscience of Resistance: Why the Brain Struggles to Change Poor Soft Skills 53

All is Not Lost 65

Our Brain is Wired to "Learn" 67

Strategies To Learn New Soft Skills 73

Role Alignment 85

Good People in Bad Roles 87

The Hidden Costs of Misalignment 97

The Car, Truck or Van 103

Chinese Food Delivery 113

Alignment Framework 117

Conducting a Role Assessment 119

The Importance of Ongoing Performance Assessments 135

Implement Comprehensive Hiring Practices 157

Invest in Training and Development 183

Encourage Role Flexibility and Mobility 197

Foster a Positive Work Environment 215
Monitor and Evaluate Alignment 229
Aligning Roles with Organizational Goals... 243
The Future of Role Alignment... 259
The Final Climb.. 275
References 281

"....If you judge a fish by its ability to climb a tree, it will live its whole life believing that it is stupid."

-Famous Quote

Introduction

The Challenges of Changing Poor Soft Skills and the Importance of Role Alignment

In the modern workplace, success often hinges on a blend of technical prowess and interpersonal finesse. While hard skills can be honed through education and training, soft skills—such as communication, empathy, and leadership—present a different challenge. This book argues that it is almost impossible to fundamentally change a person's poor soft skills at work, calling for a paradigm shift in how we approach workforce development.

Defining Soft Skills

Unlike hard skills, which are technical and job-specific, soft skills are universally applicable and significantly impact employee engagement, customer satisfaction, and overall company performance. The emphasis on soft skills can lead to a more resilient and innovative workforce, essential for thriving in today's competitive business landscape.

Let's take a closer look at the core soft skills.

Communication: Communication involves effectively conveying information and actively listening. Communication consists of the ability to convey information effectively and listen actively.

Effective communication is a cornerstone of successful interactions in both personal and professional settings. It encompasses the clarity and precision with which information is conveyed and the ability to listen attentively and respond appropriately. Good communicators can articulate their ideas clearly, whether in writing or verbally and can adapt their message to suit different audiences. They also excel in active listening, which involves fully concentrating, understanding, responding, and remembering what is being said. This skill is essential for building relationships, resolving conflicts, and ensuring mutual understanding.

Teamwork: The capacity to work well with others, collaborate, and contribute to a group effort.

Teamwork is the ability to collaborate effectively with others toward a common goal. It involves understanding team dynamics, recognizing the strengths and weaknesses of team members, and leveraging those strengths to enhance group performance. Effective team players are cooperative, supportive, and willing to share responsibility. They communicate openly, respect diverse perspectives, and contribute their fair share to the workload. Teamwork also requires navigating conflicts, providing constructive feedback, and celebrating collective achievements, fostering a sense of unity and shared purpose within the group.

Problem-Solving: Thinking critically, analyzing situations, and developing effective solutions.

Problem-solving is a critical skill that involves identifying issues, analyzing potential causes, and developing and implementing effective solutions. It requires a systematic approach to breaking down complex problems into manageable parts, evaluating options, and selecting the best action. Effective problem-solvers use critical thinking to assess situations from multiple angles, anticipate potential challenges, and devise innovative solutions. They are resourceful, resilient, and capable of making decisions under pressure. This skill is essential in navigating uncertainties and overcoming obstacles in both professional and personal contexts.

Introduction

Adaptability: The capability to adjust to new conditions and easily handle change.

Adaptability is the ability to adjust one's approach and behavior in response to changing circumstances. It involves being open to new ideas, flexible in the face of unexpected challenges, and resilient in overcoming setbacks. Adaptable individuals can quickly learn new skills, embrace new roles, and thrive in dynamic environments. They are proactive in seeking out growth opportunities and are comfortable stepping outside their comfort zones. This skill is increasingly important in today's fast-paced world, where navigating change is crucial for success.

Emotional Intelligence: The skill to recognize, understand, and manage one's own emotions and the emotions of others.

Emotional intelligence (EI) involves perceiving, understanding, and managing emotions in oneself and others. It encompasses self-awareness, self-regulation, empathy, and social skills. Self-awareness is the ability to recognize and understand one's emotions, while self-regulation involves controlling or redirecting disruptive emotions and impulses. Empathy is the ability to understand and share the feelings of others, and social skills involve managing relationships to move people in desired directions. High EI is associated with better communication, improved relationships, and effective leadership.

Time Management: The ability to effectively organize and plan how to divide time between activities.

Time management is organizing and planning how to allocate time to various tasks and activities. Effective time management involves setting clear goals, prioritizing tasks based on their importance and urgency, and creating a structured schedule to achieve these goals. It requires discipline, organization, and the ability to focus on high-priority activities while minimizing distractions. Good time managers can balance multiple responsibilities, meet deadlines, and maintain productivity, which reduces stress and enhances overall efficiency.

Leadership: The capacity to guide, motivate, and support others to achieve common goals.

Leadership is the ability to inspire and influence others toward achieving a common objective. Effective leaders possess a clear vision, communicate it compellingly, and motivate their team to pursue that vision with enthusiasm and commitment. They lead by example, demonstrating integrity, accountability, and a strong work ethic. Leaders also provide support and guidance, helping team members develop skills and overcome challenges. They foster a positive and inclusive environment, encouraging collaboration and recognizing the contributions of others. Good leadership is essential for driving team success and fostering a culture of continuous improvement.

The Myth of Malleable Soft Skills

Soft skills are often described as innate qualities that are shaped by an individual's upbringing, personality, and life experiences. Unlike hard skills, which can be taught through structured learning, soft skills are deeply ingrained and less susceptible to change. Consider the natural communicator who effortlessly engages and motivates others, compared to the technically brilliant but socially reserved individual who struggles with public speaking. While the latter can improve with practice, they are unlikely to ever match the innate charisma of the former.

Organizations invest heavily in training programs aimed at improving employees' poor soft skills. However, these initiatives almost always fall short of their goals. Employees may gain a superficial understanding of the desired behaviors, but true transformation is rare. The disconnect between the training received and the natural predispositions of the individual often leads to frustration, disillusionment, and, ultimately, disengagement. Instead of trying to change what seems unchangeable, we should focus on identifying and leveraging an individual's existing soft skill strengths.

The Power of Role Alignment

Rather than attempting to change the almost unchangeable, a more effective approach is to focus on role alignment. This involves identifying the natural strengths and soft skills of individuals and placing them in roles where these qualities are assets. When people are in roles that match their strengths, they are more likely to excel, feel satisfied, and contribute positively to the organization.

Imagine a team where each member's role perfectly aligns with their soft skills. The empathetic listener is in customer support, the persuasive speaker is in sales, and the meticulous planner is in project management. Such alignment enhances individual performance and fosters a harmonious and productive work environment.

The Empathetic Listener in Customer Support

In customer support, having an empathetic listener is invaluable. This individual naturally excels at understanding and addressing customer concerns with patience and compassion. They can read between the lines, picking up subtle cues indicating a customer's underlying emotions and needs. By genuinely empathizing with customers, they can de-escalate tense situations and turn negative experiences into positive ones. This not only improves customer satisfaction but also builds loyalty and trust in the brand.

For example, when a customer calls with a complaint, the empathetic listener doesn't just hear the words—they feel the frustration and disappointment. They respond with genuine concern, ensuring the customer feels heard and valued. This approach often leads to more effective problem resolution and a more positive overall experience for the customer.

The Persuasive Speaker in Sales

In sales, the persuasive speaker is a natural fit. This individual thrives on interaction and has the charisma to captivate and convince potential clients. Their ability to articulate the benefits of a product or service, combined with their knack for building rapport, makes them highly effective in closing deals. They understand the art of persuasion, knowing when to push for a sale and when to give the prospect space to make a decision.

Consider a sales meeting where the persuasive speaker is presenting a new product. Their enthusiasm is contagious, and their confidence reassures the potential client. They can deftly address objections, turning doubts into excitement. This skill boosts sales figures and builds long-term relationships with clients, contributing to sustained business growth.

The Meticulous Planner in Project Management

In project management, the meticulous planner is essential. This individual excels at organization, attention to detail, and foresight. They can juggle multiple tasks, set realistic timelines, and ensure that all project components align perfectly. Their ability to anticipate potential pitfalls and devise contingency plans helps keep projects on track and within budget.

Imagine a complex project with tight deadlines and numerous stakeholders. The meticulous planner can break down the project into manageable tasks, assign responsibilities, and monitor progress meticulously. They ensure that nothing falls through the cracks, leading to smooth project execution and successful outcomes. Their structured approach enhances project efficiency and reduces stress and uncertainty for the entire team.

The Synergy of Aligned Role

For example, a symphony, where each musician is perfectly attuned to their instrument, creating a harmonious masterpiece that resonates beyond individual notes. This is the power of perfect role alignment within a team—the sum of the parts becoming far greater than the whole. When each team member is in a role that matches their natural soft skills, the entire team doesn't just function; it thrives. Here's how this alignment fosters a harmonious and productive work environment:

1. **Enhanced Performance**: Individuals perform at their best when their roles align with their natural abilities. They are more engaged, motivated, and effective, leading to higher productivity and better results.

2. **Improved Collaboration**: When team members understand and appreciate each other's strengths, collaboration becomes more seamless. They can leverage each other's skills to achieve common goals, resulting in a more cohesive and efficient team.

3. **Increased Job Satisfaction**: Employees who are in roles that suit their strengths are generally more satisfied with their jobs. They experience less stress and frustration, leading to higher morale and lower turnover rates.

4. **Innovation and Creativity**: A team with diverse strengths and well-aligned roles can innovate more effectively. The creative thinker's ideas, combined with the meticulous planner's execution, the persuasive speaker's market insights, and the empathetic listener's customer feedback, create a powerful engine for innovation.

5. **Resilience and Adaptability**: When roles are well-aligned, teams are more resilient and adaptable. They can respond more effectively to challenges and changes, as each member can rely on their strengths to navigate uncertainties and find solutions.

Real-Life Implications

Throughout this book, we will explore real-life examples and case studies that illustrate the impact of role alignment on organizational success. We will examine the struggles faced by individuals forced into ill-fitting roles and the transformative effect of aligning people with positions that suit their natural abilities. These stories will provide practical insights into how organizations can implement strategies to better understand their employees' soft skills and align roles accordingly.

A New Paradigm for Success

The idea that "anyone can do anything" with enough training is a well-intentioned but misguided notion. Instead, by embracing the concept that soft skills are largely immutable, we can shift our focus to creating environments where individuals thrive in roles that match their natural dispositions. This new paradigm not only respects the inherent qualities of individuals but also leverages these qualities to drive organizational success.

As you read through the chapters of this book, I invite you to challenge the traditional views on soft skills development and consider the transformative power of role alignment. By doing so, we can create workplaces where employees are not only more effective but also more engaged, satisfied, and fulfilled.

Welcome to an exciting journey of rethinking talent management and unlocking the true superpowers of your workforce. Let's unleash greatness together!

The Critical Role of Soft Skills in the Workplace

In today's rapidly evolving work environment, the value of technical prowess and industry-specific knowledge cannot be overstated. However, as work dynamics continue to shift, the importance of soft skills has become increasingly apparent. These skills, often called interpersonal or people skills, encompass a range of abilities that facilitate effective communication, collaboration, and problem-solving. This chapter delves into the various facets of soft skills in the workplace, highlighting their significance, the challenges associated with developing them, and strategies for fostering these skills within organizational settings.

Several studies underscore the critical importance of soft skills in the workplace, highlighting their significant impact on job performance and career success. For example, a 2016 LinkedIn survey found that 58% of hiring managers believe soft skills are more important than hard ones. This sentiment is echoed across various industries, where the ability to communicate effectively, work well in teams, and adapt to changing environments is highly valued.

Furthermore, a study conducted by Harvard University, the Carnegie Foundation, and Stanford Research Center concluded that 85% of job success comes from having well-developed soft skills and people skills, while only 15% is derived from hard skills and knowledge. This finding emphasizes the disproportionate influence of soft skills on career advancement and overall job performance.

The emphasis on soft skills is further supported by a study from the National Association of Colleges and Employers (NACE), which identified teamwork, problem-solving, and communication as the top three attributes employers seek in new hires. This alignment between employer expectations and the demand for soft skills underscores individuals' need to develop and hone these abilities to remain competitive in the job market.

The Business Case for Soft Skills

1. **Enhanced Communication:** Effective communication is at the heart of organizational success. It ensures that information flows smoothly, reducing misunderstandings and fostering a collaborative environment.
2. **Improved Teamwork:** Teams that excel in soft skills such as empathy and conflict resolution can work harmoniously together, leading to higher productivity and job satisfaction.
3. **Better Leadership:** Leaders with strong soft skills can inspire and motivate their teams, manage stress, and navigate complex interpersonal dynamics, driving the organization toward its goals.
4. **Customer Relations:** Employees with excellent interpersonal skills can build better customer relationships, enhancing customer satisfaction and loyalty.

Adaptability to Change: In a world where change is constant, employees who are adaptable and open to new ideas can help organizations pivot and thrive in new environments.

Expanded Insights

The Interplay Between Soft and Hard Skills

While hard skills (hard skills) are often the primary focus during education and early career development, the importance of soft skills becomes increasingly evident as individuals advance in their careers. In many cases, an individual's technical expertise gets them the job, but it's their soft skills that ensure they thrive in the role. For instance, a brilliant engineer might struggle in leadership positions if they cannot communicate effectively or empathize with their team members.

Balancing hard and soft skills is critical. Employers look for candidates who not only excel technically but also demonstrate the ability to interact well with others, adapt to changes, and lead teams. This balance is often referred to as having a "T-shaped" skill set—broad in soft skills and deep in one or two technical areas.

While hard skills can be learned through training and practice, soft skills are often more challenging to develop, making it crucial to focus on leveraging existing strengths rather than attempting to dramatically change inherent traits.

The Global Perspective on Soft Skills

The demand for soft skills is not limited to specific regions or industries. Globally, there is a growing recognition of their importance. In a report by the World Economic Forum, skills such as complex problem-solving, critical thinking, and creativity were highlighted as essential for the future workforce. As automation and AI continue to reshape job markets, the uniquely human traits represented by soft skills become even more valuable.

Cultural differences can also influence the emphasis on certain soft skills. For example, in collectivist cultures, teamwork and harmony might be prioritized, whereas in individualist cultures, assertiveness and leadership might be more highly valued. Understanding cultural differences in soft skill emphasis can help multinational organizations tailor their training programs. This ensures that programs better fit their diverse workforce and address varying cultural priorities in soft skills.

Soft Skills in Remote Work Environments

The rise of remote work has further amplified the need for strong soft skills. Remote work requires employees to be more self-directed and proficient in virtual communication. Miscommunications can easily occur when teams are not physically together, making clear and effective communication even more critical. Similarly, emotional intelligence is essential for recognizing and addressing the unique challenges and stresses that remote work can impose on individuals.

Teamwork in a remote setting also presents new challenges. Collaborating across different time zones, maintaining team cohesion, and fostering a sense of belonging all require refined soft skills. Organizations need to provide tools and training that help remote workers develop these skills, ensuring that productivity and morale remain high even when physical proximity is not possible.

The Role of Soft Skills in Leadership

Leadership is a multifaceted role that demands a blend of various soft skills. Effective leaders must be able to communicate a clear vision, inspire and motivate their teams, and navigate the complexities of interpersonal relationships within the organization. Leaders with high emotional intelligence are better equipped to handle conflicts, provide constructive feedback, and create a positive work environment.

Moreover, leadership is not confined to those in formal managerial roles. Employees at all levels can exhibit leadership through their ability to influence and guide their peers. Encouraging a culture where leadership is seen as a shared responsibility can enhance overall organizational performance and employee engagement.

Soft skills are an essential component of workplace success, complementing technical abilities and enabling individuals to navigate complex interpersonal and organizational dynamics effectively. By recognizing the importance of soft skills and investing in their development, organizations can cultivate a more collaborative, adaptable, and resilient workforce, ultimately driving long-term success and innovation.

The Role of Social Styles in Developing Soft Skills

Most of us are aware of the various social styles and how to interact with people of said styles, but we often overlook the role that social styles have in mastering soft skills. In this chapter, we will dive deeper into this alignment.

Understanding Social Styles

Social styles refer to the behaviors that individuals exhibit in their interactions with others. These styles influence how people communicate, make decisions, and respond to various situations. The concept of social styles was popularized by the work of David Merrill and Roger Reid, who identified four primary social styles: Analytical, Driver, Expressive, and Amiable. Each style has its unique characteristics and preferred ways of interacting with others.

1. **Analytical Style**: Individuals with an Analytical social style are detail-oriented, methodical, and systematic. They prefer structure, data, and factual information. They are cautious in their decision-making, often requiring substantial evidence before forming conclusions. Analyticals value precision and accuracy, and they may come across as reserved or formal in their interactions.

2. **Driver Style**: Drivers are results-oriented, decisive, and assertive. They focus on achieving goals and prefer efficiency and productivity. Drivers are often seen as direct and task-focused, sometimes at the expense of interpersonal relationships. They value control and autonomy and are typically quick to make decisions and take action.

3. **Expressive Style**: Expressives are outgoing, enthusiastic, and persuasive. They thrive in social settings and are skilled at motivating and inspiring others. Expressives are often visionary, focusing on the big picture rather than the details. They value creativity, spontaneity, and emotional engagement, and they excel in roles that require communication and relationship-building.

4. **Amiable Style**: Amiables are supportive, cooperative, and empathetic. They prioritize harmony and positive relationships and are often seen as dependable team players. Amiables are patient and good listeners, preferring to avoid conflict and seek consensus. They value loyalty and trust and are inclined to help others and foster collaborative environments.

Understanding these social styles is crucial for mapping to soft skills because it allows individuals to tailor their communication and interaction strategies to different personality types. This enhances collaboration, reduces misunderstandings, and fosters a more inclusive and productive work environment.

Communication Skills

Effective communication is a cornerstone of soft skills. Understanding social styles helps individuals communicate more effectively by allowing them to adjust their message delivery to suit the preferences of their audience.

- **Analytical**: When communicating with an Analytical person, it is important to provide clear, concise, and well-structured information. Focus on facts, data, and logical reasoning. Avoid emotional appeals and ensure that your arguments are well-supported by evidence.

- **Driver**: With Drivers, be direct and to the point. Highlight the practical benefits and results of your proposals. Avoid unnecessary details and focus on action-oriented language. Show confidence and decisiveness in your communication.

- **Expressive**: Engage Expressives with enthusiastic and dynamic communication. Use stories, anecdotes, and visual aids to capture their interest. Emphasize the big picture and the potential for innovation and creativity. Be open to their ideas and encourage a collaborative dialogue.

- **Amiable**: When interacting with Amiables, prioritize building rapport and trust. Use a warm and friendly tone, and show genuine concern for their feelings and opinions. Be patient and take the time to listen actively. Focus on how your message aligns with their values and fosters a positive environment.

These communication strategies help place the right person in the right role by aligning their strengths with their natural communication style. For example, Analytical individuals excel in detail-oriented roles, while Drivers thrive in fast-paced, results-focused positions. Expressive employees are suited for creative tasks, and Amiable team members shine in collaborative roles. Matching roles to communication styles boosts performance and improves team cohesion.

These communication strategies are particularly valuable in customer service and sales contexts. By recognizing and adapting to a customer's social style, professionals can tailor their approach for more effective interactions. For instance, a sales representative might use data-driven arguments with an Analytical customer, focus on results with a Driver, emphasize innovative aspects with an Expressive, or build a personal connection with an Amiable customer. This adaptive communication can lead to improved customer satisfaction and more successful business outcomes.

Emotional Intelligence

Emotional intelligence (EI) involves recognizing, understanding, and managing emotions in oneself and others. Social styles enhance EI by providing insights into different emotional triggers and responses.

- **Self-awareness**: Understanding your own social style helps you become more aware of your communication preferences, strengths, and potential blind spots. This self-awareness allows you to manage your emotions more effectively and adapt your behavior in different situations.
- **Empathy**: Recognizing the social styles of others enhances empathy by allowing you to understand their perspectives and emotional needs. For example, knowing that an Analytical person values data and structure helps you appreciate their need for clarity and precision, leading to more empathetic interactions.
- **Relationship Management**: Effective relationship management involves adapting your communication and behavior to foster positive interactions. Understanding social styles helps you build rapport, resolve conflicts, and collaborate more effectively by aligning your approach with the preferences of others.

Conflict Resolution

Conflict is inevitable in any social or professional setting. Understanding social styles can help in resolving conflicts more effectively by tailoring conflict resolution strategies to the individuals involved.

- **Analytical**: Approach conflicts with Analyticals by focusing on facts and logical arguments. Avoid emotional confrontations and provide clear evidence to support your points. Be patient and give them time to process information and arrive at a decision.

- **Driver:** With Drivers, address conflicts head-on and focus on finding practical solutions. Be assertive and direct, and avoid beating around the bush. Emphasize the benefits of resolving the conflict quickly and efficiently.

- **Expressive:** Engage Expressives in a collaborative and creative problem-solving process. Use positive and optimistic language, and encourage open communication. Highlight the potential for growth and innovation that can come from resolving the conflict.

- **Amiable:** When resolving conflicts with Amiables, prioritize maintaining harmony and positive relationships. Use a gentle and empathetic approach, and seek to understand their concerns and feelings. Focus on finding mutually beneficial solutions that foster a sense of cooperation and trust.

Leadership and Teamwork

Effective leadership and teamwork are heavily influenced by an understanding of social styles. Leaders who recognize and adapt to the social styles of their team members can create a more cohesive and motivated team.

- **Leadership:** Leaders with high social style awareness can tailor their leadership approach to meet the needs of different team members. For example, they can provide detailed instructions and support to Analytical team members, while giving Drivers the autonomy and decision-making power they crave. Expressives may thrive under a leader who encourages creativity and innovation, while Amiables may appreciate a leader who fosters a supportive and collaborative environment.

- **Teamwork:** In team settings, understanding social styles helps team members appreciate diverse perspectives and work more effectively together. Teams that recognize and leverage the strengths of different social styles can enhance their problem-solving abilities, creativity, and overall performance. For example, an Analytical team member may excel at analyzing data and providing detailed insights, while an Expressive team member can inspire and motivate the team with their enthusiasm and vision.

Adaptability and Flexibility

Adaptability and flexibility are critical soft skills in today's fast-paced and dynamic work environments. Understanding social styles enhances adaptability by providing a framework for adjusting your behavior and communication in different situations.

- **Analytical**: Adapting to an Analytical social style involves being meticulous and detail-oriented. Be prepared to adjust your approach based on new information and evidence. Show flexibility in your thinking and willingness to revise your plans based on logical analysis.

- **Driver**: Flexibility with Drivers means being able to make quick decisions and take decisive action. Be open to changing your approach to achieve results more efficiently. Show adaptability by being responsive to new challenges and opportunities.

- **Expressive**: Adapting to an Expressive social style involves being open to new ideas and approaches. Embrace creativity and spontaneity, and be willing to explore innovative solutions. Show flexibility by being receptive to different perspectives and adjusting your plans to incorporate fresh insights.

- **Amiable**: Flexibility with Amiables means being sensitive to their need for stability and positive relationships. Be willing to adjust your approach to maintain harmony and build trust. Show adaptability by being patient and accommodating, and by seeking collaborative solutions that benefit everyone involved.

Practical Applications of Social Styles in Soft Skills Development

1. **Training and Development Programs**: Incorporating social styles into training and development programs can enhance the effectiveness of these initiatives. For example, communication workshops can include modules on recognizing and adapting to different social styles, helping participants develop more effective interpersonal skills.

2. **Performance Reviews and Feedback**: Understanding social styles can improve the quality of performance reviews and feedback sessions. Tailoring feedback to align with the recipient's social style can make it more constructive and motivating. For example, providing detailed, data-driven feedback to an Analytical employee, or offering positive reinforcement and encouragement to an Expressive employee.

3. **Conflict Mediation**: In conflict mediation, understanding the social styles of the parties involved can facilitate more effective resolution. Mediators can use this knowledge to guide the process, ensuring that the needs and preferences of all parties are considered and addressed.

4. **Team Building Activities**: Incorporating social styles into team-building activities can help teams understand and appreciate each other's differences. Activities that highlight the strengths and contributions of each social style can foster a more inclusive and collaborative team environment.

The role of social styles in developing soft skills cannot be overstated. By understanding and leveraging social styles, individuals can enhance their communication, emotional intelligence, conflict resolution, leadership, teamwork, and adaptability. This awareness not only improves interpersonal interactions but also contributes to personal and professional growth. As the workplace continues to evolve, the ability to navigate diverse social styles will remain a critical asset for success. Embracing the insights provided by social styles can lead to more effective and harmonious relationships, ultimately driving better outcomes for individuals and organizations alike.

The Harsh Reality

Now that we have a better understanding of soft skills and their role in the workplace, it's time to face the harsh reality. It is **almost impossible** to change poor soft skills.

Whenever I say this provocative statement in front of people, their first silent reaction tends to be disbelief. What do you mean it is almost impossible? Of course, people can change……..

Over the next several chapters, we will explore why this is so challenging.

Cockeyed Optimist

Years ago, I considered myself a cockeyed optimist when it came to helping people change their poor soft skills. I would spend countless hours mentoring and shadowing individuals at work so I could provide real-life examples for them to leverage when trying to change. But as time has passed, I have come to the realization that it is nearly impossible for someone to change their poor soft skills. This chapter delves into my experiences and reflections on the subject, exploring the inherent difficulties and emotional toll involved in attempting to improve poor soft skills.

The Optimistic Beginning

My journey began with a fervent belief that with the right guidance and support, anyone could improve their poor soft skills. I saw potential in everyone and was eager to help them realize it. Soft skills, such as communication, teamwork, and emotional intelligence, seemed to be the key to unlocking career success and personal growth. I was determined to make a difference. "Well not so fast my friend" - as Lee Corso would say. Let's look at some of my first-hand attempts to overcome these challenges.

Diego's Struggle

One of the earliest and most memorable examples was Diego. Diego was an up-and-coming high performer at the company where I worked. In fact, he was up for a big promotion. However, Diego had one significant problem: he was a horrible team player. Nobody liked to work with Diego because invariably, they would annoy him, and he would quickly escalate the situation to uncomfortable levels. While Diego had unmatched hard skills, his lack of soft skills was quickly overtaking his performance perception at the company.

In true cockeyed optimist form, I jumped at the opportunity to mentor Diego to help him overcome his soft skill gap, continue his upward trajectory, and most importantly, get promoted to the next level.

The Mentorship Process

On conference calls with Diego and others, I would take notes of how I handled situations so I could circle back with Diego afterward and go over my approach. In emails, I monitored his tone and responses to the team, using these as talking points during our one-on-ones. I discussed with him ways to handle difficult situations, emphasizing the importance of not letting the situation get the best of him and responding negatively. We went over all the coping mechanisms that are standard to many of us: don't let your emotions control you, don't email responses when angry, maintain a positive tone, etc.

I met weekly with him to go over these talking points. The progress we made during these one-on-ones was remarkable. Diego would ask me questions about my approach and agreed that it was the right one.

Over the following months, I started to notice a positive turnaround in his communication soft skills on conference calls and emails. People even came up to me to remark on the positive difference they saw in Diego. Soon, it was time for our end-of-year performance process, and Diego was up for a promotion. I was somewhat giddy, knowing that I helped turn Diego around and that he was now a shoo-in for the promotion. Diego himself remarked that he felt like a changed person and thanked me profusely for helping him close his communication soft skill gap.

The Setback

Then came the dreaded email. It was a Monday at 10:00 AM, and our HR department sent out an email to every employee indicating a change in the policy on how we were to track our time. Nothing major, just a minor policy change that seemed innocuous to all. But Diego did not think so. He proceeded to reply all and completely unload on HR, calling the change ridiculous, accusing them of being inept, and stating that he would not abide by the change.

Reading Diego's response felt like I was watching a train wreck in slow motion. I remember screaming in my head, "Noooooooooooooooo." I frantically tried to call Diego but realized the damage was done. Needless to say, Diego did not get the promotion and quit the company within a week before the ax could fall.

This experience made me realize that instead of trying to change Diego's inherent traits, I should have focused on identifying and leveraging his existing strengths while finding ways to minimize the impact of his weaknesses.

The Emotional Toll

Throughout my career, I have tried endlessly to help people like Diego close a soft skill gap. Each attempt carried an emotional weight, as I invested a great deal of time, effort, and hope into these endeavors. Unfortunately, the setback with Diego was not an isolated incident but rather a recurring theme.

Susan's Challenges

Another similar challenge was with Susan. I was Susan's line manager and had recently promoted her to a senior role in my organization. It wasn't long after I put her in the role that I started to get complaints from her team members and colleagues about her abrasive style and condescending tone. This was a complete shock to me, as I had never seen this firsthand, and none of the senior members on my team noticed this trait in Susan.

The Intervention

I confronted Susan about the complaints and mentored her in improving her communication style. She was receptive and seemed to improve for a while. However, after six months, the complaints resurfaced, leading me to realize that her change in behavior wasn't sustainable.

Over the next six months, I received positive feedback about her improvements. However, soon after, complaints started coming in again, with some team members threatening to quit. I was heartbroken. Susan was trying so hard to change, and I felt she had turned the corner. Susan herself was devastated by the complaints. Finally, realizing that her change in behavior was not going to be sustainable, I had to move her out of the role.

The Realization

For every Diego and Susan, there were others like Jim, Sally, Joe, and Jackie, whom I tried to help along my career but to no avail. I have come to the conclusion that you can't fundamentally change someone's poor soft skills. While it pains me to say it, I am 100 percent convinced of this.

The Robin Williams "Awakening" Analogy

My cockeyed optimism was like Robin Williams in the movie "Awakening." He grasped at every sign of hope that the patients had been cured, but after a while, the medication wore off, and they returned to their original state. This melancholy example mirrors the emotional drain I experienced when realizing that the people I was trying to help could not change.

Reflections on the Inevitability of Inherent Traits

Some would argue that the same soft skill challenges exist in the personal world. While my focus is on the professional setting in this book, the case could certainly be made that these challenges are pervasive in all areas of life. How many times have you heard someone's partner say, "I know he was like that when we met but I thought I could change him"?

In conclusion, my journey of trying to help individuals improve their soft skills has been a profound and eye-opening experience. Despite my unwavering optimism and dedication, I have come to understand the inherent difficulties in fundamentally changing these ingrained traits. The experiences with Diego and Susan, along with many others, have taught me that while temporary improvements are possible, sustaining these changes over the long term is often an insurmountable challenge. This realization has been both humbling and enlightening, shaping my perspective on the limitations and possibilities within talent development and interpersonal growth. As I reflect on these experiences, I recognize the importance of focusing on identifying and leveraging the natural strengths of individuals rather than attempting to overhaul their inherent characteristics. This approach not only respects the individuality of each person but also fosters a more realistic and sustainable path to personal and professional growth.

This realization has profound implications for how we approach talent management and personal development. Instead of trying to fundamentally change people's soft skills, we should focus on identifying and leveraging their existing strengths. This approach not only respects individual differences but also leads to more sustainable and authentic growth. In the following chapters, we'll explore strategies for implementing this strengths-based approach in various professional contexts.

The Challenge of Changing Poor Soft Skills at Work

Change is a constant in both our personal and professional lives, yet many individuals and organizations struggle with it. Understanding the root causes of resistance to change can help us address these challenges more effectively. This chapter delves into the psychological, organizational, and cultural factors that contribute to the inability to change, providing insights and strategies for overcoming these barriers.

The Complexity of Changing Poor Soft Skills

Improving poor soft skills is inherently complex due to several interconnected factors. This section explores three key elements that contribute to this complexity: the intrinsic nature of soft skills, the influence of personality traits, and the impact of early life experiences.

Intrinsic Nature of Soft Skills

Soft skills are deeply rooted in an individual's personality, upbringing, and life experiences. Unlike hard skills, which can be taught through formal education and training, soft skills are often developed over time through social interactions and personal experiences.

The Influence of Personality Traits

Characteristics such as introversion or extroversion can significantly influence an individual's ability to develop certain soft skills. These personality traits shape how people interact with the world around them and, consequently, how they acquire and refine various interpersonal abilities.

For instance, an introverted person may find it more challenging to develop strong communication skills compared to an extrovert. Introverts often prefer solitary activities or small group interactions, which can limit their opportunities to practice and refine their public speaking and networking abilities. Their preference for introspection and quiet environments may lead them to avoid large social gatherings or situations that require extensive verbal interaction. As a result, introverts may need to put in a more deliberate effort to develop communication skills, such as seeking out small, supportive groups for practice, using written communication to build confidence, or gradually exposing themselves to larger audiences.

Conversely, extroverts, who thrive in social settings and seek out interactions, may naturally find it easier to develop and exhibit strong communication skills. Their comfort with being around people and engaging in conversations provides them with frequent opportunities to practice speaking and listening. Extroverts often enjoy public speaking, networking events, and group activities, which can help them hone their ability to communicate effectively. They are typically more at ease with spontaneity in conversations and can quickly build rapport with others.

This does not mean introverts cannot excel in communication; it may simply require more intentional effort and practice. Introverts can leverage their strengths, such as deep thinking and active listening, to become effective communicators. By focusing on preparation, developing a unique communication style, and gradually increasing their exposure to social situations, introverts can achieve proficiency in communication skills. In fact, their ability to listen and empathize can make them particularly effective in one-on-one or small-group interactions, where deep connections and thoughtful dialogue are valued.

Overall, both introverts and extroverts have unique strengths that can be harnessed to develop strong communication skills. Understanding one's personality traits and adapting learning strategies to suit those traits can lead to successful skill development and more effective interpersonal interactions.

The Impact of Early Life Experiences

Childhood and early social interactions play a crucial role in shaping soft skills. The experiences children have during their formative years can significantly influence their ability to engage socially, empathize with others, and regulate their emotions. These foundational years set the stage for how individuals interact with the world and handle interpersonal relationships throughout their lives.

Positive early life experiences are instrumental in fostering the development of soft skills. A supportive family environment, where children feel safe and valued, provides a strong foundation for building self-confidence and social competence. In such environments, children are encouraged to express their feelings, share their thoughts, and communicate openly. This open communication helps children learn how to articulate their emotions, understand others' perspectives, and develop empathy.

Engaging in group activities is another critical aspect of positive early life experiences. Whether through sports, school projects, or community events, group activities teach children essential skills like teamwork, cooperation, and conflict resolution. These activities provide opportunities for children to interact with peers, navigate social dynamics, and learn how to work toward common goals. Through these interactions, children develop the ability to negotiate, compromise, and build relationships.

Social play is also vital in early childhood development. Play allows children to explore different social roles, experiment with communication, and learn the rules of social engagement in a low-pressure setting. Through play, children practice taking turns, sharing, and resolving disputes, which are crucial skills for successful social interactions later in life. Playful activities also encourage creativity and problem-solving, contributing to a well-rounded skill set.

Children who are encouraged to express their feelings and resolve conflicts constructively are more likely to develop strong emotional regulation and empathy. For example, when parents and caregivers model and teach constructive ways to handle disagreements, children learn how to manage their emotions and approach conflicts with a problem-solving mindset. These children grow up with a better understanding of their own emotions and the emotions of others, making them more adept at navigating complex social situations.

Conversely, negative early experiences can hinder the development of these essential soft skills. Neglect, lack of social interaction, or exposure to a hostile or unsupportive environment can significantly impact a child's social and emotional development. Children who do not receive adequate emotional support or opportunities for social engagement may struggle with self-esteem, have difficulty forming relationships, and find it challenging to manage their emotions. Without positive role models or opportunities to practice social skills, these children may face ongoing difficulties in both personal and professional settings.

For example, a child who grows up in a neglectful environment may not learn how to express their emotions appropriately or understand social cues, leading to difficulties in forming and maintaining relationships. Similarly, a lack of social interaction during critical developmental periods can result in social anxiety and a lack of confidence in social settings.

In summary, early life experiences play a pivotal role in the development of soft skills. Positive experiences, such as supportive family environments, group activities, and social play, provide children with the tools they need to develop strong social and emotional competencies. These skills are essential for navigating social and professional environments effectively. Conversely, negative early experiences can hinder the development of these skills, making it more challenging for individuals to interact successfully with others as they grow older. Therefore, creating nurturing and engaging environments for children is crucial for fostering the development of essential soft skills.

Understanding these three factors - the intrinsic nature of soft skills, personality traits, and early life experiences - helps explain why changing poor soft skills can be so challenging. It underscores the importance of focusing on individual strengths and finding ways to work with, rather than against, these deeply ingrained characteristics.

Psychological and Emotional Factors

The development of soft skills is closely linked to the following psychological and emotional factors, making them difficult to alter.

Self-Awareness and Self-Regulation: Improving soft skills requires a high level of self-awareness and the ability to regulate one's own behavior and emotions. These two aspects are fundamental in the process of personal development and social interaction, as they enable individuals to understand themselves better and adapt their actions to various situations.

Self-Awareness: Self-awareness involves recognizing one's own emotions, strengths, weaknesses, values, and motives. It is the foundation of emotional intelligence and is crucial for personal growth. Self-aware individuals can objectively assess their behavior and its impact on others, which is essential for developing and refining soft skills.

For example, someone with high self-awareness can identify when they are feeling stressed or anxious and understand how these emotions influence their interactions. This understanding allows them to take proactive steps to manage their stress, such as practicing mindfulness or seeking support, which in turn helps them maintain positive relationships and effective communication.

Self-awareness also involves recognizing one's strengths and areas for improvement. By understanding their competencies, individuals can leverage their strengths to excel in social and professional settings while also working on their weaknesses. For instance, a person who knows they are a good listener but struggles with public speaking can focus on developing their presentation skills while continuing to use their listening ability to build strong interpersonal relationships.

Self-Regulation: Self-regulation is the ability to manage one's emotions, thoughts, and behaviors in different situations. It involves staying in control, being flexible, and maintaining a positive outlook even in challenging circumstances. Self-regulation is crucial for effective communication, conflict resolution, and maintaining professionalism.

Individuals who excel in self-regulation can keep their emotions in check and respond to situations calmly and rationally. For example, in a heated discussion, a person with strong self-regulation skills can remain composed, listen actively, and respond thoughtfully rather than reacting impulsively. This ability to manage emotional responses helps prevent conflicts from escalating and promotes constructive dialogue.

Self-regulation also encompasses the ability to adapt behavior to achieve desired outcomes. For instance, someone who is aware of their tendency to procrastinate can implement strategies to stay focused and meet deadlines, such as breaking tasks into smaller steps, setting reminders, or creating a conducive work environment. This behavioral adjustment not only enhances productivity but also demonstrates reliability and commitment.

Challenges in Developing Self-Awareness and Self-Regulation

Developing self-awareness and self-regulation can be challenging, especially for individuals who lack introspective capabilities or have not been encouraged to engage in self-reflection. Without these skills, individuals may struggle to understand their emotions and behaviors, making it difficult to improve their soft skills.

Lack of self-awareness can lead to misunderstandings and conflicts in social interactions. For example, someone who is unaware of their tendency to dominate conversations may inadvertently alienate others, affecting their relationships and teamwork. Similarly, without self-regulation, individuals may react impulsively to stress or criticism, leading to negative outcomes in both personal and professional settings.

Overcoming these challenges requires intentional effort and practice. Individuals can develop self-awareness through activities such as journaling, seeking feedback, and engaging in mindfulness practices. These activities encourage reflection and provide insights into one's thoughts, emotions, and behaviors.

Developing self-regulation involves practicing self-discipline and learning to manage emotions effectively. Techniques such as deep breathing, cognitive restructuring, and setting clear goals can help individuals stay focused and calm in stressful situations. Additionally, building a supportive environment with mentors or coaches can provide guidance and accountability in the journey of personal development.

In summary, self-awareness and self-regulation are essential components in the development of soft skills. They enable individuals to understand themselves better, manage their emotions, and adapt their behaviors to various situations. Although challenging to develop, these skills can be cultivated through intentional practice and self-reflection, leading to improved interpersonal interactions and personal growth.

Fear of Vulnerability

Developing soft skills often involves stepping out of one's comfort zone and being vulnerable. This fear of vulnerability can significantly impede personal growth, as it requires individuals to confront and address aspects of themselves that may be uncomfortable or challenging.

Acknowledging Personal Biases: Improving empathy, for example, necessitates acknowledging and addressing personal biases and emotional responses. This process can be uncomfortable because it involves recognizing prejudices or preconceived notions that one might prefer to deny or ignore. Confronting these biases is crucial for developing a genuine understanding and compassion for others.

Personal biases can stem from various sources, including cultural background, upbringing, and past experiences. These biases shape how individuals perceive and interact with others. Acknowledging them requires introspection and honesty, which can be daunting. It involves admitting to oneself that their perspective is limited and potentially flawed and being open to changing long-held beliefs.

Emotional Responses: Addressing emotional responses is another aspect of vulnerability. Developing emotional intelligence, which is closely tied to soft skills, requires individuals to understand and manage their emotions effectively. This process can be uncomfortable because it involves facing emotions that might be suppressed or ignored, such as fear, anger, or sadness.

For example, improving conflict resolution skills might require an individual to confront their fear of confrontation. They need to acknowledge how their emotional responses to conflict, such as anxiety or defensiveness, affect their behavior and outcomes. This level of self-awareness is challenging because it exposes personal insecurities and requires a willingness to change habitual reactions.

Stepping Out of Comfort Zones: Stepping out of one's comfort zone is a significant aspect of overcoming the fear of vulnerability. Comfort zones provide a sense of security and predictability, but they also limit growth. Developing soft skills often involves engaging in new and unfamiliar experiences, which can be intimidating.

For instance, enhancing public speaking skills might require an individual to speak in front of large groups, which can be anxiety-inducing. The fear of making mistakes, being judged, or appearing incompetent can be overwhelming. However, it is through these experiences that individuals learn and grow. Embracing vulnerability allows them to push past their fears and build confidence.

The Role of Feedback: Receiving feedback is another area where vulnerability plays a crucial role. Constructive criticism is essential for personal and professional development, but it can also be difficult to accept. It requires individuals to acknowledge their shortcomings and be open to suggestions for improvement.

For example, a manager striving to improve their leadership skills might receive feedback about their communication style. Accepting this feedback means recognizing that their current approach may not be effective and being willing to make changes. This process can be uncomfortable because it involves admitting to imperfections and actively working to address them.

Building Resilience: Embracing vulnerability and stepping out of comfort zones build resilience. Resilience is the ability to adapt and thrive in the face of challenges and setbacks. Developing soft skills often involves encountering difficulties and learning from them. Each experience of vulnerability, whether it's receiving feedback, confronting biases, or managing emotions, contributes to a stronger, more resilient character.

For example, an individual working on their networking skills may initially find social events daunting. However, by continually pushing themselves to attend and engage, they build resilience and gradually become more comfortable and adept at networking.

Creating a Supportive Environment: Creating a supportive environment can help individuals overcome their fear of vulnerability. Encouragement from mentors, colleagues, or peers provides reassurance and motivation. A safe and non-judgmental space allows individuals to express their thoughts and feelings openly, making it easier to confront and address areas of vulnerability.

For example, a team that fosters open communication and values diverse perspectives creates an environment where individuals feel safe to share their ideas and experiences. This support enables them to take risks, make mistakes, and learn from them, ultimately leading to personal and collective growth.

In summary, the fear of vulnerability is a significant barrier to developing soft skills. Overcoming this fear requires individuals to step out of their comfort zones, confront personal biases, manage emotional responses, and embrace feedback. By doing so, they build resilience and create opportunities for growth. A supportive environment further facilitates this process, providing the encouragement and safety needed to navigate the challenges of personal development.

Organizational Challenges in Improving Soft Skills

Beyond the individual complexities, organizational factors also contribute to the difficulty of improving soft skills.

Cultural Barriers

The culture of an organization plays a crucial role in the development and reinforcement of soft skills.

Existing Beliefs and Values: In organizations with a rigid hierarchical structure or a culture that does not prioritize soft skills, employees may find it challenging to develop these abilities. An organization's beliefs and values significantly influence employee behavior and development. When a culture values hard skills over interpersonal skills, it can hinder efforts to improve soft skills, such as communication, teamwork, and emotional intelligence.

Rigid Hierarchical Structures: Rigid hierarchical structures often emphasize top-down communication and decision-making, which can limit opportunities for employees to practice and develop soft skills. In such environments, the focus tends to be on following directives rather than engaging in open dialogue and collaboration. This can stifle creativity and innovation, as employees may feel discouraged from sharing ideas or providing feedback.

For example, in a company where decisions are made solely by senior management, lower-level employees may have limited opportunities to participate in discussions, offer suggestions, or engage in problem-solving activities. This lack of engagement can hinder the development of communication skills and reduce the motivation to build relationships within the organization.

Hard Skills Over Interpersonal Skills

When organizations prioritize technical expertise over interpersonal skills, employees may perceive soft skills as undervalued or irrelevant to their career advancement.. This can lead to a focus on developing hard skills, such as technical knowledge and problem-solving abilities while neglecting the importance of effective communication, empathy, and collaboration.

For instance, in a technology-driven company where success is measured by technical achievements and innovation, employees may prioritize learning new software or improving technical capabilities over developing leadership or teamwork skills. As a result, the organization may struggle with issues such as poor team dynamics, communication breakdowns, and low employee morale.

Impact on Employee Development

The lack of emphasis on soft skills within an organization can have several negative impacts on employee development and overall organizational performance. Employees may struggle to build effective working relationships, leading to conflicts and misunderstandings. Additionally, the absence of strong communication and collaboration skills can hinder project success and reduce productivity.

For example, in a project-based environment, the ability to work effectively in teams is crucial. If team members lack the necessary interpersonal skills to communicate and collaborate, projects may face delays, quality issues, and a lack of cohesion. This can ultimately affect the organization's ability to deliver successful outcomes and maintain a competitive edge.

In conclusion, the challenge of changing poor soft skills is multifaceted, involving deeply ingrained personal habits, psychological barriers, and organizational culture. However, by understanding these complexities, individuals and organizations can adopt targeted strategies to address these deficient skills. In the following chapters, we will discuss how to offset these challenges and take advantage of opportunities for growth, focusing on the power of proper role alignment within your workforce.

The Diet Analogy

As we have read in the previous chapters, change is a difficult, often grueling process. While attempting to improve one's poor soft skills, the journey is fraught with challenges, setbacks, and a profound sense of discomfort. This chapter draws a parallel with the well-known struggle of maintaining a diet.

When someone embarks on the journey to improve their poor soft skills, they are essentially trying to rewire their natural tendencies and behavioral patterns. This is akin to attempting to change the way one inherently processes emotions and interacts with the world. It's no surprise that this is an incredibly challenging task.

The Diet Analogy

Consider the common scenario of someone trying to lose weight. Initially, the motivation is high, and the commitment to a new diet and exercise regimen is strong. However, as time goes on, the initial excitement wanes and the true challenge begins: maintaining the new lifestyle in the face of cravings, social pressures, and ingrained eating habits.

Research indicates that approximately 80% of people who lose weight on a diet will eventually regain it (*Obesity Reviews*). This high failure rate underscores the difficulty of maintaining long-term behavioral changes in eating habits. Similarly, the process of changing poor soft skills starts with enthusiasm. One might attend workshops, read books, and actively practice new behaviors. However, over time, old habits begin to resurface. The comfort of familiar behavior is hard to resist, just as the allure of a favorite comfort food is difficult to ignore.

A study published in *The American Journal of Clinical Nutrition* found that while 80% of dieters show high levels of motivation and adherence in the initial stages of their diet, more than 50% begin to drop off by the third month. This decline in adherence parallels the waning commitment seen correcting poor soft skills. Much like dieting, the initial excitement of attending workshops and actively practicing new behaviors can fade as old habits resurface.

About 60% of dieters cite cravings and social eating situations as major challenges that derail their progress. Similarly, individuals working on poor soft skills improvement often face setbacks due to the comfort of reverting to old, familiar behaviors and the influence of established social dynamics at work.

The saying "old habits die hard" underscores the difficulty of changing deeply ingrained behaviors, whether related to diet or interpersonal skills. Both processes require more than initial enthusiasm; they demand sustained commitment, resilience in the face of setbacks, and effective strategies to adjust over the long term.

While this chapter highlights the challenges of changing poor soft skills, it's important to note that a more effective approach might be to focus on leveraging existing strengths rather than trying to drastically change inherent traits. Just as successful diets often involve finding healthier alternatives that align with one's preferences, improving soft skills can involve finding ways to use one's natural tendencies more effectively in various situations.

The Emotional Component

Just like with a diet, there are emotional components tied to the changing of poor soft skills and also involves a significant emotional component. For instance, someone who has always been introverted might find it emotionally taxing to adopt more extroverted behaviors. This emotional resistance is similar to the comfort and identity people find in their eating habits.

Emotional Triggers and Responses

Self-Doubt: Self-doubt often accompanies efforts to change poor soft skills. Individuals may question their ability to make lasting changes, leading to a lack of confidence in their efforts. This self-doubt can create a vicious cycle where the individual feels discouraged and less motivated to continue their improvement efforts. For instance, someone trying to improve their assertiveness may struggle with the fear of being perceived as aggressive, leading to second-guessing and inconsistent behavior.

Dieting Example: Consider someone who has struggled with weight loss for years and has tried multiple diets without long-term success. When they start a new diet, they might be filled with initial enthusiasm, but underlying self-doubt can quickly undermine their efforts.

As they begin the diet, they may constantly question whether they have the willpower to stick with it. Every minor slip-up—such as indulging in a dessert at a social event or skipping a workout—feeds their self-doubt. They start thinking, "I've failed so many times before, why would this time be any different?" This lack of confidence in their ability to make lasting changes leads to feelings of discouragement.

This self-doubt can create a vicious cycle. When they doubt their ability to succeed, their motivation wanes. They might skip meal planning, avoid exercise, or give in to unhealthy cravings more easily. These actions then reinforce their belief that they cannot stick to a diet, further decreasing their confidence.

For example, after an initial slip-up, they might think, "I knew I couldn't do this," and this thought pattern leads them to make more poor dietary choices, such as eating junk food for comfort. The inconsistency in their adherence to the diet grows, and before long, they abandon their efforts entirely, reverting to old eating habits.

This cycle of self-doubt and discouragement highlights how challenging it is to make and sustain dietary changes, as the psychological barriers often prove to be as significant as the physical ones.

Emotional Fatigue: The process of changing soft skills can lead to emotional fatigue. Constantly pushing oneself to behave in ways that do not come naturally can drain emotional energy. For example, someone who is naturally reserved may find it exhausting to continuously engage in extroverted behaviors, such as networking or participating in group discussions. Over time, this emotional strain can lead to burnout and a return to old habits.

Dieting Example: Consider someone who is trying to maintain a strict diet that requires them to avoid their favorite foods and adhere to a regimented eating schedule. Initially, they might be able to stick to the diet with determination and willpower. However, as time goes on, the constant effort required to resist cravings, plan meals, and stay within the dietary guidelines begins to take a toll on their emotional energy.

For instance, someone who loves social dining might find it emotionally draining to continuously decline invitations to eat out with friends or to navigate social situations where unhealthy food is present. The emotional fatigue from always having to make the "right" food choice can accumulate, making the person feel stressed and deprived.

Over time, this emotional strain can lead to burnout. The dieter might start to feel that the effort required to maintain their diet is unsustainable. This fatigue can cause them to revert to old eating habits, seeking comfort in familiar foods that provide emotional satisfaction but do not align with their dietary goals.

For example, after weeks of strict dieting, the emotional fatigue might culminate in a scenario where the dieter, feeling overwhelmed and exhausted, gives in to the temptation of a favorite high-calorie treat. This lapse can be the first step back into old habits, as the relief from the emotional strain is immediate. The dieter might think, "I've been so good for so long, I deserve this," and this thought can open the door to more frequent indulgences.

The cycle of emotional fatigue and burnout illustrates how difficult it is to sustain dietary changes. The constant emotional effort to adhere to new eating patterns can be draining, leading individuals to eventually seek relief by returning to their old, more comforting habits.

Mind over Matter

Beyond the emotional components, there are significant psychological barriers that make changing poor soft skills similar to dieting.

Cognitive Dissonance: When individuals try to change poor soft skills behaviors that are fundamentally at odds with their self-image, they experience cognitive dissonance. This psychological discomfort can be overwhelming and often leads to rationalizing or justifying the old behaviors rather than embracing new ones.

Dieting Example: Imagine someone who has always seen themselves as a "foodie"—someone who loves to indulge in rich, flavorful foods and views eating as one of life's greatest pleasures. This self-image is deeply ingrained and closely tied to their identity. When this person decides to embark on a strict diet to lose weight, they are attempting to adopt behaviors that conflict with their self-perception.

As they try to adhere to their new diet, they might find themselves experiencing significant psychological discomfort. The restrictive eating plan feels like a denial of who they are. This cognitive dissonance creates a sense of inner turmoil, as they struggle between their desire to lose weight and their identity as a foodie.

To alleviate this discomfort, they might start rationalizing their old eating habits. For example, they might tell themselves, "Life is too short to deprive myself of the foods I love," or "I deserve to enjoy my meals after a hard day." These rationalizations help them justify straying from their diet and returning to their previous eating behaviors.

This cognitive dissonance makes it extremely challenging to maintain the new, healthier eating habits, as the psychological tension pushes them back toward their comforting, familiar patterns of behavior. Thus, despite their initial commitment and motivation, the internal conflict caused by cognitive dissonance often leads to a relapse into old habits, undermining their dieting efforts.

Habituation: Humans are creatures of habit. Behaviors, when learned and repeated, become automatic and ingrained. Breaking these habitual responses requires significant conscious effort, which can be exhausting and demotivating over time.

Dieting Example: Consider someone who has developed the habit of having a dessert every evening after dinner. Over the years, this behavior has become automatic and ingrained in their daily routine. When they decide to embark on a new diet that excludes sweets, they must break this long-standing habit.

Initially, the person might manage to resist the urge to have dessert through sheer willpower and motivation. However, as the days and weeks pass, the constant effort required to override this habitual response starts to wear them down. Each evening, they face the same challenge: resisting the automatic impulse to reach for a sweet treat. This repeated effort can be mentally exhausting.

For example, the dieter might find that, at the end of a long day, their resolve is weakest. The habitual urge for dessert becomes particularly strong because it is associated with relaxation and reward after a day's work. The mental energy required to consistently say no to this ingrained habit can lead to fatigue and decreased motivation.

Over time, the effort to break this habit might become demotivating. The dieter could start to feel that the constant battle against their automatic behaviors is too much to sustain. They might begin to rationalize occasional indulgences, thinking, "One dessert won't hurt," but this can quickly lead to more frequent lapses as the old habit reasserts itself.

The cycle of habituation and the challenge of breaking ingrained behaviors illustrate why it is so difficult to maintain dietary changes. The automatic nature of habitual responses requires significant conscious effort to overcome, and this effort can be both exhausting and demotivating over time.

Behavioral Inertia: The tendency to continue doing what one has always done is a powerful force. Changing poor soft skills requires overcoming this inertia, which involves not only the initial push to start new behaviors but also the sustained effort to maintain them.

Dieting Example: Consider someone accustomed to fast food lunches might initially switch to homemade meals but struggle to maintain this change long-term. The familiarity and convenience of the old habit exert a strong pull, especially during busy or stressful times. This illustrates how behavioral inertia can undermine efforts to change, whether in dieting or improving soft skills.

Initially, the person might be motivated to prepare and bring healthier meals from home. The first few days or weeks might go well as the novelty of the new behavior provides a boost of enthusiasm. However, as time goes on, the powerful pull of their established routine starts to reassert itself.

For instance, on a particularly busy day, the convenience of stopping by the fast-food restaurant they've frequented for years becomes tempting. The effort required to prepare a healthy meal feels daunting compared to the ease of slipping back into the familiar habit. The psychological and logistical challenge of maintaining the new behavior in the face of stress and time constraints can be significant.

Overcoming this behavioral inertia involves a two-step process. First, there is the initial push to start the new behavior—deciding to bring a healthy lunch instead of buying fast food. Second, and more challenging, is the sustained effort to maintain this change. This means consistently preparing meals, planning ahead, and resisting the ease and familiarity of the old routine.

As days turn into weeks, the initial motivation might wane, and the person could find themselves slipping back into their old habits. The convenience and comfort of the fast-food routine have a strong pull, and without sustained effort and perhaps additional support, the individual may struggle to stick to their new dietary goals.

This struggle illustrates the concept of behavioral inertia in dieting. The initial effort to change is often overcome by the established momentum of old habits, requiring continuous and sustained effort to maintain new behaviors. The difficulty in maintaining this effort is a significant reason why many people find it challenging to stick to dietary changes over the long term.

The Diet Analogy

In conclusion, the journey to improve poor soft skills is a nearly impossible task, akin to the struggle of adhering to a stringent diet. Both efforts require immense willpower to overcome ingrained behaviors, with slim odds of long-term success. Initial enthusiasm and commitment often give way to the powerful pull of old habits and comfort zones. The emotional and psychological hurdles make the process even more challenging. Just as the majority of dieters ultimately revert to their previous eating patterns, individuals attempting to change their poor soft skills frequently fall back into familiar behaviors. Recognizing the profound difficulty of this journey can help set more realistic expectations.

The Neuroscience of Resistance: Why the Brain Struggles to Change Poor Soft Skills

Despite the countless training programs, development initiatives, and mentoring efforts, our brain is wired in a way that makes it extremely challenging to significantly alter these skills. I could certainly write an entire book exploring each of the topics below in depth, but for simplicity's sake, I will cover the neuroscience behind this at a surface level.

This chapter delves into the neuroscience behind this resistance, exploring the brain's structure, function, and the psychological principles that make changing soft skills a formidable task.

The Brain's Structure and Function

To understand why the brain resists changing soft skills, it's essential to first grasp the basic structure and function of the brain. The brain is composed of various regions, each responsible for different cognitive and emotional processes. These regions collectively contribute to the development, reinforcement, and modification of soft skills, making the task of changing these skills a formidable challenge.

The Prefrontal Cortex

The prefrontal cortex, located at the front of the brain, is crucial for higher-order cognitive functions such as decision-making, problem-solving, and impulse control. This region is heavily involved in regulating behavior and managing complex social interactions, making it essential for the development and application of soft skills.

Executive Functions: The prefrontal cortex is responsible for planning, organizing, and executing tasks. These executive functions are integral to soft skills such as effective communication, leadership, and teamwork. For example, when leading a team, the ability to plan strategically and organize tasks efficiently is paramount. This involves setting goals, anticipating challenges, and coordinating efforts, all of which are mediated by the prefrontal cortex. Without a well-functioning prefrontal cortex, individuals may struggle to structure their thoughts and actions in a way that facilitates effective collaboration and leadership.

Behavioral Regulation: This area helps control impulses and emotional responses, which are critical for maintaining professional composure and demonstrating empathy. When someone feels anger or frustration in a workplace setting, the prefrontal cortex helps manage these emotions, ensuring that responses remain appropriate and measured. This regulatory function is vital for soft skills such as conflict resolution, where the ability to stay calm and empathetic under pressure can determine the outcome of a disagreement. By managing impulses and emotions, the prefrontal cortex enables individuals to navigate social interactions with greater skill and poise.

The Limbic System

The limbic system, which includes structures like the amygdala and hippocampus, is involved in emotional processing and memory formation. These structures play a significant role in how we perceive, react to, and remember social and emotional stimuli, deeply influencing our soft skills.

Emotional Responses: The amygdala processes emotional reactions, influencing how we respond to social cues and stress. It is deeply involved in the development of emotional intelligence, empathy, and other interpersonal skills. For instance, when faced with a stressful situation, the amygdala's activation can lead to a fight-or-flight response.

A well-regulated amygdala, however, helps an individual remain calm and empathetic, enabling them to handle stress with greater emotional intelligence. The ability to manage one's emotions in social settings is crucial for building strong interpersonal relationships and effectively navigating workplace dynamics.

Memory and Learning: The hippocampus is vital for forming and retrieving memories, which affects how we learn from past experiences and apply that knowledge in social interactions. Memories of past interactions, whether positive or negative, shape our future behavior and responses in similar situations. This is crucial for developing social skills and understanding social dynamics. For example, remembering a successful negotiation can help an individual apply similar strategies in future interactions, while recalling a past miscommunication can prompt them to adjust their approach to avoid repeating the same mistakes.

Neural Pathways and Habit Formation

Neural pathways are the connections between neurons that facilitate communication within the brain. These pathways are strengthened through repetition, leading to the formation of habits. Once these habits are established, they become automatic responses, deeply ingrained in the brain's structure.

Basal Ganglia: This group of nuclei is essential for habit formation. Once a behavior becomes habitual, it requires less conscious effort to perform, making it difficult to change established patterns. For example, if someone has developed the habit of reacting defensively to criticism, this behavior becomes ingrained in the basal ganglia. As a result, adopting a more constructive response requires significant effort and practice to create new neural pathways that override the old habits. The basal ganglia's role in habit formation explains why changing soft skills, which often involve altering long-established patterns of behavior, is so challenging.

The Difficulty of Changing poor soft skills

Soft skills are deeply ingrained in our neural circuitry, shaped by a combination of genetics, early life experiences, and repetitive social interactions. Several factors contribute to the brain's resistance to changing these skills.

The Plasticity of the Adult Brain

Neuroplasticity is the brain's capacity to form new neural connections, allowing it to reorganize itself. Though this ability persists throughout life, it decreases with age.

Developmental Plasticity: During childhood and adolescence, the brain is highly adaptable, allowing for rapid learning and development of new skills. This period is crucial for the formation of soft skills. For instance, a child learning to share and communicate effectively with peers develops these skills relatively easily because their brain is highly malleable. However, these early-formed habits and responses become deeply embedded over time.

Adult Plasticity: In adulthood, the rate of neuroplastic change slows down. The established neural pathways for existing behaviors become more entrenched, making it challenging to develop new soft skills or alter existing ones. For example, an adult who has spent years avoiding confrontation may struggle to adopt assertive communication techniques because their brain is used to the established pattern of behavior. Learning to be assertive would require significant effort and persistence to rewire these neural pathways.

The Power of Habits

Habits are automatic behaviors reinforced through repetition. The basal ganglia play a significant role in the formation and reinforcement of these habits, including those related to soft skills.

Automaticity: Once a behavior becomes habitual, it operates on autopilot, reducing the cognitive effort required. This efficiency is beneficial for routine tasks but poses a challenge when trying to change ingrained behaviors. For example, if someone habitually avoids eye contact during conversations, breaking this habit to improve their interpersonal communication skills requires ongoing, conscious effort. This is challenging because the automatic behavior is deeply entrenched.

Resistance to Change: Changing a habit involves disrupting established neural pathways and creating new ones, which requires sustained effort and can be mentally exhausting. For instance, a person who has developed the habit of giving terse responses might need to work hard to adopt a more engaging and conversational style. This change requires constant vigilance and practice, often leading to mental fatigue and frustration.

Emotional Responses and Social Conditioning

Emotional responses and social conditioning are critical factors in the development of soft skills. The amygdala processes emotional reactions and helps encode memories associated with social interactions.

Automatic Emotional Responses: Over time, emotional responses to social stimuli become automatic, influencing how we react in social situations. Changing these responses requires not only cognitive effort but also emotional regulation. For example, someone who instinctively reacts defensively to constructive criticism may struggle to adopt a more open and receptive attitude. This automatic defensive response is difficult to override because it is rooted in emotional conditioning.

Social Conditioning: Early life experiences and social conditioning shape our soft skills. These deeply ingrained behaviors are resistant to change because they are reinforced by long-standing neural pathways. For instance, if a person was raised in an environment where showing vulnerability was discouraged, they might find it challenging to develop empathetic listening skills. Their conditioned response to maintain emotional distance becomes a barrier to changing their interpersonal behavior.

The Science of Resistance to Change

The brain's resistance to change is not merely a matter of willpower or motivation; it is rooted in its biological and functional design. Several scientific principles explain this resistance.

Cognitive Load Theory

Cognitive load theory posits that the brain can only process a limited amount of information at once. This concept, first introduced by John Sweller in the 1980s, has profound implications for learning and behavior change, particularly in the context of developing new skills or modifying existing ones.

Mental Fatigue: Mental fatigue is a state of exhaustion that occurs when the brain is overworked and unable to maintain high levels of cognitive function. This condition can significantly impede the process of changing soft skills, which often require sustained cognitive effort, patience, and consistent practice. For instance, someone trying to improve their active listening skills may find it mentally exhausting to focus intently on conversations all day, leading to lapses in attention and eventual regression to old habits.

Overload: Overload occurs when the cognitive load—the total amount of mental effort being used—exceeds the brain's capacity to process information effectively. This state of cognitive overload can have significant negative impacts on an individual's ability to maintain focus, sustain effort, and successfully learn new skills or change existing behaviors. For example, a manager trying to adopt a more inclusive leadership style might struggle to balance this effort with the demands of their job, leading to inconsistent application of the new behavior.

The Role of Dopamine

Dopamine is a neurotransmitter associated with reward and pleasure. It plays a crucial role in motivation and reinforcement learning.

Reinforcement Learning: Behaviors that lead to positive outcomes are reinforced by dopamine release, making them more likely to be repeated. Changing soft skills often involves unlearning behaviors that have been reinforced by dopamine, which can be challenging. For instance, if interrupting others has previously led to being heard and acknowledged, this behavior is reinforced. Unlearning it means overcoming the lack of immediate dopamine rewards that the old behavior provided.

Motivation: Dopamine also affects motivation. The effort required to change established behaviors may not provide immediate rewards, leading to decreased motivation. When learning new soft skills, delayed gratification can make it difficult to stay committed to the change. For instance, an employee working on becoming more patient with colleagues may not see immediate positive feedback, leading to a drop in motivation to continue the effort.

Fear and the Status Quo Bias

The brain prioritizes safety and predictability. The amygdala, responsible for processing fear, can trigger anxiety when facing uncertainty or potential failure.

Fear Response: The fear response reinforces the status quo bias, a cognitive bias that leads individuals to prefer familiar routines and resist change. The fear of making mistakes or facing negative consequences can deter individuals from trying to change their soft skills. For example, someone might avoid taking on a leadership role because they fear failure and the potential negative feedback that comes with it.

Avoidance of Uncertainty: The brain's preference for predictability and routine makes it difficult to embrace new behaviors, even when recognizing the potential benefits. The discomfort associated with stepping out of one's comfort zone to practice new soft skills often results in reverting to familiar, ingrained behaviors. For instance, an employee might resist adopting a new conflict-resolution approach because the old way, though less effective, feels safer and more predictable.

Case Studies: The Impact of Neuroscience on Soft Skills Development

Emily's Journey:

Emily, a mid-level manager at a tech firm, was known for her technical expertise but often struggled with effective communication. Her tendency to deliver information in a blunt, technical manner sometimes caused misunderstandings with her team and peers. Despite recognizing the importance of soft skills, Emily found it challenging to change her communication style. Over the years, she attended numerous communication workshops, but these interventions seemed to have little lasting impact.

Neural Pathways

One of the primary reasons for Emily's difficulty in improving her communication skills lies in the concept of neural pathways. Our brains form neural pathways based on repeated behaviors and experiences, which become the default patterns for how we think, feel, and act. For Emily, her communication habits had been reinforced over many years, becoming deeply ingrained neural pathways. Changing these established pathways requires significant cognitive effort and time, as the brain tends to revert to familiar patterns, especially under stress or pressure.

Emily's struggle to improve her communication skills illustrates how neuroscience explains our brain's resistance to change, highlighting the challenges of altering deeply ingrained behaviors.

Our journey to improve poor soft skills, despite the numerous training programs, development initiatives, and mentoring efforts, is a challenging endeavor deeply rooted in the brain's structure and function. This chapter has explored the neuroscience behind this resistance, highlighting the significant obstacles posed by the brain's inherent wiring.

Understanding the complexity of the brain's structure and function is crucial to comprehending why changing soft skills is so arduous. The prefrontal cortex, responsible for higher-order cognitive functions, plays a vital role in regulating behavior and managing complex social interactions. However, its involvement in executive functions and behavioral regulation underscores the difficulty of altering established patterns, particularly when those patterns have been reinforced over years of repetition.

The limbic system, including the amygdala and hippocampus, further complicates the process of change. The amygdala's role in emotional processing means that our reactions to social stimuli and stress are deeply ingrained. The hippocampus's involvement in memory formation ensures that our past experiences continue to influence our present behavior.

Together, these structures create powerful emotional responses and memories that make changing soft skills a challenging task.

Neural pathways and habit formation also play a significant role in this resistance. The basal ganglia's involvement in habit formation means that once a behavior becomes automatic, it requires less conscious effort to perform, making it difficult to change established patterns. This automaticity, while efficient for routine tasks, poses a substantial challenge when trying to develop new soft skills or alter existing ones.

The difficulty of changing soft skills is further compounded by the brain's plasticity. While the brain remains capable of forming new neural connections throughout life, this plasticity diminishes with age. The entrenched neural pathways for existing behaviors make it challenging for adults to develop new skills or modify old ones.

The power of habits and the emotional responses tied to social conditioning also contribute to the brain's resistance to change. Habits operate on autopilot, reducing the cognitive effort required to perform them but making it difficult to disrupt established patterns. Emotional responses, processed by the amygdala, become automatic over time, influencing how we react in social situations and adding another layer of complexity to the process of change.

Scientific principles such as cognitive load theory and the role of dopamine further explain this resistance. The brain's limited capacity for processing information means that it can become overwhelmed by the effort required to change behaviors. Dopamine's role in reinforcement learning and motivation means that changing behaviors that have been positively reinforced is particularly challenging. Additionally, the brain's fear response and status quo bias lead to a preference for familiar routines, making it difficult to embrace new behaviors.

In conclusion, the brain's resistance to changing soft skills is a multifaceted issue involving biological, cognitive, and emotional factors. This resistance is not merely a matter of willpower or motivation but is deeply rooted in the brain's structure and function. Recognizing the profound difficulty of this journey can help set more realistic expectations and provide valuable insights into human behavior and the complexities of personal development. Understanding the neuroscience behind this resistance can offer a more compassionate and informed approach to the challenge of improving soft skills, highlighting the need for sustained effort, resilience, and realistic goals in the pursuit of personal and professional growth.

All is Not Lost

Up to now, we have learned about soft skills and the challenges of changing poor soft skills. Fortunately these same challenges do not exist when learning new soft skills or further developing positive soft skills. Over the next few chapters we will explore the science behind this as well as other contributing factors.

Our Brain is Wired to "Learn"

Understanding the neuroscience behind our ability to learn and enhance soft skills versus the difficulty of changing poor soft skills provides valuable insights into human behavior and development. This section delves into the neurological mechanisms that facilitate the acquisition and improvement of soft skills.

While this chapter explores the brain's capacity for learning, it's important to note that this primarily applies to acquiring new skills or enhancing existing strengths. Changing deeply ingrained poor soft skills remains challenging, as discussed in previous chapters. The strategies presented here are most effective when applied to developing new skills or improving already positive traits, rather than attempting to drastically alter established negative behaviors.

The Brain's Plasticity and Learning New Skills

The brain's plasticity, or neuroplasticity, refers to its ability to reorganize itself by forming new neural connections throughout life. In the previous chapter, we learned that this part of the brain makes it challenging to change poor soft skills. However this part of our brain is perfectly suited to learn new skills or enhance existing positive skills, including soft skills. Neuroplasticity is most prominent in certain brain regions involved in learning and memory, such as the hippocampus and the prefrontal cortex.

Neuroplasticity and Skill Acquisition

When learning a new soft skill, such as effective communication or emotional intelligence, the brain undergoes significant structural and functional changes. Here are some key aspects of how this process works:

Strengthening Synaptic Connections: The brain reinforces synaptic connections through repeated practice and engagement in skill-promoting activities. This process, known as long-term potentiation (LTP), increases the strength of synapses based on recent patterns of activity, thereby enhancing the brain's ability to retain and utilize new information. LTP is crucial because it forms the biological basis for learning and memory, allowing new skills to become more ingrained with continuous practice.

Formation of New Neural Pathways: Learning new skills involves the formation of new neural pathways. These pathways are created through the brain's ability to adapt and reorganize, allowing for the incorporation of new behaviors and responses into our cognitive framework. This adaptability is what enables us to learn new skills and improve existing ones, as the brain continually refines and optimizes its network of connections.

Role of Dopamine: Dopamine, a neurotransmitter linked to motivation, reward, and learning, is crucial in this process. Positive reinforcement and rewarding experiences related to practicing new soft skills can enhance dopamine release. This reinforcement makes the behavior more likely to be repeated, which is essential for the acquisition and enhancement of new soft skills. Dopamine's role in the brain's reward system is vital for sustaining motivation and reinforcement learning.

Myelination: Myelination is the process of forming a myelin sheath around the axons of neurons, which increases the speed and efficiency of neural transmission. Repeated practice of new soft skills leads to improved myelination, enhancing communication between brain regions involved in these skills. This improved connectivity supports the development and refinement of new soft skills, making neural processes more efficient and effective over time.

Enhancing Positive Soft Skills Through Targeted Interventions

While altering deeply ingrained poor soft skills is challenging, enhancing positive soft skills through targeted interventions is achievable. Here are some neuroscience-backed strategies:

Mindfulness and Emotional Regulation

Research shows that mindfulness practices like meditation increase prefrontal cortex activity and enhance emotional regulation. Regular mindfulness practice helps individuals develop greater self-awareness and control over their emotional responses, thereby enhancing soft skills like empathy and emotional intelligence. Mindfulness can lead to structural changes in the brain, such as increased gray matter density in areas associated with learning and memory, which supports overall cognitive and emotional functioning.

Cognitive Behavioral Techniques

Cognitive-behavioral techniques (CBT) focus on identifying and changing negative thought patterns and behaviors. By reprogramming cognitive biases and developing new ways of thinking, individuals can enhance their soft skills. CBT has been shown to create lasting changes in brain structure and function, particularly in regions involved in emotion regulation and executive function. This approach helps individuals develop more adaptive responses and improve their interpersonal interactions.

Role-Playing and Simulation

Engaging in role-playing and simulation exercises allows individuals to practice and refine their soft skills in a safe and controlled environment. These activities stimulate the brain's learning centers and promote the formation of new neural pathways. Over time, repeated practice in these simulated environments can lead to the integration of these skills into everyday behavior. Role-playing helps individuals build confidence and improve their ability to handle real-world situations effectively.

Feedback and Reflective Practice

Receiving constructive feedback and engaging in reflective practice can enhance soft skills by promoting self-awareness and continuous improvement. Feedback helps individuals identify areas for growth, while reflection allows them to consolidate learning and reinforce positive behaviors. Reflective practice involves regularly reviewing one's actions and experiences to gain insights and make adjustments. This iterative process supports the development of more effective communication, problem-solving, and interpersonal skills.

These interventions are most effective when used to enhance existing strengths or develop new skills, rather than attempting to fundamentally change deeply ingrained poor soft skills.

Practical Applications in the Workplace

Implementing these strategies in the workplace can facilitate the development and enhancement of soft skills among employees. Organizations can foster a culture of continuous learning and improvement by integrating neuroscience-based approaches into their training and development programs. Here are some practical applications:

Leadership Development

Invest in leadership development programs that emphasize emotional intelligence, mindfulness, and cognitive-behavioral techniques. Leaders play a crucial role in shaping organizational culture and can set an example for continuous learning and development.

Peer Support and Mentoring

Establish peer support and mentoring programs that encourage collaboration and knowledge sharing. Peer support can provide valuable feedback and reinforcement, while mentoring can guide individuals through the process of developing new soft skills.

Structured Training and Continuous Learning Opportunities

Develop structured training programs that incorporate principles of neuroplasticity, incremental change, and positive reinforcement. These programs should gradually introduce new skills, offer opportunities for practice and feedback, and reinforce learning through positive experiences. Additionally, provide continuous learning opportunities through workshops, seminars, and online courses. Encourage employees to engage in reflective practice, seek regular feedback, and make learning resources readily available and accessible to all.

Measuring and Tracking Progress

Implement systems to measure and track progress in soft skills development. Use assessments, surveys, and performance metrics to monitor improvements and identify areas for further development. Regularly review and adjust training programs based on feedback and performance data.

Understanding the neuroscience behind learning new soft skills and enhancing positive ones underscores the brain's remarkable capacity for change and adaptation. While deeply ingrained poor soft skills are difficult to alter due to established neural pathways, emotional responses, and cognitive biases, it is possible to acquire new soft skills and improve existing ones through targeted interventions. By leveraging neuroplasticity, positive reinforcement, and deliberate practice, individuals can develop the soft skills necessary for personal and professional success. Understanding these neurological mechanisms provides a foundation for more effective strategies in soft skills development and highlights the importance of a proactive approach to continuous learning and growth.

Strategies To Learn New Soft Skills

In the following chapter, we will discuss one's potential to learn new soft skills. We will delve into psychological insights, behavioral patterns, and practical strategies to navigate the dynamics of learning new soft skills.

It's important to note that while this chapter focuses on learning new soft skills, this process is distinct from attempting to change deeply ingrained poor soft skills. Learning new skills allows us to build on our strengths and expand our capabilities, whereas changing existing poor skills often proves more challenging and less effective.

Facilitators of Learning New Soft Skills

Fresh Start and Open Mindset: One of the most powerful facilitators in learning new soft skills is approaching challenges with a beginner's mindset. This mindset encourages curiosity and receptivity to feedback, essential components for exploring alternative approaches and discovering new ways to interact and communicate. By fostering curiosity, individuals can explore various ways to approach problems, interact with colleagues, and handle complex situations, paving the way for continuous development.

The Essence of a Beginner's Mindset

A beginner's mindset is characterized by the willingness to see things from a fresh perspective, free from preconceived notions and judgments. This openness is crucial for embracing new ideas and methods that can enhance one's soft skills. When individuals adopt a beginner's mindset, they approach each new experience as a learning opportunity, unburdened by the fear of making mistakes or the pressure of having to know everything. This attitude fosters an environment where learning and growth can flourish.

Openness to New Experiences: An open mindset allows individuals to view challenges not as insurmountable obstacles but as opportunities for growth and learning. This perspective is vital in the realm of soft skills, where adaptability and flexibility are often more valuable than rigid adherence to established methods. For instance, someone learning active listening must set aside their habitual ways of communicating and genuinely focus on understanding and responding to others. This openness to new experiences enables individuals to absorb different techniques and strategies that can improve their interpersonal interactions.

Curiosity and Exploration: Curiosity is a driving force behind a beginner's mindset. It motivates individuals to explore various ways to approach problems, interact with colleagues, and handle complex situations. This sense of curiosity leads to a deeper understanding of the nuances of soft skills and encourages continuous development. By being curious, individuals are more likely to ask questions, seek out new information, and experiment with different approaches, all of which contribute to the growth of their soft skills.

Receptivity to Feedback: Another critical component of a beginner's mindset is the receptivity to feedback. Constructive feedback provides valuable insights into one's strengths and areas for improvement. When individuals are open to feedback, they can make informed adjustments to their behaviors and strategies, leading to enhanced soft skills. This receptivity is essential for continuous learning and development.

Embracing Feedback as a Tool for Growth: Feedback should be viewed as a tool for growth rather than a critique of one's abilities. A beginner's mindset fosters an attitude that embraces feedback, understanding that it is an integral part of the learning process. By welcoming feedback, individuals can gain new perspectives on their actions and behaviors, which can lead to significant improvements in their soft skills. This openness to feedback also promotes a culture of learning and development within teams and organizations.

Viewing Challenges as Opportunities

A beginner's mindset transforms the perception of challenges. Instead of seeing obstacles as roadblocks, individuals with this mindset view them as opportunities for growth and learning. This shift in perspective is particularly important when developing soft skills, which often require navigating complex social and emotional dynamics.

Overcoming Fear of Failure: One of the biggest barriers to learning new skills is the fear of failure. A beginner's mindset helps mitigate this fear by emphasizing the value of the learning process itself, rather than the outcome. When individuals are not afraid to fail, they are more willing to take risks, try new approaches, and learn from their mistakes. This resilience and willingness to learn from failure are crucial for developing robust soft skills.

Motivation and Enthusiasm: Intrinsic motivation plays a crucial role in the pursuit of new soft skills. Personal growth aspirations and professional development goals often drive this motivation, fueling perseverance and a proactive attitude. When individuals are enthusiastic about learning, they are more likely to remain committed and resilient in the face of challenges. This motivation can stem from a desire to advance in one's career, improve relationships with colleagues, or simply become a more effective communicator or leader. Enthusiasm for learning can lead to sustained effort, even when progress seems slow or difficult.

The Role of Intrinsic Motivation

Intrinsic motivation refers to the drive to engage in activities for their inherent satisfaction rather than for some separable consequence. This type of motivation is characterized by a genuine interest and enjoyment in the task itself, leading individuals to pursue new skills because they find the process rewarding. When it comes to learning new soft skills, intrinsic motivation is a powerful force that can significantly enhance one's ability to persevere and succeed.

Personal Growth Aspirations: One of the key drivers of intrinsic motivation is the desire for personal growth. Many individuals are motivated by the prospect of self-improvement and the attainment of new competencies. This desire to become better versions of themselves encourages them to take on the challenge of learning new soft skills, despite the potential difficulties involved.

For instance, someone who wishes to enhance their emotional intelligence might be driven by the aspiration to better understand and manage their emotions, improve their interpersonal relationships, and increase their overall well-being. This personal growth aspiration can provide a strong incentive to engage in the learning process with enthusiasm and dedication.

Professional Development Goals: In addition to personal growth aspirations, professional development goals also play a significant role in motivating individuals to learn new soft skills. Career advancement often requires the acquisition of new competencies, particularly those related to effective communication, leadership, and teamwork. Individuals who are motivated by the desire to advance in their careers are more likely to invest time and effort into developing these skills.

For example, an employee aiming for a promotion to a managerial position may recognize the need to improve their leadership abilities. This professional development goal can serve as a powerful motivator, driving them to seek out training opportunities, engage in practice exercises, and apply new skills in the workplace.

Sustaining Effort Through Enthusiasm

Enthusiasm for learning is another critical factor that contributes to the sustained effort required to develop new soft skills. When individuals are genuinely excited about the learning process, they are more likely to stay focused on their goals and remain resilient in the face of challenges.

The Power of Enthusiasm: Enthusiasm can transform the learning experience, making it more enjoyable and rewarding. When individuals approach the task of learning new soft skills with a positive attitude, they are more likely to embrace challenges as opportunities for growth rather than obstacles. This enthusiastic mindset can help them maintain momentum and continue making progress, even when the going gets tough.

Commitment to Long-Term Success: Motivation and enthusiasm also help individuals stay focused on their long-term goals. Developing new soft skills often requires sustained effort over an extended period. During this time, individuals may encounter setbacks, experience slow progress, or face moments of self-doubt. However, those who are driven by a deep desire to improve are more likely to persevere through these difficulties.

For example, someone who is determined to become a more effective public speaker may face initial anxiety and self-consciousness. However, their intrinsic motivation and enthusiasm for mastering this skill can help them push through these challenges, continuously seeking out opportunities to practice and improve.

The Role of Motivation in Overcoming Obstacles

Intrinsic motivation not only fuels the pursuit of new skills but also plays a crucial role in overcoming obstacles. When individuals are driven by a strong internal desire to improve, they are more likely to seek out resources, practice diligently, and find creative solutions to the challenges they encounter.

Seeking Out Resources: Motivated individuals are proactive in seeking out resources that can aid in their skill development. They may attend workshops, enroll in courses, read books, or participate in online forums and communities. This proactive approach to learning ensures that they have access to the tools and information needed to succeed.

Diligent Practice: The development of new soft skills requires consistent practice. Individuals who are motivated and enthusiastic about learning are more likely to engage in regular practice sessions, applying their new skills in various contexts to reinforce their learning. This diligent practice helps them build proficiency and confidence over time.

Overcoming Challenges: Learning new soft skills often involves facing and overcoming various challenges. Motivated individuals are more likely to view these challenges as opportunities for growth rather than insurmountable obstacles. Their intrinsic drive to succeed encourages them to find creative solutions, seek feedback, and make necessary adjustments to their approach.

Structured Learning Opportunities: Access to structured learning environments is a significant facilitator of soft skill development. Workshops, courses, mentoring programs, and online resources provide systematic frameworks that guide the learning process. These opportunities offer practical exercises, feedback mechanisms, and the necessary support to help individuals achieve their learning objectives. Structured learning can help break down complex soft skills into manageable components, allowing individuals to focus on one aspect at a time and gradually build their competencies.

The Role of Systematic Frameworks in Learning

Structured learning environments offer systematic frameworks that provide a clear roadmap for skill development. These frameworks are essential for breaking down the complexities of soft skills into manageable and understandable components. By following a structured approach, individuals can systematically address each aspect of a soft skill, ensuring a comprehensive understanding and mastery over time.

Workshops, courses, mentoring programs, and online resources offer systematic frameworks that guide the learning process. These opportunities provide practical exercises, feedback, and support to help individuals achieve their learning objectives. By breaking down complex soft skills into manageable components, structured learning enables individuals to focus on each aspect progressively, building their competencies over time. Below are some other opportunities and their benefits.

Role Modeling: Mentors serve as role models, demonstrating effective soft skills in real-world contexts. Observing and interacting with mentors allows learners to see how soft skills are applied in professional settings, providing a practical reference for their own development.

Online Resources: The digital age has made a wealth of online resources available for soft skill development. These resources offer flexibility and convenience, allowing individuals to learn at their own pace and from any location. Online resources include webinars, podcasts, e-learning platforms, and digital libraries.

Webinars and Podcasts: Webinars and podcasts provide access to expert insights and discussions on various soft skills. They offer a platform for continuous learning, where individuals can stay updated with the latest trends, techniques, and best practices in soft skill development.

E-Learning Platforms: E-learning platforms offer structured courses and training programs that cover a wide range of soft skills. These platforms often include interactive modules, quizzes, and progress tracking features that enhance the learning experience.

Digital Libraries: Digital libraries provide access to a vast array of books, articles, and research papers on soft skills. Learners can explore different perspectives, theories, and case studies to deepen their understanding of soft skills.

Absence of Preexisting Habits: Unlike trying to change existing soft skills, learning new ones involves starting from a blank slate. Without the need to unlearn entrenched behaviors or biases, individuals can experiment, adapt, and refine new skills more freely. This absence of preexisting habits allows for a more fluid and iterative approach to skill development. Starting with a clean slate can make it easier to adopt new behaviors, as there are no old habits to overcome. This can lead to a more positive and rewarding learning experience.

When individuals are not burdened by previous patterns of behavior, they can approach learning with a sense of freedom and creativity. This openness allows them to try new techniques and approaches without the fear of reverting to old habits. It also provides a unique opportunity to build a strong foundation of soft skills that can be further developed and refined over time.

Case Study: Embracing Emotional Intelligence

Background

David, a project leader, recognized the importance of emotional intelligence (EI) in enhancing team dynamics and client relationships. He realized that to be more effective in his role, he needed to learn how to manage emotions, understand the perspectives of others, and navigate social complexities.

Approach

David enrolled in an EI certification program, participated in self-assessment exercises, and applied EI frameworks in team meetings and client interactions. The program provided a structured learning environment where David could gain insights into his emotional strengths. He engaged in practical exercises, such as role-playing and scenario analysis, to apply the concepts he learned.

Results

Over time, David demonstrated significant understanding in managing interpersonal dynamics, resolving conflicts constructively, and inspiring team collaboration. His proactive approach to learning EI skills contributed to enhanced project outcomes and stakeholder satisfaction. David's commitment to developing his emotional intelligence not only improved his professional effectiveness but also strengthened his relationships with colleagues and clients.

Strategies for Learning New Soft Skills

Effective strategies facilitate the acquisition and integration of new soft skills into professional practice, promoting continuous growth and adaptability.

Identify Skill Relevance: The first step in learning new soft skills is to evaluate their relevance to professional objectives, career aspirations, and organizational roles. Focusing on skills that match personal and organizational needs allows individuals to maximize their learning impact. Understanding the relevance of specific skills can also enhance motivation and engagement in the learning process.

For example, a manager may identify that learning conflict resolution skills is crucial for maintaining a harmonious work environment. By recognizing the importance of this skill, they can prioritize their learning efforts and seek out relevant resources and training opportunities.

Set SMART Goals: Establishing SMART (Specific, Measurable, Achievable, Relevant, Time-bound) goals is essential for clarifying learning objectives, tracking progress, and maintaining accountability. SMART goals provide a clear roadmap for the skill development process, helping individuals stay focused and motivated. Setting specific goals can also make it easier to measure progress and make necessary adjustments along the way.

For instance, an individual aiming to learn public speaking skills might set a SMART goal to deliver three presentations within the next six months, each with increasing complexity and audience size. This approach ensures that the learning process is structured and progress is measurable.

Access Learning Resources: Exploring diverse learning resources is crucial for acquiring new soft skills. Workshops, seminars, webinars, online courses, podcasts, and professional literature offer a wealth of practical insights, case studies, and interactive learning experiences. Utilizing these resources can provide a well-rounded approach to skill development. Accessing a variety of learning materials can also help reinforce new concepts and provide different perspectives on how to apply soft skills in various contexts.

By engaging with multiple resources, individuals can learn new soft skills and gain exposure to different teaching methods and practical applications. This comprehensive approach can enhance the learning experience and provide valuable tools for skill development.

Practice Application: Applying new soft skills in daily work and interactions is crucial for improving proficiency and adaptability. Practicing these skills in various contexts helps reinforce learning and build confidence. Regular practice can also help solidify new behaviors, making them more natural and automatic over time.

For example, someone learning active listening can make a conscious effort to practice this skill during team meetings, client interactions, and casual conversations with colleagues. By consistently applying the skill, they can improve their ability to listen effectively and respond appropriately in different situations.

Solicit Feedback and Reflection: Engaging in ongoing self-assessment and seeking feedback from mentors, peers, supervisors, and stakeholders is crucial for refining skill application strategies. Reflecting on performance outcomes, identifying areas for improvement, and making necessary adjustments can significantly enhance the learning process. Feedback from others can provide valuable insights into how new behaviors are perceived and highlight areas where further improvement is needed.

Regular reflection and feedback can help individuals stay on track with their learning goals and make informed decisions about how to adjust their approach. This iterative process ensures continuous improvement and long-term success in developing new soft skills.

In conclusion, learning new soft skills is a journey that requires a combination of curiosity, motivation, structured learning, and consistent practice. By fostering an open mindset and leveraging various resources and strategies, individuals can develop new soft skills that enhance their professional effectiveness and personal growth. Grasping the psychological and behavioral aspects of soft skills is key to navigating skill development. While changing existing soft skills may be challenging, the potential to learn and acquire new ones offers a viable pathway for continuous growth and adaptation.

Role Alignment

Ok, now that we have explored the challenges of changing poor soft skills and our ability to learn new soft skills, let's look at solving these challenges and leveraging the new skills through the power of Role Alignment. This is the true paradox of the book's title: setting the right expectations of the "fish" based on what we know. We have to stop putting square pegs in round holes—or, in the book's case, stop expecting the fish to climb the tree.

Good People in Bad Roles

Throughout my career journey, employees are often labeled as "bad performers" when they fail to meet expectations. This chapter challenges the notion that poor performance is an inherent trait, proposing instead that mismatches between individuals and their roles are the primary cause. By aligning people's strengths with suitable roles, organizations can unlock their potential and foster a thriving workplace.

The Myth of the Bad Performer: The concept of a "bad performer" is pervasive in corporate culture, often leading to negative outcomes for both the employee and the organization. Many organizations quickly label employees as poor performers without considering whether their roles align with their strengths. This premature judgment can lead to a cycle of disengagement and under performance; and ultimately lead to the employee being exited from the organization. Let's take a look at 2 case studies that demonstrate the power of role alignment.

Luis the "Underperformer": I once was asked to take over for a colleague who was struggling in his role. After the knowledge transfer period, Luis had a two-week trip planned with his family over the holidays. I learned that my management was planning to exit Luis from the firm when he returned based on his performance.

While Luis was away during the holidays, I was getting acclimated to my new role. During this time, I quickly realized that Luis was not a bad performer; he was just in the wrong role. He had a lot of very positive soft and hard skills that I could leverage as part of my team when he got back.

Recognizing the Misalignment: As I delved deeper into the responsibilities and tasks of my new role, I noticed a pattern in the issues that Luis had been facing. The tasks he struggled with required a high degree of attention to detail, which did not align with his strengths. Instead, Luis excelled in areas that required strong interpersonal skills. His outstanding communication abilities and natural rapport with people were valuable assets.

This discovery prompted me to look more closely at Luis' past performance reviews and speak with his colleagues and clients. What I found was enlightening. Luis consistently received positive feedback on his ability to build and maintain strong relationships with clients. His clients trusted him and often sought his advice and support. His colleagues appreciated his team spirit and willingness to help out whenever needed.

Making the Case for Luis: Armed with this new understanding, I quickly advocated for Luis' reassignment. I presented my findings to management, emphasizing Luis' strengths and how they could be better utilized. Fortunately, they agreed to give Luis another chance, trusting my judgment.

Luis' Transformation: When Luis returned from his holiday, I sat down with him to discuss his new role. I explained that his previous position required a level of detail orientation that was not aligned with his strengths. Instead, I placed him in a client-facing role that leveraged his ability to build strong relationships. Luis' new responsibilities included managing client accounts, addressing client concerns, and ensuring client satisfaction.

The transformation was immediate and remarkable. In his new role, Luis thrived. His natural ability to connect with people shone through, and he quickly became a favorite among clients. He was able to use his excellent communication skills to understand client needs, address their concerns, and build lasting relationships.

Success Beyond Expectations: Luis' success led to multiple promotions. He adapted and excelled in each new role, becoming one of the most successful executives in the firm's history, generating hundreds of millions of dollars in revenue over his career

Lessons for Organizations

Luis' story offers valuable lessons for organizations:

1. **Identify Strengths and Weaknesses**: Regularly assess employees' strengths and weaknesses. Use tools like performance reviews, feedback from colleagues and clients, and self-assessments to get a comprehensive understanding of each employee's abilities.

2. **Flexible Role Assignments**: Be willing to reassign roles based on employees' strengths. If someone is struggling in their current role, consider whether a different role might be a better fit before making the decision to terminate their employment.

3. **Supportive Management**: Management should be supportive and open to feedback from their teams. Trusting managers to make decisions about role alignment can lead to better outcomes for both the employees and the organization.

4. **Continuous Development**: Provide opportunities for continuous development and growth. Encourage employees to develop their skills and pursue roles that align with their strengths and interests.

5. **Create a Positive Work Environment**: Foster a work environment where employees feel valued and supported. When employees know that their strengths are recognized and appreciated, they are more likely to be engaged and committed to their work.

Reflections on Role Alignment: Had I not recognized that Luis was not aligned to the right role, Luis and the firm would have never achieved the success they had without one another. This experience highlights the importance of understanding each employee's unique strengths and aligning their roles accordingly. Organizations that invest in role alignment can unlock the full potential of their workforce, leading to increased productivity, higher employee satisfaction, and greater overall success.

Of course, not all stories have a happy ending for the company as many people are not put in the right role to succeed. How many times have you seen someone from your organization get let go as an "underperformer" and land at another company and be wildly successful at their new company? I have seen this a plethora of times - more than I'd like to count.

One such example is Tony.

Tony - The Starting Pitcher: Tony, a day-one employee at my previous company, quickly rose from an entry-level position to become a world-renowned expert in his field. He was a legend, much like an All-World Shortstop in baseball. Tony's journey was marked by exceptional achievements, and his expertise was highly regarded both within the company and in the broader industry.

A New Challenge: Tony was asked to move into a new, unfamiliar role based on his past success. This transition was like asking an All-World Shortstop to become an All-World Starting Pitcher. Despite the significant shift in skills and mindset required, Tony eagerly accepted the challenge, approaching it with enthusiasm and determination.

Good, Not Great: Tony quickly adapted to his new role, bringing unique perspectives and valuable insights. However, despite his hard work, his performance was good but not great. The new position didn't fully leverage his core strengths, preventing him from reaching the same heights as in his previous role.

A Leadership Misstep: Instead of recognizing this misalignment and moving Tony back to a role where he could excel, leadership decided to exit him from the organization. This decision was a significant misstep. It overlooked Tony's immense potential and the value he had brought to the company. Rather than finding a way to leverage Tony's strengths, the company chose to part ways with one of its most valuable assets.

The Aftermath: Unsurprisingly, it didn't take long for Tony to land with a new company. His reputation as the best shortstop in the world preceded him, and he quickly re-established himself as a top performer in his field. Tony's new team recognized his talents and placed him in a role that fully utilized his skills and expertise. He thrived in this new environment, once again achieving greatness and making significant contributions to his new organization.

Lessons Learned

Tony's story is a powerful reminder of the importance of role alignment in the workplace. It highlights the critical need for organizations to recognize and leverage the unique strengths of their employees. Here are some key lessons to be learned from Tony's experience:

1. **Recognize and Leverage Strengths:** Tony excelled as a shortstop because it was a role that perfectly matched his skills and strengths. When he was moved to a position that did not align with these strengths, his performance, while still good, did not reach its full potential. Organizations must take the time to understand the unique strengths of their employees and place them in roles where they can excel.

2. **Provide Support and Training:** When employees are asked to move into new roles, it is essential to provide them with the necessary support and training to succeed. This includes not only technical

training but also ongoing mentorship and guidance. While Tony quickly adapted to his new role, additional support and resources might have helped him bridge the gap between good and great performance.

3. **Be Willing to Reassess and Adjust:** Organizations should be flexible and willing to reassess and adjust role assignments based on performance and alignment. If an employee is not thriving in a new role, it is important to consider whether a different position might be a better fit. Rather than exiting valuable employees, companies should explore all possible options to leverage their talents.

4. **Appreciate and Retain Talent:** Losing a top performer like Tony can have a significant impact on an organization. It is crucial to appreciate and retain talent by creating a supportive environment where employees feel valued and recognized for their contributions. This includes not only competitive compensation and benefits but also opportunities for growth and development.

5. **Understand the Costs of Misalignment:** The costs of misalignment can be significant, both in terms of lost productivity and the impact on employee morale. When employees are not in roles that align with their strengths, they are less likely to be engaged and motivated. This can lead to decreased performance, increased turnover, and ultimately, a negative impact on the organization's bottom line.

To this day, I stay in contact with Tony. While I am happy that he has once again found his passion and is thriving in his new role, it pains me to know that we once had the best shortstop in the world on our team. Tony's success at his new company serves as a constant reminder of the importance of role alignment and the potential that can be unlocked when employees are placed in positions that fully leverage their strengths.

Finally, I'd like to close a loose end that I created previously in my book

Susan - The Story Doesn't End There: If you read the chapter on me being a Cockeyed Optimist, you will have come across the story of Susan. Well, the story doesn't end there. I finished that tale by mentioning that I had to assign her a new role. Susan is another excellent example of someone who was a good performer in a bad role.

Susan's case demonstrates that rather than trying to change her soft skills to fit a leadership role, it was more effective to find a role that aligned with her existing strengths.

Recognizing the Misalignment: Susan had been in a leadership position for a significant period, but over time, her strengths evolved. Recognizing that the leadership role was no longer a great fit, I reassigned her to a position that played to her strengths, particularly her attention to detail and strong work ethic.

Embracing the New Role: In her new role, Susan hit the ground running. She quickly became an expert in her field, with her attention to detail becoming her defining trait. Her meticulous nature ensured that every task she undertook was executed flawlessly. Susan transformed into a "fire and forget" type of employee. Anything assigned to her was completed with precision and excellence, and I never had to follow up with her. This reliability and independence were invaluable to our team and the organization.

Flourishing in the Right Environment: As each day passed, it became evident that Susan was thriving. You could see the pride in her eyes as she realized she was performing at her best. Gone were the days of feeling inadequate while trying to improve team leadership skills that were not her natural strength. Susan's new role allowed her to leverage her innate abilities and experience true job satisfaction.

The Impact on Team Dynamics: Susan's transformation had a ripple effect on the entire team. Her confidence, expertise, and precision inspired colleagues and set a high standard. Her reliability allowed team members to focus on their tasks, improving overall productivity. Susan's success story became a motivational tale within the organization, illustrating the importance of proper role alignment.

The Long-Term Benefits: To this day, Susan remains the hardest-working person I have ever met. Her dedication and precision in her work have only grown stronger. She often thanks me profusely for taking a chance on her and putting her in a position to succeed. But in truth, it was her willingness to embrace change and her determination to excel that paved the way for her success.

Susan's story underscores several important lessons for both employees and employers:

1. **Self-Awareness and Acceptance**: Susan's ability to recognize that a leadership role was no longer the right fit for her was crucial. Accepting that her strengths had evolved allowed her to embrace a role where she could truly excel.

2. **Role Flexibility**: Organizations must be flexible in their approach to role assignments. Just because an employee excelled in a role early in their career does not mean they will always be the best fit for that role. Continuous assessment and flexibility can lead to better alignment and job satisfaction.

3. **Leveraging Strengths**: Identifying and leveraging an employee's strengths can lead to remarkable outcomes. Placing Susan in a role that utilized her exceptional thoroughness and diligence transformed her performance and job satisfaction.

4. **Supportive Management**: As managers, it is our responsibility to recognize when an employee is not in the right role and to take action to address it. This might involve difficult conversations and changes, but the long-term benefits far outweigh the challenges.

5. **Employee Morale and Productivity**: When employees are in roles that align with their strengths, their morale and productivity improve significantly. Susan's pride in her work and her consistent performance were direct results of this alignment.

Reflections and Future Considerations: Susan's journey also highlights the dynamic nature of careers. People's strengths and interests evolve over time, and organizations must be attuned to these changes. By fostering an environment that values continuous development and role reassessment, companies can retain top talent and ensure that their employees are always in positions where they can perform at their best.

Moreover, Susan's experience serves as a reminder that professional growth is not always linear. Sometimes, stepping back from a leadership role can lead to greater personal and professional fulfillment. This is an important consideration for both employees and managers when planning career paths and development opportunities.

Susan's Continued Success: Today, Susan continues to excel in her role. Her attention to detail, work ethic, and ability to execute tasks with precision have made her an invaluable asset to the organization. Her journey from a misaligned leadership role to her current position is a testament to the power of role alignment and the impact it can have on an individual's career.

The story of Susan is a testament to the profound impact that role alignment can have on an individual's performance and job satisfaction. By recognizing her strengths and placing her in a role that leveraged those strengths, we were able to transform her from a good performer in a bad role to an exceptional performer in the right role. Susan's journey highlights the importance of self-awareness, flexibility, and supportive management in achieving role alignment.

Luis, Tony, and Susan's stories demonstrate how proper role alignment significantly impacts individual and organizational success. *By identifying and utilizing employees' strengths, offering support and training, and being open to reassessing and adjusting role assignments, organizations can foster an environment where employees excel. As leaders, it is our duty to ensure that we position our employees in roles that allow them to perform at their highest potential.*

The Hidden Costs of Misalignment

The misalignment of employees to roles they are ill-suited for can lead to a cascade of negative outcomes. These include decreased productivity, increased absenteeism, higher turnover rates, lower overall employee morale, and detrimental impacts on team dynamics. Misalignment disrupts the workplace on multiple levels, affecting both individual and team performance. Understanding these costs is essential for businesses to recognize the importance of role alignment. The following sections explore key areas impacted by misalignment.

The True Cost of Misalignment: The concept of role misalignment goes beyond simple job dissatisfaction. It touches on the fundamental mismatch between an employee's skills, interests, and the demands of their position. This misalignment can lead to a series of cascading negative effects that ultimately affect the overall health and performance of an organization. Misalignment can be seen as a silent killer of workplace productivity and morale, often undetected until its negative impacts become severe.

Impact on Productivity: One of the most immediate and tangible effects of misalignment is decreased productivity. When employees are placed in roles that do not match their strengths, they are less likely to be engaged and motivated. This lack of engagement can lead to a significant drop in productivity as employees struggle to perform tasks that do not suit their skill set.

For instance, an employee with strong analytical skills but weak interpersonal skills might struggle in a customer-facing role. Their discomfort and lack of enthusiasm for the job can lead to frequent mistakes, missed deadlines, and overall poor performance. On the other hand, placing the same employee in a role that leverages their analytical skills can lead to increased job satisfaction and higher productivity.

Gallup's State of the Global Workplace report highlights that only 21% of employees worldwide are engaged at work. Engagement is closely linked to how well an employee's role aligns with their skills and interests. Disengaged employees often exhibit lower levels of motivation, creativity, and initiative, leading to overall reduced productivity.

Increased Stress and Burnout: Misalignment can also lead to increased stress and burnout among employees. When individuals are continuously tasked with responsibilities that do not align with their strengths, they are more likely to experience frustration and stress. This chronic stress can result in burnout, a state of physical, emotional, and mental exhaustion caused by prolonged stress and overwork.

The American Institute of Stress reports that workplace stress costs U.S. employers over $300 billion annually due to absenteeism, turnover, diminished productivity, and medical, legal, and insurance costs. Employees working in roles that do not suit them are more likely to experience stress and burnout, leading to higher absenteeism rates and lower overall output. Stressed employees are less capable of maintaining consistent performance levels, which can further exacerbate productivity issues.

Higher Turnover Rates: Employee turnover is another costly consequence of misalignment. When employees are not in the right roles, they are more likely to leave the organization, either voluntarily or involuntarily. High turnover rates can have several detrimental effects on an organization, including increased recruitment and training costs, lost productivity, and a negative impact on team dynamics and morale.

The Society for Human Resource Management (SHRM) estimates that the average cost to replace an employee is six to nine months of their salary. For high-level positions, this cost can be even higher. Replacing an employee involves significant costs, including advertising the position, interviewing candidates, and training new hires. Additionally, the loss of an employee often means the loss of valuable institutional knowledge and experience, which can hinder organizational efficiency and disrupt workflow continuity.

When an employee leaves, their workload must be redistributed among remaining staff or temporarily left unfulfilled. This can lead to decreased productivity as remaining employees may become overwhelmed or struggle to take on additional responsibilities. High turnover rates can also negatively affect employee morale, as remaining staff may feel uncertain about their own job security or burdened by increased workloads. This can lead to a vicious cycle of further turnover and decreased productivity.

Impact on Team Dynamics

Misalignment and the subsequent turnover disrupt team cohesion and dynamics. Teams function best when there is stability and trust among members. Frequent changes in team composition can lead to a lack of trust and increased friction among team members, further impacting productivity and morale.

Effective teams rely on the strengths and contributions of each member. When there is a mismatch in roles, it can create an imbalance, causing some team members to compensate for others' deficiencies. This not only puts additional strain on those individuals but can also lead to resentment and decreased collaboration within the team. The overall effectiveness of the team is compromised, which can affect the quality and timeliness of the work produced.

Financial Impact of Misalignment: The financial impact of misalignment extends beyond immediate productivity losses and turnover costs. Misalignment can also affect long-term organizational performance and profitability. Key areas of financial impact include reduced revenue, increased operational costs, and lower employee engagement and retention.

According to a McKinsey report, companies that fail to align their workforce correctly can experience a revenue reduction of up to 25%. Decreased productivity and high turnover rates can lead to missed sales opportunities, delayed product launches, and suboptimal customer service. These factors can directly impact revenue generation and overall profitability.

Inefficiencies arising from misaligned roles can lead to higher operational costs. This includes costs associated with correcting errors, managing increased absenteeism, and addressing quality issues. Moreover, misalignment can lead to lower employee engagement and retention rates, resulting in higher costs associated with ongoing recruitment, training, and onboarding of new hires.

To illustrate the tangible costs of misalignment, consider the following case studies and examples

Case Study 1: TechCorp's Sales Team Misalignment TechCorp, a mid-sized technology company, experienced significant turnover in its sales department. Upon investigation, it was found that many sales representatives were misaligned with their roles. High-performing individuals with strong technical backgrounds were placed in customer-facing roles, while those with strong interpersonal skills but limited technical knowledge were tasked with technical sales.

Productivity decreased as technical experts struggled with customer interactions, while those with strong people skills lacked the technical knowledge to close deals. This misalignment led to a 15% drop in sales revenue over six months and a turnover rate of 30% within the sales team.

The cost to TechCorp included not only lost sales but also the expenses related to recruiting, hiring, and training new sales representatives.

Additionally, the company had to invest in team-building and role reassessment exercises to realign employees to more suitable roles. The total financial impact was estimated to be over $500,000 within a year.

Case Study 2: HealthMed's Nursing Staff Realignment HealthMed, a healthcare provider, faced high turnover rates among its nursing staff, leading to staffing shortages and increased operational costs. A detailed assessment revealed that many nurses were assigned to roles that did not align with their skills and interests. For instance, nurses with strong administrative and organizational skills were placed in direct patient care roles, while those with a passion for patient interaction were assigned to administrative tasks.

The misalignment resulted in increased stress and burnout among nurses, leading to a turnover rate of 25% annually. To address this issue, HealthMed conducted a comprehensive role realignment exercise, matching nurses to roles that better suited their skills and preferences. This led to a significant reduction in turnover rates, improved patient care, and increased overall job satisfaction among nurses.

The cost savings from reduced turnover and improved productivity were substantial. HealthMed estimated that the realignment exercise saved the organization approximately $1 million annually in recruitment, training, and operational costs.

The costs of misalignment in the workplace are significant and multifaceted, impacting productivity, turnover rates, team dynamics, and overall organizational performance. By recognizing the importance of aligning employees to the right roles and implementing strategies to ensure proper alignment, organizations can mitigate these costs and create a more engaged, productive, and satisfied workforce.

Proper alignment boosts individual and team performance, driving long-term organizational success. Investing in comprehensive hiring practices, ongoing performance assessments, career development, role flexibility, employee engagement, and leadership development can help organizations unlock the full potential of their workforce and achieve sustainable growth and profitability.

As we have learned, the costs of misalignment in the workplace are significant and multifaceted, affecting numerous aspects of organizational health and performance. When employees are not well-suited to their roles, it can lead to decreased productivity, higher turnover rates, strained team dynamics, and overall diminished organizational performance. Misalignment often results in employees feeling undervalued, unmotivated, and disengaged, which exacerbates these negative outcomes.

Recognizing the importance of aligning employees to the right roles is crucial for mitigating these costs. Implementing strategies to ensure proper alignment can transform the workplace into a more engaged, productive, and satisfied environment. This requires a proactive approach to understanding employees' strengths, skills, and career aspirations, and matching them with appropriate roles that capitalize on these attributes.

Proper alignment enhances individual and team performance by ensuring that employees are not only capable but also motivated to perform their tasks. When employees feel that their roles are a good fit, they are more likely to be engaged and committed to their work, which boosts overall productivity and job satisfaction. Moreover, well-aligned teams can collaborate more effectively, leveraging each member's strengths to achieve common goals.

The Car, Truck or Van

Earlier in my career, I was moved into a role that ran a P&L for a division of my company. As such, all the sellers within this division reported to me. As time went on, I had this one seller (Jimmy) who was starting to annoy me. He would never put in his monthly forecasts or update his sales close plans like the rest of the sales team. At times, he would have a negative edge on our team calls. His saving grace was that he was exceeding his sales targets every month. Having my "Cockeyed Optimist" years behind me, I knew there was no way for him to change these soft skills. I had an epiphany one day, success in the workplace doesn't come from having a team of identical personalities; it arises from recognizing and leveraging the unique strengths each team member brings to the table. Instead of trying to change Jimmy's inherent soft skills, I realized the key was to leverage his unique strengths in a role that suited him best.

This chapter uses the analogy of a sales team compared to vehicles, emphasizing the importance of matching the right person with the right situation for optimal performance. Just as different vehicles are suited to different tasks, team members with various soft skills excel in distinct roles. Jimmy was a "Truck" and I was trying to make him a "Car". Once I realized this, my appreciation for what Jimmy was able to do increased exponentially.

The Analogy: Vehicles for Different Purposes

Imagine a sales team as a fleet of vehicles, each designed for a specific purpose:

- **Trucks**: Robust and capable of carrying heavy loads, ideal for tasks requiring strength and endurance.
- **Vans**: Spacious and reliable, perfect for transporting multiple people or items efficiently.
- **Sports Cars**: Fast and agile, designed to win races with their speed and precision.

Similarly, team members have unique social styles that make them particularly suited to certain tasks. Recognizing and leveraging these differences can drive the team toward success.

The Sales Team: A Blend of Social Styles: In a sales team, different social styles can be equated to the vehicles in our analogy. Each style brings distinct advantages to the team, and understanding these can help leaders assign the right roles to the right people.

The Truck: The Driver: Drivers, like trucks in a sales team, are strong and decisive. They excel in high-pressure situations and handle heavy workloads effortlessly.

Strengths: Decisive: Quickly Make Decisions and Take Action

Decisiveness is the ability to make quick, clear decisions and take action with confidence. This skill is crucial in dynamic environments where rapid responses are often required. Decisive individuals can navigate uncertainty, make informed choices swiftly, and implement solutions effectively.

Key Characteristics:

- **Clarity:** Decisive individuals can assess situations quickly, identifying key factors and potential outcomes.
- **Confidence:** They possess the self-assurance to make decisions without unnecessary hesitation.

- **Action-Oriented:** Once a decision is made, they promptly take steps to implement it.

Goal-Oriented: Focused on Achieving Results and Meeting Targets

Goal orientation refers to a strong focus on achieving specific outcomes and meeting targets. This skill is essential for maintaining motivation, driving progress, and ensuring that efforts are aligned with strategic objectives.

Key Characteristics:

- **Vision:** Goal-oriented individuals have a clear understanding of what they want to achieve.
- **Motivation:** They possess a strong internal drive to pursue their goals.
- **Persistence:** They remain committed to their objectives despite obstacles and setbacks.

Resilient: Handle Stress and Challenges with Determination

Resilience is the ability to withstand and recover from adversity, stress, and challenges. This skill is critical for maintaining mental health and performance in high-pressure environments. Resilient individuals can navigate difficult situations, adapt to change, and emerge stronger.

Key Characteristics:

- **Adaptability:** Resilient individuals can adjust to new circumstances and find solutions in changing environments.
- **Emotional Regulation:** They manage their emotions effectively, preventing stress from overwhelming them.
- **Persistence:** They maintain their efforts despite setbacks, showing determination and endurance.

Weaknesses

- **Impatient**: May become frustrated with delays or obstacles.
- **Insensitive**: Can overlook the feelings and contributions of others.
- **Autocratic**: Their assertiveness can sometimes come across as domineering.

Best Suited For

- **Closing Deals**: Drivers excel in high-stakes situations where decisiveness and persistence are key.
- **Leading Projects**: Their focus and determination make them effective project leaders.

The Van: The Amiable: Amiables in a sales team are akin to vans. They are reliable, cooperative, and great at building relationships. They ensure smooth operations and maintain harmony within the team.

Strengths

- **Empathetic**: Skilled at understanding and responding to clients' needs.
- **Team-Oriented**: Foster a collaborative and supportive work environment.
- **Patient**: Manage stress and conflict with a calm demeanor.

Weaknesses

- **Conflict-Avoidant**: May avoid necessary confrontations or difficult decisions.
- **Indecisive**: Their focus on consensus can lead to delays.

- **Overly Accommodating**: Can prioritize others' needs over their own, leading to burnout.

Best Suited For

- **Customer Relations**: Amiables excel in roles requiring empathy and relationship-building.
- **Team Coordination**: Their collaborative nature helps maintain team cohesion and morale.

The Sports Car: The Expressive: Expressives in a sales team are like sports cars. They are fast, enthusiastic, and innovative. They bring energy and creativity, helping the team stay dynamic and forward-thinking.

Strengths

- **Charismatic**: Engage and inspire clients and team members.
- **Innovative**: Generate creative ideas and solutions.
- **Socially Skilled**: Build networks and relationships with ease.

Weaknesses

- **Disorganized**: May neglect details and organization.
- **Impulsive**: Can make decisions based on emotion rather than logic.
- **Overly Optimistic**: Their enthusiasm can lead to unrealistic expectations.

Best Suited For

- **Networking Events**: Expressives shine in social settings where charisma and enthusiasm are key.
- **Creative Projects**: Their innovation and energy drive creative endeavors and campaigns.

The Importance of Recognizing Differences: Just as you wouldn't use a sports car to haul lumber or a truck to win a race, it's crucial to recognize the different strengths of each social style in your team. Misalignment of roles can lead to frustration and inefficiency, while proper alignment enhances performance and satisfaction.

Leveraging Social Styles in the Sales Team: To maximize the effectiveness of a sales team, leaders should strategically assign roles based on each member's social style. Here are some strategies for leveraging diverse social styles:

Matching Roles to Styles

- **Drivers**: Assign to roles that require quick decision-making and goal-oriented focus, such as closing high-stakes deals or leading sales initiatives.
- **Amiables**: Place in positions where building and maintaining relationships is crucial, such as customer service or team coordination.
- **Expressives**: Utilize in roles that benefit from creativity and social interaction, like networking events or innovative marketing campaigns.

Balancing the Team: Creating a balanced team with a mix of social styles ensures that all strengths are represented and weaknesses are mitigated. For example, pairing a Driver with an Amiable can combine decisiveness with empathy, while an Expressive can bring creativity to a team led by a detail-oriented Analytical.

Effective Communication: Tailoring communication to suit different social styles can improve understanding and collaboration:

- **Drivers**: Be direct and focus on results and objectives.
- **Amiables**: Emphasize harmony and build consensus.
- **Expressives**: Engage with enthusiasm and highlight the big picture.

Case Study: Diverse Sales Team Success: Stellar Sales Inc., a dynamic player in the competitive sales industry, faced significant challenges with team performance. Despite having talented individuals, the lack of role alignment and utilization of team members' strengths hindered their overall effectiveness and efficiency.

Identifying the Problem: Stellar Sales Inc. noticed their team's performance was lagging due to a mismatch between individual strengths and assigned roles. This mismatch led to inefficiencies, missed opportunities, and ultimately, a decrease in overall team performance.

Assessment and Restructuring: To address these challenges, Stellar Sales Inc. conducted a thorough assessment of their team members' social styles and strengths. This assessment revealed distinct social styles among team members, which could be leveraged to optimize team performance.

- **John (Driver):**
- **Previous Role:** Involved in general sales tasks without a specific focus.
- **Revised Role:** Assigned to lead high-stakes sales projects requiring decisive action and goal orientation.
- **Impact:** John's new role resulted in a remarkable 20% increase in closed deals. His ability to make quick decisions and drive toward goals proved instrumental in closing complex sales.
- **Mary (Amiable):**
- **Previous Role:** Engaged in routine sales activities without utilizing her empathetic strengths.
- **Revised Role:** Transitioned to a customer relations role focused on enhancing client satisfaction.

- **Impact:** Mary's role change led to a significant improvement, with client satisfaction scores soaring by 30%. Her empathetic approach and patience played a crucial role in building strong client relationships and resolving customer issues effectively.

Steve (Expressive):

Previous Role: Part of the sales team without specific responsibilities aligned with his expressive personality.

Revised Role: Tasked with leading creative marketing campaigns aimed at boosting brand engagement.

Impact: Steve's shift to leading marketing initiatives resulted in a notable 25% increase in brand engagement. His creativity and ability to connect with audiences effectively translated into successful marketing campaigns that resonated with the target market.

Implementation and Results: The restructuring at Stellar Sales Inc. was not merely about reshuffling roles but aligning responsibilities with individual strengths and social styles. This strategic realignment allowed each team member to leverage their innate abilities more effectively, leading to tangible improvements in key performance indicators:

- **Team Collaboration:** By aligning roles with social styles, Stellar Sales Inc. fostered a more collaborative environment where team members complemented each other's strengths and worked synergistically toward common goals.
- **Performance Metrics:** The measurable impact of the role restructuring was evident in key performance metrics such as closed deals, client satisfaction scores, and brand engagement. These improvements underscored the effectiveness of matching roles with individual strengths.

- **Employee Satisfaction:** Beyond performance metrics, the restructuring also enhanced employee satisfaction and morale. Team members felt more valued and motivated in roles that aligned with their strengths, leading to higher job satisfaction and reduced turnover.

A successful team thrives on diverse personalities with complementary strengths. *By recognizing and leveraging the unique social styles of team members, leaders can create a dynamic and effective team. Just as different vehicles serve different purposes, understanding the distinct capabilities of each social style allows for strategic role alignment, driving the team toward collective success.*

Chinese Food Delivery

As discussed previously, misalignment in the workplace can have detrimental effects on productivity, employee satisfaction, and overall organizational performance. In addition to addressing misalignment, it's important to consider how leveraging positive soft skills can lead to unexpected career opportunities. This chapter will provide a comprehensive guide on evaluating the current alignment of roles within your organization, identifying areas where misalignment may be impacting productivity and morale, and implementing strategies to realign roles for optimal performance. It will also explore how recognizing and utilizing existing soft skills, as demonstrated in Boris's journey from delivering Chinese food to becoming a Senior IT Engineer, can open doors to new career paths.

The Tale of Boris - From Delivering Chinese Food on his Bicycle to Sr. IT Engineer

Back in the 90s, New York City was a buzzing hub of activity, innovation, and relentless ambition. Amidst this whirlwind, I found myself at the helm of the IT department for one of the city's largest advertising companies. As the Director of IT, my days were filled with the challenges and opportunities that came with managing technology in a rapidly evolving industry. It was during this exciting yet tumultuous period that I encountered Boris, a young man whose journey from delivering Chinese food on a bicycle to becoming a Senior Network Engineer would become a testament to the power of determination, hard work, and the right opportunities.

One brisk spring day, Ivan, one of my most dedicated employees, walked into my office with a request that would set off a chain of events leading to an extraordinary story. Ivan was a talented and diligent worker, having joined our team a few years earlier. His work ethic and technical prowess had quickly earned him a place of respect within the company. That day, however, he wasn't there to discuss a project or request time off. He had come to ask if his younger brother, Boris, could intern for me.

Ivan's request took me by surprise. Naturally, my first question was about Boris's experience in IT. Ivan's response was as unexpected as it was intriguing: Boris had no IT experience whatsoever. This raised my curiosity about what Boris did for a living. Ivan explained that Boris was currently delivering Chinese food on his bicycle in Brooklyn. The image of a young man navigating the bustling streets of Brooklyn on a bicycle, braving traffic and weather to make ends meet, painted a vivid picture of resilience and determination.

I delved deeper into their backstory. Both Ivan and Boris had only been in the United States for a few years, having migrated from Russia. Their journey to America was far from straightforward. They had traversed through more than five different countries before finally reaching the US, a testament to their perseverance and desire for a better life. Ivan, being three years older, had managed to secure a better education and had quickly adapted to his new environment. Boris, on the other hand, had taken a different path, one that involved more immediate and practical means of survival.

Understanding the challenges they had faced, I felt a sense of empathy for their situation. I decided to meet Boris to gauge his potential. Setting up the interview, I had no expectations, but I was open to being impressed.

The day of the interview arrived, and as soon as Boris walked into my office, I was struck by his humble demeanor. He was visibly nervous but determined to make a good impression. As we talked, his sincerity and eagerness to learn became evident. He was honest about his lack of experience but expressed a genuine desire to work hard and prove himself. This honesty and humility resonated with me, reminding me of my own early days in the industry when all I had was a passion for technology and a willingness to learn.

I decided to give Boris a chance. I laid out my expectations clearly: he had to be the first one in the office and the last one to leave. He had to give 110% effort, tackling every assignment with enthusiasm and diligence, no matter how trivial it seemed. In return, I promised to teach him about our networks and provide firsthand experience in installing and troubleshooting complex networking protocols.

Boris's progress was inspiring. He absorbed knowledge rapidly, constantly asking questions, seeking feedback, and embracing challenges. His tenacity and determination were palpable, and they began to pay off. Boris's progress was not just about gaining hard skills; it was about growing as a person, building confidence, and forging a path toward a brighter future.

One particularly memorable project involved the installation of a new network infrastructure for our new building. This was no small feat, as it required meticulous planning, coordination, and execution. Boris volunteered to assist, eager to gain hands-on experience. His role started with seemingly menial tasks, such as running cables and setting up workstations, but his attention to detail and willingness to learn quickly earned him more responsibilities.

As the project progressed, Boris's contributions became increasingly significant. He learned to configure routers and switches, troubleshoot connectivity issues, and ensure the security of the network. His problem-solving skills improved with each challenge, and he developed a keen understanding of how various components of the network interacted. By the end of the project, Boris had transformed from a novice into a competent and reliable team member.

His performance did not go unnoticed. Our leadership was impressed with the efficiency and reliability of the new network, and our team received accolades for the successful implementation. Boris's role in the project was a testament to his hard work and dedication, and it further solidified his place within our team.

As summer turned to fall, Boris excitedly shared that he'd received an entry-level networking offer from a major media company. I felt a swell of pride, much like a parent watching their child take their first steps toward independence. Boris's achievement was a testament to his hard work and dedication, and it was immensely satisfying to see him succeed.

Over the years, I kept in touch with Boris. His career trajectory was nothing short of remarkable. Within five years, he had been promoted several times, eventually becoming a Senior Network Engineer for the media company. His success was a powerful reminder of the impact of perseverance, hard work, and the right opportunities.

Reflecting on Boris's journey, I often pondered what made him so successful. It wasn't just his hard skills, though he certainly developed those rapidly. It was his soft skills—his work ethic, his humility, his willingness to learn, and his unwavering determination—that set him apart. Boris had the right attitude and approach, which allowed him to master the hard skills necessary for success in the IT field.

Boris's story vividly illustrates how opportunity and determination can help individuals overcome obstacles and achieve success. His journey from delivering Chinese food on a bicycle in Brooklyn to becoming a Senior Network Engineer is a testament to the resilience and potential within all of us.

Throughout my career, I've encountered many talented individuals, but Boris's story holds a special place in my heart. It reinforces the importance of giving people a chance, even when they lack conventional qualifications. It's about recognizing potential, nurturing it, and watching it flourish.

Alignment Framework

As we delve deeper into the principles and practices of aligning employees with their roles, the following chapters will provide a comprehensive framework designed to ensure that your organization not only achieves optimal role alignment but also maintains this alignment continuously. This framework will address various aspects of role alignment, from the initial hiring process to ongoing assessments and future planning.

It's important to note that while some organizations may already have implemented certain aspects of this framework, the power lies in its comprehensive nature. Each component of the Alignment Framework is designed to work synergistically with the others, creating a holistic approach to role alignment. Whether your organization is starting from scratch or looking to enhance existing practices, the insights and strategies presented in these chapters offer valuable opportunities for improvement and optimization. We encourage you to approach each section with an open mind, considering how it can complement and strengthen your current processes.

Conducting a Role Assessment

In the previous chapters, we've explored the challenges of misalignment through real-life stories like those of Luis, Tony, and Boris. These narratives highlighted the profound impact that proper role alignment can have on individual success and organizational performance. Now, we turn our attention to a systematic approach for identifying and addressing misalignment within your own organization.

While the stories we've shared demonstrate the power of intuitive role assessment and adjustment, many organizations require a more structured method to effectively evaluate and realign their workforce. This chapter provides a comprehensive guide to conducting role assessments, allowing you to apply the insights gained from our earlier discussions in a practical, scalable manner.

As discussed previously, misalignment in the workplace can have detrimental effects on productivity, employee satisfaction, and overall organizational performance. To address this issue effectively, it is essential to conduct a thorough role assessment. This chapter will provide a comprehensive guide on how to evaluate the current alignment of roles within your organization, identify areas where misalignment may be impacting productivity and employee satisfaction, and implement strategies to realign roles for optimal performance.

By following this systematic approach, you'll be better equipped to identify your own 'Luiss' and 'Borises' - employees whose potential may be hidden by misalignment - and create opportunities for them to thrive in roles that match their strengths."

Understanding Role Assessment: Role assessment is a systematic process of evaluating how well employees' roles align with their skills, strengths, and interests. It involves examining the duties and responsibilities of each role, the qualifications and capabilities of the individuals occupying those roles, and the overall impact on organizational performance. The goal is to identify misalignment and develop strategies to ensure that employees are placed in roles that maximize their potential and contribute to the organization's success.

The Importance of Role Assessment: Conducting a role assessment is a fundamental process for organizations striving for excellence and efficiency. It involves evaluating how well employees' roles align with their skills, interests, and the overall objectives of the organization. This assessment has far-reaching implications for productivity, employee satisfaction, organizational performance, training, and career development.

Here's an in-depth look at the importance and benefits of conducting a role assessment:

Maximizing Productivity: Maximizing Productivity is one of the primary benefits of conducting role assessments. When employees are well-aligned with their roles, they are more likely to perform at their best. This alignment leads to increased productivity, higher quality of work, and greater efficiency. Here's how:

- **Optimal Utilization of Skills:** Ensuring that employees are placed in roles that match their skills means that tasks are performed more efficiently and effectively. Employees are able to use their strengths to the fullest, leading to higher productivity.

- **Reduced Mistakes and Errors:** When employees are well-suited for their roles, they make fewer mistakes. This reduction in errors improves overall work quality and reduces the time spent on corrections and rework.

- **Increased Focus and Efficiency:** Employees who understand their roles and responsibilities can focus on their tasks without confusion or misdirection. This clarity leads to streamlined workflows and improved efficiency.

Enhancing Employee Satisfaction: Enhancing Employee Satisfaction is another critical benefit of role assessments. Employees who are in roles that match their skills and interests are more likely to be engaged, motivated, and satisfied with their work. This satisfaction can lead to lower turnover rates and higher overall job satisfaction. Here's why:

- **Increased Engagement:** Employees who feel that their skills are well-utilized and that their work is meaningful are more engaged. This engagement leads to higher motivation and commitment to the organization.

- **Reduced Turnover:** When employees are satisfied with their roles, they are less likely to seek opportunities elsewhere. This retention reduces the costs associated with hiring and training new employees.

- **Positive Work Environment:** High levels of job satisfaction contribute to a positive work environment. Satisfied employees are more likely to collaborate effectively and support their colleagues, fostering a cohesive and productive team.

Improving Organizational Performance: Improving Organizational Performance is a significant outcome of effective role alignment. Proper role alignment ensures that the right people are in the right positions, leading to better decision-making, improved teamwork, and enhanced organizational performance. Here's how:

- **Strategic Decision-Making:** When employees are well-suited to their roles, they are more likely to make informed and strategic decisions that benefit the organization.

- **Enhanced Teamwork:** Role clarity and alignment improve teamwork by ensuring that each team member understands their responsibilities and how they contribute to the team's objectives. This clarity fosters collaboration and reduces conflicts.

- **Increased Innovation:** Employees who are engaged and satisfied with their roles are more likely to contribute innovative ideas. This creativity drives organizational growth and competitiveness.

Identifying Training Needs: Identifying Training Needs is another crucial aspect of role assessments. By evaluating the alignment between employees' skills and their roles, organizations can identify gaps in skills and knowledge. Addressing these gaps through targeted training and development programs is essential for maintaining a competitive and capable workforce. Here's why:

- **Skill Development:** Role assessments highlight areas where employees may need additional training to perform their duties effectively. This identification allows for targeted skill development initiatives.

- **Continuous Improvement:** Regular training keeps employees up-to-date with the latest industry trends and technologies, fostering a culture of continuous improvement.

- **Enhanced Competence:** Targeted training ensures that employees have the necessary skills and knowledge to excel in their roles, leading to improved performance and productivity.

Supporting Career Development: Supporting Career Development is a vital benefit of conducting role assessments. By understanding employees' strengths and interests, organizations can provide opportunities for career growth and advancement. This support leads to higher retention rates and a more skilled workforce. Here's how:

- **Career Pathing:** Role assessments help in creating clear career paths for employees. Understanding their skills and aspirations allows for strategic career planning and progression.

- **Professional Growth:** Providing opportunities for employees to develop new skills and advance in their careers fosters a culture of professional growth. This culture attracts top talent and retains existing employees.

- **Employee Loyalty:** When employees see a clear path for career advancement within the organization, they are more likely to stay and contribute to its success. This loyalty reduces turnover and builds a stable and experienced workforce.

Strategies for Promoting Role Assessments: To conduct a comprehensive role assessment, follow these steps:

1. **Define the Scope and Objectives**
2. **Collect Data**
3. **Analyze Roles and Responsibilities**
4. **Evaluate Employee Skills and Strengths**
5. **Identify Misalignment**
6. **Develop Realignment Strategies**
7. **Implement Changes**
8. **Monitor and Evaluate**

1. **Define the Scope and Objectives:** Before beginning the role assessment, it is essential to define the scope and objectives of the process. This involves identifying the departments, teams, or roles to be assessed and determining the specific goals of the assessment. Common objectives include improving productivity, enhancing

employee satisfaction, reducing turnover rates, and identifying training needs.

Key Components of Defining the Scope and Objectives

Identifying Departments, Teams, or Roles: Determine which areas of the organization will be assessed.

Setting Clear Objectives: Outline specific goals for what the assessment aims to achieve.

Understanding Current Performance Levels: Gather baseline data on current performance metrics.

Determining Key Focus Areas: Identify key areas that need improvement or further development.

Engaging Stakeholders: Involve key stakeholders in defining the scope and objectives to ensure alignment and buy-in.

Example Objective

Improve Productivity:

- Increase sales volume by 20% within six months.
- Reduce the sales cycle time by 15%.
- Improve the lead conversion rate by 10%.

Enhance Employee Satisfaction:

- Increase employee satisfaction scores by 25% in annual surveys.
- Reduce voluntary turnover in the sales department by 30%.
- Achieve a 90% retention rate for top performers.

2. **Collect Data:** Data collection is a critical step in the role assessment process. This involves gathering information on current roles, responsibilities, and employee performance. Data can be collected through various methods.

   Key components of Collect Data
   1. **Job Descriptions**: Review existing job descriptions to understand the duties and responsibilities of each role.
   2. **Performance Reviews**: Analyze past performance reviews to assess employees' strengths, weaknesses, and areas for improvement.
   3. **Employee Surveys**: Conduct surveys to gather feedback from employees about their current roles, job satisfaction, and career aspirations.
   4. **Interviews**: Conduct one-on-one interviews with employees and managers to gain deeper insights into their experiences and perspectives.
   5. **Observation**: Observe employees in their roles to understand how they perform their tasks and interact with colleagues.

   Example Data Collection Methods
   - Review job descriptions for all roles in the sales department.
   - Analyze the last two years of performance reviews for sales team members.
   - Conduct an anonymous survey to gather feedback from sales employees.
   - Interview sales managers and team leaders to understand their perspectives.
   - Observe sales team members during client meetings and internal discussions.

3. **Analyze Roles and Responsibilities:** Once data is collected, the next step is to analyze the roles and responsibilities of each position. This involves examining the tasks and duties assigned to each role, the skills and qualifications required, and the expected outcomes. The goal is to identify any discrepancies between the role requirements and the actual capabilities of the employees.

   Key components of Analyze Roles and Responsibilities

   1. **Compare Job Descriptions with Actual Duties**: Ensure that job descriptions accurately reflect the tasks and responsibilities performed by employees. Identify any discrepancies and update job descriptions as needed.

   2. **Assess Role Requirements**: Evaluate the skills, qualifications, and experience required for each role. Compare these requirements with the actual capabilities of the employees currently occupying these roles.

   Example Analysis

   - Compare the job description of a sales representative with the actual tasks performed by current sales representatives.
   - Assess the skills and qualifications required for a sales manager and compare them with the skills and experience of the current sales managers.

4. **Evaluate Employee Skills and Strengths:** To determine how well employees align with their roles, it is essential to evaluate their skills, strengths, and interests. This can be done through various methods.

   Key Components of Evaluating Employee Skills and Strengths

   1. **Skill Assessments**: Conduct skill assessments to evaluate employees' competencies and identify areas where they excel.

2. **Strengths-Based Assessments**: Use tools like the CliftonStrengths assessment to identify employees' top strengths and how they can be leveraged in their roles.

3. **Performance Data**: Analyze performance data to identify employees who consistently excel in their tasks and responsibilities.

4. **Employee Feedback**: Gather feedback from employees about their skills, interests, and career aspirations.

Example Evaluation Methods:

- Conduct a skill assessment for all sales team members to evaluate their competencies.
- Use the CliftonStrengths assessment to identify the top strengths of sales representatives.
- Analyze performance data to identify high-performing sales representatives.
- Gather feedback from sales employees about their skills and career goals.

5. **Identify Misalignment: Once roles and employees have been evaluated, the next step is to identify areas of misalignment.** This involves comparing the requirements of each role with the skills, strengths, and interests of the employees currently occupying these roles. Misalignment can occur in several ways.

Key Components of Identity Misalignment

1. **Skill Gaps**: Employees may lack the necessary skills or qualifications for their roles.

2. **Underutilization of Strengths**: Employees' strengths and talents may not be fully utilized in their current roles.

3. **Lack of Interest or Engagement**: Employees may not be interested or engaged in their current tasks and responsibilities.

4. **Misfit with Role Requirements**: Employees may not fit well with the specific requirements of their roles, such as the need for strong interpersonal skills or technical expertise.

Example Misalignment Identification

- Identify sales representatives who lack the necessary technical knowledge for their roles.
- Identify sales managers whose strengths in leadership and team management are underutilized.
- Identify sales team members who express a lack of interest in their current tasks and responsibilities.
- Identify sales employees who do not fit well with the customer-facing requirements of their roles.

6. **Develop Realignment Strategies:** After identifying areas of misalignment, the next step is to develop strategies to realign roles and employees. This involves creating a plan to address skill gaps, leverage employees' strengths, and ensure that employees are placed in roles that match their skills and interests.

Key Components of Developing Realignment Strategies

1. **Role Redefinition**: Redefine roles and responsibilities to better align with employees' skills and strengths.

2. **Training and Development**: Implement targeted training and development programs to address skill gaps and enhance employees' competencies.

3. **Role Transition**: Transition employees to roles that better match their skills, strengths, and interests.

4. **Job Enrichment**: Enrich current roles by adding tasks and responsibilities that align with employees' strengths and interests.

5. **Mentorship and Coaching**: Provide mentorship and coaching to support employees in their new roles and help them succeed.

Example Realignment Strategies

- Redefine the role of sales representatives to include more customer interaction for those with strong interpersonal skills.

- Implement a technical training program for sales representatives to enhance their technical knowledge.

- Transition a sales manager with strong leadership skills to a team leader role to better utilize their strengths.

- Enrich the role of a sales representative with additional responsibilities in client relationship management.

- Provide coaching to support sales employees transitioning to new roles.

7. **Implement Changes: Implement changes through careful planning and clear communication, ensuring all stakeholders are informed and involved**

Key Components of Implement Changes

1. **Communicate the Plan**: Clearly communicate the realignment plan to all employees and stakeholders. Explain the reasons for the changes and how they will benefit the organization and employees.

2. **Provide Support**: Offer support and resources to help employees transition to their new roles. This may include training, mentorship, and ongoing feedback.

3. **Monitor Progress**: Monitor the progress of the realignment process to ensure that it is on track and that employees are adjusting well to their new roles.

4. **Address Challenges**: Be prepared to address any challenges or resistance that may arise during the implementation process. Provide additional support as needed to help employees succeed.

Example Implementation Steps

- Hold a meeting with the sales team to explain the realignment plan and its benefits.
- Provide training and mentorship to support sales representatives transitioning to new roles.
- Monitor the progress of sales team members in their new roles and provide ongoing feedback.
- Address any challenges or concerns raised by sales employees during the transition process.

8. **Monitor and Evaluate**: After implementing the changes, it is essential to monitor and evaluate the impact of the realignment process. This involves assessing the effectiveness of the changes and making any necessary adjustments.

Key Components of Monitor and Evaluate

1. **Evaluate Performance**: Assess the performance of employees in their new roles to determine if the realignment has improved productivity and job satisfaction.

2. **Gather Feedback**: Collect feedback from employees and managers about their experiences with the realignment process and its impact on their roles.

3. **Make Adjustments**: Based on the evaluation and feedback, make any necessary adjustments to the realignment plan to ensure its continued success.

4. **Continuous Improvement**: Continuously monitor and evaluate role alignment to ensure that employees remain well-suited to their roles as the organization evolves.

Example Monitoring and Evaluation

- Evaluate the performance of sales representatives in their new roles after six months.
- Gather feedback from sales employees and managers about their experiences with the realignment process.
- Make adjustments to the realignment plan based on performance data and feedback.
- Continuously monitor role alignment to ensure ongoing productivity and job satisfaction.

The Long-Term Benefits of Conducting a Role Assessment

Conducting regular role assessments is essential for organizations aiming to maximize productivity, enhance employee satisfaction, and improve overall performance. By ensuring that employees are well-aligned with their roles, organizations can create a more efficient, motivated, and resilient workforce, leading to sustained success and growth.

Maximizing Productivity

Optimal Utilization of Skills: Regular role assessments help ensure that employees are placed in roles that match their skills and strengths. This alignment allows employees to perform tasks more efficiently and effectively, leading to higher productivity.

Reduced Mistakes and Errors: When employees' skills and roles are well-matched, the likelihood of mistakes and errors decreases. This not only improves the quality of work but also reduces the time spent on corrections and rework, enhancing overall efficiency.

Increased Focus and Efficiency: Role clarity achieved through assessments allows employees to focus on their tasks without confusion or misdirection. This focus leads to streamlined workflows, better time management, and increased efficiency.

Enhancing Employee Satisfaction

Increased Engagement: Employees who feel that their skills are well-utilized and that their work is meaningful are more engaged. This engagement leads to higher motivation and commitment to the organization.

Reduced Turnover: Satisfied employees are less likely to seek opportunities elsewhere, reducing turnover rates. Lower turnover minimizes the costs associated with hiring and training new employees and maintains organizational stability.

Positive Work Environment: High levels of job satisfaction contribute to a positive work environment. Satisfied employees are more likely to collaborate effectively and support their colleagues, fostering a cohesive and productive team.

Improving Organizational Performance

Strategic Decision-Making: When employees are well-suited to their roles, they are more likely to make informed and strategic decisions that benefit the organization. Role alignment ensures that employees are equipped to handle their responsibilities effectively.

Enhanced Teamwork: Role clarity and alignment improve teamwork by ensuring that each team member understands their responsibilities and how they contribute to the team's objectives. This clarity fosters collaboration and reduces conflicts.

Increased Innovation: Engaged and satisfied employees are more likely to contribute innovative ideas. This creativity drives organizational growth and competitiveness, leading to better performance and long-term success.

Identifying Training Needs

Targeted Skill Development: Role assessments highlight areas where employees may need additional training to perform their duties effectively. This identification allows for targeted skill development initiatives, ensuring that training efforts are focused and impactful.

Continuous Improvement: Regular training keeps employees up-to-date with the latest industry trends and technologies, fostering a culture of continuous improvement. This ongoing development helps maintain a competitive and capable workforce.

Enhanced Competence: Targeted training ensures that employees have the necessary skills and knowledge to excel in their roles. This competence leads to improved performance, productivity, and job satisfaction.

Supporting Career Development

Career Pathing: Role assessments help in creating clear career paths for employees. Understanding their skills and aspirations allows for strategic career planning and progression, which is essential for retaining top talent.

Professional Growth: Providing opportunities for employees to develop new skills and advance in their careers fosters a culture of professional growth. This culture attracts top talent and retains existing employees, enhancing the organization's overall capabilities.

Employee Loyalty: When employees see a clear path for career advancement within the organization, they are more likely to stay and contribute to its success. This loyalty reduces turnover and builds a stable and experienced workforce.

Conducting a role assessment is a critical step in addressing misalignment within an organization. By evaluating the current alignment of roles, identifying areas of misalignment, and implementing targeted strategies to realign roles, organizations can improve productivity, enhance employee satisfaction, and achieve better overall performance. This chapter has provided a comprehensive guide on how to conduct a role assessment, including defining the scope and objectives, collecting data, analyzing roles and responsibilities, evaluating employee skills and strengths, identifying misalignment, developing realignment strategies, implementing changes, and monitoring and evaluating the impact. By following these steps, organizations can ensure that employees are placed in roles that maximize their potential and contribute to the organization's success.

The Importance of Ongoing Performance Assessments

In the previous chapter, we explored the process of conducting initial role assessments to identify and address misalignment within an organization. While these assessments provide a crucial starting point, the dynamic nature of both individuals and organizations necessitates a continuous evaluation process. This chapter builds upon the foundation of role assessments by examining the importance of ongoing performance assessments.

Ongoing performance assessments are crucial in ensuring that employees are well-aligned with their roles. These assessments not only help in evaluating performance metrics but also play a significant role in identifying issues related to employee engagement and job satisfaction. By regularly monitoring and providing feedback, organizations can address misalignment issues early, thereby enhancing productivity and retaining top talent. This chapter will delve into the importance of ongoing performance assessments, the key elements to focus on, and strategies for effective implementation.

The Need for Ongoing Performance Assessments: Ongoing performance assessments play a crucial role in maintaining and enhancing the overall productivity, engagement, and alignment of employees within an organization. These assessments, conducted regularly, provide multiple benefits that contribute to both individual and organizational growth. Here's an in-depth exploration of why ongoing performance assessments are essential and how they contribute to organizational success.

Continuous Improvement: Continuous Improvement is a fundamental benefit of regular performance assessments. These assessments provide ongoing opportunities for employees to receive feedback, refine their skills, and enhance their performance. Here's how continuous improvement is fostered through ongoing performance assessments:

- **Regular Feedback:** Frequent assessments ensure that employees receive timely and constructive feedback. This immediate feedback allows employees to make adjustments and improvements in their performance without delay, fostering a culture of continuous learning and growth.

- **Skill Development:** Ongoing assessments help identify areas where employees may need additional training or development. This targeted approach ensures that employees continually develop their skills, keeping pace with the evolving demands of their roles and the industry.

- **Performance Benchmarks:** Regular assessments establish clear performance benchmarks. Employees can track their progress against these benchmarks, setting personal goals for improvement and striving to achieve higher standards of performance.

- **Motivation and Morale:** Knowing that their performance will be regularly assessed and acknowledged motivates employees to consistently perform at their best. This regular recognition of effort and achievement boosts morale and encourages a positive work environment.

Early Identification of Issues: Early Identification of Issues is another critical advantage of ongoing performance assessments. By consistently evaluating performance, organizations can detect and address potential misalignment issues before they escalate into significant problems. Here's how this early identification process works:

- **Proactive Problem Solving:** Regular assessments enable managers to spot performance issues early. This proactive approach allows for timely interventions, such as additional training, mentoring, or changes in job responsibilities, to address and resolve issues before they affect overall productivity.

- **Preventing Escalation:** Identifying issues early prevents minor performance problems from escalating into major disruptions. This early intervention helps maintain a smooth workflow and prevents the negative impact on team dynamics and organizational efficiency.

- **Employee Support:** Early detection of performance issues ensures that employees receive the support they need to overcome challenges. This support can include additional resources, one-on-one coaching, or adjustments in workload to help employees improve their performance.

- **Goal Realignment:** Regular assessments help ensure that employees' goals remain aligned with organizational objectives. If any misalignment is detected, corrective measures can be taken promptly to realign goals and expectations.

Enhanced Employee Engagement: Enhanced Employee Engagement is a significant benefit of regular performance assessments. Continuous feedback and recognition keep employees engaged, motivated, and satisfied with their jobs. Here's how ongoing assessments contribute to enhanced employee engagement:

- **Clear Communication:** Regular performance assessments provide a platform for open and transparent communication between employees and managers. This ongoing dialogue ensures that employees understand what is expected of them and how their efforts contribute to the organization's success.

- **Recognition and Reward:** Frequent assessments provide opportunities to recognize and reward employees for their achievements. This recognition fosters a sense of accomplishment and motivates employees to maintain high performance levels.

- **Goal Setting and Achievement:** Ongoing assessments involve setting and reviewing individual goals. This process helps employees stay focused and motivated as they work toward achieving their personal and professional objectives.

- **Employee Involvement:** Regular assessments involve employees in their performance evaluation process. This involvement gives employees a sense of ownership and accountability for their performance, enhancing their engagement and commitment to their roles.

Alignment with Organizational Goals: Alignment with Organizational Goals is a crucial benefit of ongoing performance assessments. These assessments ensure that employees' activities and efforts are consistently aligned with the broader organizational objectives. Here's how alignment is achieved through regular performance assessments:

- **Clear Objectives:** Regular assessments help communicate the organization's goals and objectives to employees. This clear communication ensures that employees understand how their roles and responsibilities contribute to the overall success of the organization.

- **Strategic Focus:** Ongoing assessments ensure that employees stay focused on strategic priorities. By aligning individual goals with organizational objectives, employees can prioritize their tasks and efforts to support the company's mission and vision.

- **Performance Metrics:** Regular assessments use performance metrics to track progress toward organizational goals. These metrics provide a quantifiable measure of how well employees are contributing to the achievement of these goals.

- **Adjustments and Realignments:** Regular performance assessments allow for adjustments and realignments of goals as needed. If organizational priorities change, these assessments ensure that employees' goals and efforts are updated to reflect the new direction.

Strategies for Promoting Effective Performance Assessments: To effectively identify and address misalignment issues, performance assessments should focus on several key elements:

1. Performance Metrics
2. Employee Engagement
3. Job Satisfaction
4. Skill Development
5. Goal Alignment

1. **Performance Metrics:** Performance metrics are quantifiable measures that provide a clear and objective way to evaluate an employee's effectiveness in their role. By establishing specific key performance indicators (KPIs) aligned with the organization's goals, businesses can gain valuable insights into employee performance and organizational health. Regularly reviewing these metrics helps in several crucial areas, ensuring that employees remain focused and aligned with the company's strategic objectives.

Key Components of Performance Metrics

Tracking Progress and Identifying Areas for Improvement: One of the primary benefits of performance metrics is the ability to track an employee's progress over time. By continuously monitoring these metrics, managers and employees can identify trends and patterns in performance, which helps in recognizing both strengths and areas that need improvement. This continuous tracking allows for proactive management and timely interventions to support employee development.

For example, if a sales representative consistently meets or exceeds their sales targets, it indicates strong performance and effectiveness in their role. Conversely, if they frequently fall short of these targets, it may signal the need for additional training or support. Similarly, tracking customer satisfaction scores can reveal insights into how well customer service teams are meeting client expectations and where improvements might be necessary.

Setting Realistic and Achievable Goals: Performance metrics provide a concrete basis for setting realistic and achievable goals. By understanding current performance levels, managers can set targets that challenge employees while still being attainable. This balance is crucial for maintaining motivation and ensuring continuous improvement.

For instance, if a project manager has a history of completing 80% of projects on time, setting a goal to increase this rate to 90% within the next quarter is both challenging and achievable. This goal-setting process is informed by past performance data, making it grounded in reality rather than arbitrary expectations. Setting clear, measurable goals also allows employees to understand what is expected of them and how they can contribute to the organization's success.

Providing a Basis for Constructive Feedback: Constructive feedback is essential for employee development and performance improvement. Performance metrics offer an objective foundation for these feedback conversations, helping to depersonalize critiques and focus on specific, measurable outcomes.

When discussing performance with an employee, referencing concrete metrics such as sales targets or project completion rates makes the feedback more tangible and actionable. For example, a manager can say, "You've met your sales target 70% of the time this quarter, which is a solid effort. Let's work on strategies to increase this to 85% next quarter." This type of feedback is clear, objective, and directed toward future improvement, fostering a positive and productive dialogue.

Example Metrics and Their Applications

Different roles within an organization require different performance metrics to accurately measure effectiveness. Here are some example metrics for various roles:

Sales Targets for Sales Teams: Sales targets are a common performance metric for sales teams. These targets typically include specific goals for the number of units sold, revenue generated, or new customers acquired within a given timeframe.

- **Units Sold**: The total number of products or services sold. This metric helps assess the volume of sales activity.

- **Revenue Generated**: The total income from sales, providing insight into the financial impact of sales efforts.

- **New Customers Acquired**: The number of new clients brought on board, indicating the team's success in expanding the customer base.

By setting and tracking these targets, sales managers can gauge individual and team performance, identify top performers, and determine areas needing improvement.

Customer Satisfaction Scores for Customer Service Teams: Customer satisfaction scores (CSAT) are a vital metric for customer service teams, reflecting how well the team meets customer needs and expectations.

- **CSAT Surveys**: Customers rate their satisfaction with a recent service interaction, typically on a scale from 1 to 5. High scores indicate successful service delivery.

- **Net Promoter Score (NPS)**: Measures customer loyalty by asking how likely customers are to recommend the company to others. A high NPS suggests strong customer satisfaction and loyalty.

- **Resolution Time**: The average time taken to resolve customer issues. Faster resolution times generally correlate with higher satisfaction levels.

Project Completion Rates for Project Managers: Project completion rates are a key metric for project managers, reflecting the efficiency and effectiveness of project execution.

- **On-Time Completion**: The percentage of projects completed by the deadline. High rates suggest effective time management and project planning.

- **Budget Adherence**: The percentage of projects completed within the allocated budget. Staying within budget indicates good financial management and resource allocation.

- **Scope Achievement**: The extent to which project goals and deliverables are met. High achievement rates indicate successful project planning and execution.

2. **Employee Engagement: A Measure of Commitment and Motivation: Employee engagement measures commitment and motivation to work and the organization.** High engagement often leads to better productivity and lower turnover.. Assessing engagement involves multiple strategies to gauge employee sentiments, participation, and day-to-day interactions.

Key Components of Employee Engagement

Regular Surveys and Feedback Sessions: Conducting regular surveys and feedback sessions is crucial for understanding employee engagement levels. These tools provide employees with a platform to express their thoughts, concerns, and suggestions, fostering a culture of openness and transparency.

- **Engagement Surveys**: Regularly scheduled surveys can measure various aspects of engagement, such as job satisfaction, commitment to the organization, and overall morale.

- **Feedback Sessions**: One-on-one or group feedback sessions allow for more detailed discussions about engagement and provide an opportunity for employees to voice their opinions directly.

I challenge you to not only think about employee engagement at the organization level but also at the individual employee level for those targeted employees.

Monitoring Participation in Team Activities and Company Events: Employee engagement can also be assessed by monitoring participation rates in team activities and company events. High participation levels often indicate strong engagement and a positive organizational culture.

- **Team Activities**: Participation in team-building exercises, workshops, and training sessions can provide insights into engagement levels.

- **Company Events**: Attendance at social events, company meetings, and other gatherings can reflect how connected employees feel to the organization.

Observing Day-to-Day Interactions and Enthusiasm for Tasks: Day-to-day interactions and enthusiasm for tasks are strong indicators of employee engagement. Observing how employees interact with each other, approach their work, and demonstrate commitment can provide valuable qualitative data.

- **Interactions**: Positive interactions, collaboration, and teamwork suggest high engagement.
- **Enthusiasm**: An employee's enthusiasm for their tasks, willingness to go above and beyond, and proactive attitude are signs of strong engagement.

Example Employee Engagement

Boost Commitment:

- Increase employee Net Promoter Score (eNPS) by 20%.
- Achieve a 90% participation rate in employee engagement surveys.
- Improve retention rates by reducing voluntary turnover by 15%.

Enhance Motivation:

- Raise employee satisfaction scores by 25% in annual surveys.
- Increase participation in professional development programs by 30%.
- Improve overall team performance metrics by 10%.

3. **Job Satisfaction: Understanding Employee Contentment:** Job satisfaction refers to how content employees are with their roles, responsibilities, and work environment. Satisfied employees are more likely to stay with the organization and perform well. Assessing job satisfaction involves several methods to gain a comprehensive understanding of employee experiences and concerns.

The Importance of Ongoing Performance Assessments

Key components of Job Satisfaction

Conducting Regular Job Satisfaction Surveys: Regular job satisfaction surveys are essential for gauging how employees feel about their jobs. These surveys should cover various aspects of job satisfaction, including work environment, role clarity, compensation, and career development opportunities.

- **Satisfaction Surveys**: These can be conducted annually or semi-annually to track changes and trends in job satisfaction over time.

- **Pulse Surveys**: Shorter, more frequent surveys can provide real-time insights into employee satisfaction and quickly identify any emerging issues.

Holding One-on-One Meetings: One-on-one meetings between employees and managers provide an opportunity to discuss individual experiences and concerns in detail. These meetings can help identify specific factors affecting job satisfaction and allow for personalized support and interventions.

- **Regular Check-ins**: Scheduled check-ins create a consistent platform for employees to share their thoughts and for managers to offer guidance and support.

- **Open Dialogue**: Encouraging open and honest dialogue helps build trust and ensures that employees feel heard and valued.

Analyzing Turnover Rates and Reasons for Employee Departures: Analyzing turnover rates and reasons for employee departures can provide insights into job satisfaction levels within the organization. Understanding why employees leave can highlight systemic issues that need to be addressed to improve overall satisfaction.

- **Turnover Analysis**: Regularly review turnover data to identify patterns and trends.

- **Exit Interviews**: Conduct thorough exit interviews to gather feedback on why employees are leaving and what could be improved.

Example of Job Satisfaction

Enhance Role Contentment:

- Improve job satisfaction scores by 25% in annual surveys.
- Reduce employee turnover rates by 20%.
- Achieve a 90% completion rate for annual satisfaction surveys.

Improve Work Environment:

- Increase positive feedback on the work environment in surveys by 30%.
- Enhance facilities and workplace amenities based on employee feedback.
- Raise overall employee well-being scores by 20%.

4. **Skill Development: Fostering Continuous Learning and Growth:** Ongoing performance assessments should also focus on the development of employees' skills and competencies. This helps in identifying training needs and career development opportunities, ensuring that employees continue to grow and contribute to the organization's success.

Key components of Skill Development

Regularly Reviewing Employee Training and Development Progress: Regular reviews of employee training and development progress are essential for tracking skill enhancement and identifying areas that require further attention.

- **Training Progress Reviews**: Schedule periodic reviews to assess the completion and effectiveness of training programs.
- **Development Plans**: Create and review individual development plans to ensure that employees are on track with their career growth.

Identifying Skill Gaps and Providing Targeted Training Programs: Identifying skill gaps through performance assessments and providing targeted training programs can help bridge these gaps, enhancing overall competency levels within the organization.

- **Skill Assessments**: Conduct regular skill assessments to identify gaps and areas for improvement.
- **Targeted Training**: Develop and offer training programs specifically designed to address identified skill gaps.

Encouraging Continuous Learning and Professional Growth: Encouraging a culture of continuous learning and professional growth ensures that employees remain engaged and motivated to improve their skills.

- **Learning Opportunities**: Provide access to a variety of learning resources, such as online courses, workshops, and seminars.
- **Growth Incentives**: Offer incentives for employees who actively engage in professional development activities.

Example of Skill Development

Identify and Address Skill Gaps:

- Conduct skills assessments to identify gaps in 100% of the workforce annually.

- Develop targeted training programs to address identified gaps, aiming for a 90% completion rate.
- Improve skill proficiency scores by 25% across the organization.

Promote Continuous Learning:

- Increase employee participation in professional development programs by 40%.
- Ensure that 85% of employees engage in at least one learning activity per quarter.
- Achieve a 95% satisfaction rate with training programs offered.

5. **Goal Alignment: Ensuring Strategic Focus and Performance: Aligning employee goals with organizational objectives is crucial for success. Regular reviews help maintain focus and drive performance**

Key components of Goal Alignment

Setting and Reviewing Individual and Team Goals: Setting and regularly reviewing individual and team goals ensures that everyone is working toward the same strategic objectives.

- **Goal Setting**: Involve employees in the goal-setting process to ensure that their goals are meaningful and aligned with organizational priorities.
- **Regular Reviews**: Schedule regular reviews to assess progress and make necessary adjustments.

Ensuring Goals are SMART: SMART goals (Specific, Measurable, Achievable, Relevant, Time-bound) provide a clear framework for setting and achieving objectives.

- **Specific**: Clearly define what is to be achieved.

- **Measurable**: Establish criteria for measuring progress and success.
- **Achievable**: Ensure that goals are realistic and attainable.
- **Relevant**: Align goals with broader organizational objectives.
- **Time-bound**: Set a clear timeline for achieving the goals.

Aligning Employee Performance with Organizational Strategies: Aligning employee performance with organizational strategies ensures that individual efforts contribute to the overall success of the company.

- **Strategic Alignment**: Ensure that employee goals and performance metrics support the company's strategic objectives.
- **Performance Reviews**: Use performance reviews to assess how well employees' efforts align with organizational strategies.

Strategies for Effective Implementation: Implementing ongoing performance assessments requires a structured approach and commitment from both management and employees. Here are some strategies for effective implementation:

Foster a Feedback Culture: Creating a culture that values and encourages feedback is essential for effective performance assessments.

- **Open Communication**: Encourage **open** and **honest** communication between employees and managers.
- **Regular Feedback**: Provide regular, constructive feedback that focuses on both strengths and areas for improvement.
- **Recognition**: Recognize and reward achievements to motivate and engage employees.

Utilize Technology for Assessments: Technology can streamline the performance assessment process and provide valuable insights.

- **Performance Management Software**: Use software to track and analyze performance data.

- **Engagement Platforms**: Implement platforms for conducting surveys and gathering feedback.

- **Learning Management Systems**: Utilize online training platforms for continuous skill development.

Train Managers and Employees: Proper training ensures that both managers and employees understand the importance of ongoing performance assessments and how to conduct them effectively.

- **Communication Training**: Offer workshops on effective communication and feedback.

- **Goal Setting Training**: Provide seminars on setting and achieving SMART goals.

- **Assessment Tools Training**: Conduct sessions on using performance management and engagement tools.

Monitor and Review the Process: Continuous monitoring and regular reviews of the performance assessment process are essential to ensure its effectiveness.

- **Regular Reviews**: Schedule quarterly reviews of the performance assessment framework.

- **Data Analysis**: Analyze survey results and feedback data to identify patterns and issues.

- **Focus Groups**: Hold focus groups with employees and managers to gather insights and suggestions.

Example of Goal Alignment

Set Clear and Aligned Goals:

- Define SMART (Specific, Measurable, Achievable, Relevant, Time-bound) goals for 100% of employees that align with organizational objectives.
- Ensure that 90% of individual goals are directly linked to the company's strategic priorities.
- Increase the alignment score between individual and organizational goals by 20% annually.

Regularly Review and Adjust Goals:

- Conduct quarterly reviews to assess the alignment and progress of goals.
- Achieve a 95% participation rate in goal review meetings.
- Implement necessary adjustments to goals within two weeks of each review.

Enhance Communication and Transparency:

- Ensure that 85% of employees understand how their goals contribute to organizational success.
- Improve the frequency and quality of communication about goals and progress through monthly updates.
- Increase employee satisfaction with goal-setting processes by 30%.

Monitor and Measure Performance:

- Use performance metrics to track progress toward individual and organizational goals.
- Achieve a 90% accuracy rate in performance tracking and reporting.
- Provide timely feedback to 100% of employees on their progress.

The Long-Term Benefits of Ongoing Performance Assessments

Implementing ongoing performance assessments provides substantial long-term benefits for both employees and the organization as a whole. These assessments foster a culture of continuous improvement, enhance employee engagement, and ensure alignment with organizational goals, ultimately driving sustained success and growth.

Continuous Improvement and Skill Development

Fostering a Learning Culture: Ongoing performance assessments promote a culture of continuous learning and improvement. Regular feedback and evaluations encourage employees to continually develop their skills, adapt to new challenges, and strive for higher levels of performance.

Addressing Skill Gaps: By regularly assessing performance, organizations can identify skill gaps and provide targeted training and development opportunities. This proactive approach ensures that employees have the necessary skills to meet evolving job requirements and industry standards, enhancing overall competency and productivity.

Enhanced Adaptability: Continuous improvement through regular assessments helps employees become more adaptable and resilient. As they receive ongoing feedback and engage in continuous learning, they are better prepared to handle changes and new challenges, contributing to a more agile and responsive organization.

Increased Employee Engagement and Retention

Higher Engagement Levels: Regular performance assessments keep employees engaged by providing them with clear goals, consistent feedback, and recognition of their achievements. Engaged employees are more motivated, committed, and enthusiastic about their work, leading to higher levels of job satisfaction and productivity.

Personal and Professional Growth: Ongoing assessments support employees' personal and professional growth by identifying areas for development and providing opportunities for advancement. When employees see a clear path for career progression and receive the necessary support to achieve their goals, they are more likely to remain loyal to the organization.

Reduced Turnover Rates: High levels of employee engagement and satisfaction contribute to lower turnover rates. By fostering a positive work environment and addressing performance issues proactively, organizations can retain their top talent, reducing the costs and disruptions associated with high turnover.

Enhanced Organizational Performance

Strategic Alignment: Regular performance assessments ensure that individual goals and activities are aligned with the organization's strategic objectives. This alignment drives a cohesive effort toward achieving the company's mission and vision, enhancing overall organizational performance.

Improved Decision-Making: With ongoing assessments, managers have access to up-to-date performance data, enabling them to make informed decisions. This data-driven approach helps identify trends, anticipate challenges, and allocate resources more effectively, leading to better strategic planning and execution.

Increased Accountability: Continuous performance evaluations establish a culture of accountability. Employees are held responsible for their performance, and managers are accountable for providing the necessary support and resources. This mutual accountability drives higher performance standards and a stronger commitment to achieving organizational goals.

Enhanced Employee Well-Being

Timely Support and Intervention: Regular assessments allow for early identification of performance issues and provide timely support and intervention. This proactive approach prevents minor problems from escalating into major issues, reducing stress and enhancing employee well-being.

Recognition and Reward: Ongoing performance assessments provide opportunities for recognizing and rewarding employees' efforts and achievements. Regular recognition boosts morale, fosters a positive work environment, and reinforces desired behaviors, contributing to overall employee well-being.

Work-Life Balance: By identifying workload imbalances and performance challenges, ongoing assessments help managers address issues that may impact employees' work-life balance. Ensuring that employees are not overburdened and have the support they need enhances their overall quality of life and job satisfaction.

Long-Term Organizational Growth

Sustained Competitive Advantage: Organizations that invest in ongoing performance assessments are better positioned for long-term success. Continuous improvement, skill development, and strategic alignment contribute to sustained competitive advantage, enabling the organization to adapt to market changes and stay ahead of competitors.

Building a High-Performance Culture: Regular performance evaluations foster a high-performance culture where excellence is the norm. Employees are motivated to perform at their best, and the organization continuously strives for improvement and innovation, driving long-term growth and success.

Enhanced Reputation: Organizations that prioritize ongoing performance assessments and employee development build a reputation as employers of choice. This positive reputation attracts top talent, fosters customer trust, and enhances the organization's brand image, contributing to long-term success.

Regular performance assessments are key to identifying and addressing misalignment. By evaluating metrics, engagement, satisfaction, skills, and goals, organizations ensure employees are in suitable roles and motivated to excel.. *Implementing a comprehensive assessment framework, fostering a feedback culture, utilizing technology, training managers and employees, and continuously monitoring the process are essential strategies for effective performance assessments. Through regular evaluations and feedback, organizations can enhance productivity, retain top talent, and achieve long-term success.*

Implement Comprehensive Hiring Practices

Effective hiring practices are the cornerstone of building a successful organization. Ensuring that new hires are well-aligned with their roles from the outset can significantly impact productivity, employee satisfaction, and retention. This chapter explores the importance of comprehensive hiring practices, the key elements involved, and actionable steps to enhance your hiring process to ensure candidates' skills, strengths, and cultural fit align with your organization's needs.

The Importance of Comprehensive Hiring Practices: Comprehensive hiring practices are crucial for building a capable, cohesive, and committed workforce. Here's an in-depth look at why these practices are essential and how they benefit organizations.

Ensuring Role Alignment: One of the primary goals of comprehensive hiring practices is to ensure role alignment, meaning that the candidates selected for a job have the skills, experience, and strengths that match the requirements of the role.

- **Accurate Job Descriptions:** Detailed job descriptions are vital as they help potential candidates understand what is expected of them. This clarity ensures that applicants self-select for roles where they believe they can succeed.

- **Skill Assessments:** Incorporating skill assessments in the hiring process allows employers to objectively evaluate a candidate's abilities. This helps in identifying candidates who not only have the necessary qualifications but also the specific skills required for the job.

- **Behavioral Interviews:** Using behavioral interview techniques helps in assessing whether candidates have demonstrated the required competencies in their past roles. This predictive method increases the likelihood of selecting candidates who will perform well in the new role.

- **Role-Specific Scenarios:** Presenting candidates with role-specific scenarios during the interview process can help gauge their problem-solving abilities and their approach to real-world challenges they would face in the role.

Ensuring role alignment from the beginning not only increases the chances of job performance but also reduces the time and resources spent on training and development to bring new hires up to speed.

Reducing Turnover: Employee turnover can be costly and disruptive. Comprehensive hiring practices help in reducing turnover by ensuring that new hires are a good fit for their roles and the organization.

- **Cultural Fit Assessments:** Evaluating whether a candidate aligns with the organizational culture can reduce turnover. Employees who fit well with the company culture are more likely to stay and thrive in the organization.

- **Realistic Job Previews:** Providing candidates with a realistic job preview, including potential challenges and day-to-day responsibilities, ensures that they have a clear understanding of what the job entails. This transparency helps in managing expectations and reducing the likelihood of early turnover.

- **Probationary Periods:** Implementing a probationary period allows both the employer and the new hire to assess fit and performance before making a long-term commitment. This period can act as a safety net to ensure mutual satisfaction.

By focusing on reducing turnover through these methods, organizations can save on the costs associated with hiring and training new employees, as well as minimize the disruption to operations.

Enhancing Productivity: Productivity is closely linked to how well employees are suited to their roles. When employees have the right skills and are engaged in work that plays to their strengths, productivity naturally increases.

- **Targeted Recruitment:** Using targeted recruitment strategies to find candidates with the specific skills and experience needed for the role ensures that new hires can hit the ground running and contribute quickly.

- **Onboarding Programs:** Comprehensive onboarding programs that provide new hires with the tools, knowledge, and support they need to succeed can significantly boost productivity. Effective onboarding includes training on company systems, processes, and culture.

- **Continuous Development:** Offering continuous development opportunities ensures that employees keep improving and remain productive over time. This includes regular training sessions, workshops, and access to learning resources.

Enhancing productivity through comprehensive hiring practices ensures that the organization remains competitive and can achieve its strategic goals.

Fostering Cultural Fit: Ensuring that new hires align with the organizational culture is vital for maintaining a positive work environment and achieving long-term success.

- **Cultural Competency Interviews:** Including questions that assess a candidate's values, beliefs, and work style helps in determining whether they will fit in with the existing team and organizational culture.

- **Team Involvement:** Involving team members in the hiring process can provide additional perspectives on whether a candidate will fit in. Team-based interviews or panel discussions can reveal how well a candidate interacts with potential colleagues.

- **Company Values:** Clearly communicating the organization's values and culture during the hiring process helps candidates understand whether the company is the right fit for them. This can include discussions about work-life balance, company mission, and workplace norms.

Fostering cultural fit not only helps in creating a cohesive and harmonious work environment but also enhances employee engagement and retention.

Strategies for promoting Comprehensive Hiring Practices: To effectively assess candidates and ensure alignment with roles, comprehensive hiring practices should focus on several key elements:

1. **Detailed Job Descriptions**
2. **Robust Screening Processes**
3. **Behavioral Interviews**
4. **Skills Assessments**
5. **Cultural Fit Evaluation**

1. **Detailed Job Descriptions:** Detailed job descriptions are the foundation of effective hiring practices. They provide clarity on the role's requirements and help attract suitable candidates.

Key components of a Detailed Job Description

Role Overview: The role overview is a concise summary that outlines the primary purpose and significance of the position within the organization. It provides potential candidates with a high-level understanding of how the role contributes to the overall goals and mission of the company. This section typically includes the job title, department, and a brief description of how the role interacts with other parts of the organization. By offering a snapshot of the position's importance, the role overview helps candidates quickly grasp the essence of the job and its impact on the company's success.

Key Responsibilities: This section offers a detailed enumeration of the tasks and duties that the role entails. It should comprehensively list the core activities that the employee will be responsible for on a daily, weekly, or monthly basis. The key responsibilities section provides clarity on what is expected from the candidate and helps them assess their suitability for the role. It may also include information on the scope of the role, such as supervisory responsibilities, cross-functional collaborations, and specific projects or initiatives that the candidate will be involved in. A thorough outline of responsibilities ensures that candidates have a realistic understanding of the job and can better envision themselves performing these tasks.

Required Skills and Qualifications: This part of the job description delineates the specific skills, experience, and educational background necessary for the role. It includes both hard skills, such as technical abilities and certifications, and soft skills, such as communication and problem-solving capabilities. By clearly stating these requirements, this section helps filter out candidates who do not meet the minimum criteria, ensuring that only qualified individuals apply. The required skills and qualifications section also serves as a benchmark for evaluating candidates' resumes and application materials, making the screening process more efficient and effective. It may also highlight preferred qualifications, which are desirable but not essential, giving candidates a sense of what additional attributes would be beneficial.

Performance Expectations: The performance expectations section sets out the specific metrics, goals, and outcomes that the employee is expected to achieve. This can include key performance indicators (KPIs), targets, and other measurable objectives that define success in the role. Providing clear performance expectations helps candidates understand what will be required of them once they are on the job and sets the stage for how their performance will be evaluated. This section is crucial for aligning candidates' understanding with the organization's standards and expectations, ensuring that they are prepared to meet or exceed these benchmarks. It also helps to establish accountability and provides a framework for ongoing performance reviews and professional development.

Working Conditions: This component outlines the physical and environmental conditions associated with the role. It includes information about the work setting, such as whether the job is office-based, remote, or requires travel. Details on working hours, including any requirements for overtime, shift work, or on-call duties, are also included. By providing this information, candidates can assess whether the working conditions align with their preferences and lifestyle, helping to set realistic expectations about the job.

Company Culture and Values: This section describes the organization's culture, values, and mission. It provides candidates with insight into the company's ethos and work environment, helping them determine if they would be a good cultural fit. Highlighting the company's commitment to certain values, such as diversity, innovation, or community engagement, can attract candidates who share these principles and are motivated to contribute to the organization's broader goals.

Advancement Opportunities: Detailing potential career paths and advancement opportunities within the organization can attract ambitious candidates who are looking for long-term growth. This section can include information about promotion prospects, professional development programs, and opportunities for acquiring new skills and responsibilities. By outlining a clear trajectory for career advancement, the job description can motivate candidates to see the role as a stepping stone in their professional journey.

Compensation and Benefits: While not always included in a public job description, providing information about the compensation package and benefits can be a significant factor in attracting top talent. This section can outline salary ranges, bonus structures, health benefits, retirement plans, and other perks such as flexible working hours, wellness programs, and professional development support. Transparency in compensation and benefits helps candidates make informed decisions about whether to pursue the opportunity.

Application Process: This final component provides candidates with clear instructions on how to apply for the role. It includes details on the application deadline, required documents (such as a resume, cover letter, or portfolio), and any specific instructions for submitting their application. This section may also outline the stages of the hiring process, such as initial screenings, interviews, and assessments, giving candidates an understanding of what to expect and how to prepare.

Example Job Description Structure

- **Job Title**: Senior Software Engineer
- **Role Overview**: Responsible for developing and maintaining software applications, ensuring high performance and responsiveness.

Key Responsibilities:

- Design and implement software applications.
- Collaborate with cross-functional teams to define and achieve project goals.
- Maintain and improve code quality through regular testing and reviews.

Required Skills and Qualifications:

- Bachelor's degree in Computer Science or related field.
- At least 5 years of experience in software development.
- Proficiency in programming languages such as Java, Python, or C++.

Performance Expectations:

- Complete assigned projects within deadlines.
- Maintain a code quality score of 90% or higher.
- Achieve a customer satisfaction rating of at least 4.5 out of 5.

2. **Robust Screening Processes:** A robust screening process ensures that only the most suitable candidates proceed to the interview stage.

Key Components of Robust Screening Processes

Resume Screening: The process of resume screening involves meticulously reviewing the resumes submitted by applicants to identify those who meet the basic qualifications required for the role. This initial step is critical for efficiently filtering out unqualified candidates, allowing the recruitment team to focus their efforts on individuals who possess the necessary educational background, work experience, and specific skills pertinent to the job. Effective resume screening helps streamline the hiring process, ensuring that only the most relevant candidates move forward to the next stages.

Initial Phone Screens: Conducting initial phone screens serves as a preliminary interview phase where recruiters can assess candidates' experience, skills, and genuine interest in the role. This step is designed to further narrow down the candidate pool by providing a quick and cost-effective method to gauge whether an applicant's qualifications and career aspirations align with the job requirements and organizational culture. During these brief interviews, recruiters can clarify details from the resume, ask about career motivations, and evaluate communication skills, thereby identifying strong candidates for in-depth evaluation.

Pre-Employment Assessments: Utilizing pre-employment assessments is a vital component of the screening process, providing objective data to support hiring decisions. These assessments can encompass a variety of tests, including those that measure hard skills, cognitive abilities, personality traits, and cultural fit. By implementing standardized assessments, organizations can gain insights into a candidate's potential performance and compatibility with the company's values and work environment. These evaluations help ensure that the selection process is not solely based on subjective judgments, thereby enhancing the reliability and fairness of hiring decisions.

Behavioral Assessments: Incorporating behavioral assessments into the screening process allows recruiters to understand a candidate's typical behavior in various work-related scenarios. These assessments often focus on traits such as leadership, teamwork, stress management, and problem-solving abilities. By evaluating these attributes, organizations can predict how candidates are likely to behave in real-world situations, ensuring a better fit with the company's culture and team dynamics. This step is particularly important for roles that require specific interpersonal skills and behavioral competencies.

Background Checks: Conducting thorough background checks is an essential part of robust screening processes, aimed at verifying the accuracy of the information provided by candidates and ensuring their suitability for the role. Background checks can include verification of employment history, educational credentials, and professional licenses, as well as checks for criminal records and financial stability. This step helps mitigate risks associated with hiring by confirming that candidates have been truthful in their applications and possess a clean record, which is particularly important for roles with significant responsibilities or access to sensitive information.

Reference Checks: Performing reference checks involves contacting previous employers, colleagues, or other professional contacts provided by the candidate to gather insights into their past job performance, work ethic, and overall suitability for the role. Reference checks serve as an additional layer of validation, offering a third-party perspective on the candidate's capabilities and reliability. This step can provide valuable information that may not be evident from resumes, interviews, or assessments alone, helping to ensure a comprehensive evaluation of each candidate.

Job Simulations and Work Samples: Implementing job simulations and work samples as part of the screening process allows candidates to demonstrate their abilities in a controlled environment that mimics real job tasks. These exercises provide a practical assessment of a candidate's skills, problem-solving approaches, and decision-making processes. By observing how candidates handle specific job-related scenarios, recruiters can gain a deeper understanding of their practical competencies and potential fit for the role. This step is particularly useful for positions that require technical expertise or complex problem-solving skills.

Structured Interviews: Utilizing structured interviews, where each candidate is asked a consistent set of questions, ensures a fair and standardized evaluation process. Structured interviews help reduce bias by providing a uniform framework for comparing candidates' responses and assessing their qualifications against predetermined criteria. This approach enhances the reliability and validity of the interview process, making it easier to identify the most suitable candidates based on objective, job-relevant factors.

Talent Pools and Pipelines: Maintaining active talent pools and pipelines involves creating a database of potential candidates who have expressed interest in the organization or who possess desirable skills and qualifications. This proactive approach allows organizations to quickly identify and engage with qualified candidates when job openings arise. By nurturing relationships with potential candidates, companies can streamline the screening process and ensure a steady supply of top talent, reducing time-to-hire and improving overall recruitment efficiency.

Continuous Improvement and Metrics: Implementing a continuous improvement approach to the screening process involves regularly reviewing and refining screening methods and criteria based on performance metrics and feedback. By analyzing data on the effectiveness of different screening tools and processes, organizations can identify areas for improvement and make evidence-based adjustments. This ongoing optimization ensures that the screening process remains efficient, effective, and aligned with the organization's evolving hiring needs and goals.

Example Screening Steps

- Develop a checklist of required qualifications and skills.
- Use applicant tracking systems (ATS) to filter resumes.
- Conduct 15-minute phone screens to gauge candidates' suitability.

3. **Behavioral Interviews: Behavioral interviews assess past behavior to predict future performance by asking about specific experiences and how candidates handled them.**

Key Components of Behavioral Interviews

Competency-Based Questions: The foundation of behavioral interviews lies in asking competency-based questions. These questions are designed to evaluate the specific competencies required for the job role. By focusing on the key skills and abilities that are critical for success in the position, employers can assess whether the candidate possesses the necessary competencies. This approach ensures that the interview process is directly aligned with the job requirements and helps in identifying candidates who are likely to perform well in the role.

STAR Method: The STAR method (Situation, Task, Action, Result) is a widely-used framework in behavioral interviews. It provides a structured way for candidates to articulate their experiences and for interviewers to evaluate their responses. By asking candidates to describe a specific situation, the task they were responsible for, the actions they took, and the results of those actions, interviewers can gain a clear and detailed understanding of the candidate's past behavior and performance. This method helps in identifying how candidates have handled similar situations in the past and their potential for future success.

Past Experience Focus: Behavioral interviews emphasize past experiences because past behavior is often a good predictor of future performance. By asking candidates to provide specific examples from their previous work experiences, interviewers can gather concrete evidence of the candidate's skills and abilities. This focus on past experiences allows interviewers to assess how candidates have applied their competencies in real-world situations and to evaluate their problem-solving abilities, decision-making skills, and overall effectiveness.

Situational Consistency: Ensuring that interview questions are relevant to the situations the candidate will encounter in the new role is crucial for an effective behavioral interview. This situational consistency helps interviewers to assess how well the candidate's past experiences align with the demands of the job. By asking questions that mirror the challenges and tasks the candidate will face in the role, interviewers can better predict how the candidate will perform and adapt to the new environment.

Behavioral Indicators: Identifying specific behaviors that indicate the candidate's competencies and skills is a key component of behavioral interviews. Behavioral indicators are the observable actions and outcomes that demonstrate a candidate's proficiency in a particular competency. By looking for these indicators in the candidate's responses, interviewers can assess whether the candidate has the necessary skills and behaviors to succeed in the role. This approach ensures that the evaluation is based on concrete evidence rather than subjective impressions.

Follow-Up Questions: Using follow-up questions to delve deeper into the candidate's responses is essential for gaining a comprehensive understanding of their experiences and competencies. Follow-up questions help interviewers to clarify details, probe for additional information, and explore the candidate's thought processes and decision-making strategies. This deeper level of inquiry allows interviewers to assess the candidate's depth of experience, critical thinking abilities, and overall suitability for the role.

Consistency Across Interviews: Asking the same core questions to all candidates ensures a fair and standardized interview process. Consistency across interviews allows for an objective comparison of candidates and helps to eliminate bias. By evaluating each candidate against the same set of criteria, interviewers can make more informed and equitable hiring decisions. This consistency also enhances the reliability and validity of the interview process.

Note-Taking: Taking detailed notes during the interview is crucial for capturing key points and behaviors. Accurate and comprehensive notes provide a record of the candidate's responses and help interviewers to remember important details after the interview has concluded. These notes are valuable for the evaluation and decision-making process, allowing interviewers to compare candidates objectively and to provide specific feedback if needed.

Assessment of Soft Skills: Evaluating essential soft skills such as communication, teamwork, and adaptability is a critical aspect of behavioral interviews. Soft skills are often as important as technical skills for job performance and success. By focusing on these skills during the interview, employers can assess how well candidates will fit into the organizational culture, interact with colleagues, and handle the interpersonal aspects of the job. This assessment helps in identifying candidates who not only have the technical competencies but also the interpersonal skills necessary for effective collaboration and leadership.

Example Behavioral Interview Questions

- Describe a time when you had to meet a tight deadline. How did you manage it?
- Tell me about a challenging project you worked on. What was the outcome?
- Give an example of how you dealt with a conflict within your team.

4. **Skills Assessments:** Skills assessments provide objective data on candidates' abilities.

Key Components of Skills Assessments

Technical Tests: Technical tests are designed to evaluate a candidate's hard skills and technical knowledge relevant to the job role. These tests are often standardized and focus on specific competencies required for the position. They provide an objective measure of a candidate's abilities and can cover a range of areas, from coding and engineering skills to proficiency in software applications or understanding of financial principles. The primary goal is to ascertain whether the candidate possesses the technical expertise needed to perform the job effectively.

Problem-Solving Exercises: Problem-solving exercises are critical for assessing a candidate's ability to think critically, analyze situations, and develop effective solutions. These exercises can be customized to reflect the actual challenges and scenarios the candidate might encounter in the role. They test not only the candidate's cognitive abilities but also their approach to problem-solving, their creativity in developing solutions, and their ability to work under pressure. This type of assessment helps employers understand how candidates tackle complex problems and whether they have the strategic thinking skills necessary for the position.

Work Samples: Work samples are practical tasks or projects that simulate the kind of work the candidate would be expected to perform in the role. By completing these tasks, candidates demonstrate their practical abilities, work ethic, and approach to completing assignments. Work samples provide a tangible indication of a candidate's capabilities and their potential to contribute to the organization. This assessment method allows employers to evaluate not just theoretical knowledge but also the application of skills in a real-world context.

Simulations: Simulations are advanced assessments that mimic the actual working environment and the specific tasks candidates will face. They provide a realistic and immersive experience that allows candidates to demonstrate their skills, decision-making abilities, and behavioral responses in a controlled setting. Simulations can range from virtual scenarios to interactive role-plays, offering insights into how candidates perform in realistic situations.

Cognitive Ability Tests: Cognitive ability tests measure general mental capabilities such as reasoning, memory, and problem-solving skills. These tests help predict a candidate's potential for learning and performing in the role. They are valuable for assessing whether a candidate can grasp new concepts quickly and apply their cognitive skills effectively to various tasks.

Situational Judgment Tests: Situational judgment tests present candidates with hypothetical scenarios relevant to the job and ask them to choose the best course of action from a set of options. These tests assess a candidate's judgment, decision-making skills, and ability to navigate complex situations. They are particularly useful for roles that require strong interpersonal skills and the ability to handle challenging situations.

Behavioral Assessments: Behavioral assessments focus on evaluating a candidate's personality traits, work style, and cultural fit with the organization. These assessments help determine whether a candidate's behavioral tendencies align with the job requirements and the organization's values. They can provide insights into how a candidate will interact with colleagues, manage stress, and approach their work.

Performance Tasks: Performance tasks are specific assignments that candidates complete to demonstrate their skills and competencies. These tasks can include presentations, written reports, or practical demonstrations of their abilities. Performance tasks allow employers to assess the quality of a candidate's work, their attention to detail, and their ability to meet deadlines.

Skills Gap Analysis: Skills gap analysis involves comparing a candidate's current skills with the skills required for the role. This analysis helps identify any gaps in the candidate's competencies and determine whether additional training or development is needed. It provides a comprehensive understanding of the candidate's strengths and areas for improvement.

Competency-Based Interviews: Competency-based interviews complement skills assessments by probing deeper into the candidate's experiences and how they have demonstrated key competencies in the past. These interviews provide a qualitative assessment of a candidate's abilities and help verify the results of technical tests and other assessments.

Comprehensive Evaluation: A comprehensive evaluation combines multiple assessment methods to provide a holistic view of a candidate's abilities. This approach ensures that all relevant skills and competencies are thoroughly assessed, reducing the risk of hiring decisions based on incomplete information.

Benchmarking: Benchmarking involves comparing a candidate's assessment results with those of top performers in similar roles. This process helps identify candidates who have the potential to excel and contribute significantly to the organization. Benchmarking provides a standard for evaluating candidate performance and making informed hiring decisions.

Feedback Mechanisms: Providing candidates with feedback on their assessment performance is an essential component of the assessment process. Feedback helps candidates understand their strengths and areas for improvement, contributing to their professional development. It also demonstrates the organization's commitment to a fair and transparent hiring process.

Example Skills Assessment Tools

- Coding challenges for software development roles.
- Case studies for consulting roles.
- Writing samples for content creation roles.

5. **Cultural Fit Evaluation: Cultural fit evaluation ensures new hires align with organizational values and work environment.**

Key Components of Cultural Fit Evaluation

Values-Based Interviews: Values-based interviews focus on understanding a candidate's personal values and how they align with the organization's core values. During these interviews, questions are designed to elicit responses that reveal the candidate's beliefs, motivations, and ethical standards. This type of interview helps employers gauge whether a candidate will thrive in the company's environment and contribute positively to its culture. By ensuring alignment between individual and organizational values, companies can foster a more cohesive and motivated workforce.

Team Interviews: Team interviews involve multiple team members in the interview process to evaluate how well a candidate might integrate with the existing team dynamics. This method provides a broader perspective on the candidate's potential fit within the team and the organization as a whole. Team interviews can reveal insights into a candidate's interpersonal skills, collaboration style, and adaptability. The collective feedback from various team members helps in making a more informed hiring decision, ensuring that new hires will complement the team's strengths and work harmoniously with their colleagues.

Cultural Fit Assessments: Cultural fit assessments are tools used to measure a candidate's compatibility with the organization's culture. These assessments can take various forms, such as personality tests, situational judgment tests, and behavioral assessments. They provide a structured way to evaluate how well a candidate's attitudes, behaviors, and work style align with the cultural norms and expectations of the organization. Cultural fit assessments help identify candidates who are likely to resonate with the company's work environment, values, and practices, thereby enhancing employee satisfaction and retention.

Behavioral Questions: Incorporating behavioral questions into the interview process helps assess how a candidate has handled past situations that are relevant to the company's culture. These questions often follow the STAR (Situation, Task, Action, Result) method, allowing candidates to provide specific examples of their past behavior and decision-making processes. Evaluating these responses gives insight into how a candidate might react to similar situations within the organization, indicating their potential fit with the company's culture.

Organizational Scenario Discussions: Presenting candidates with hypothetical scenarios that reflect real-life situations in the organization can be a useful tool in cultural fit evaluation. Candidates are asked to describe how they would handle these scenarios, which helps employers understand their problem-solving approaches and whether their methods align with the company's cultural expectations. This approach provides a practical assessment of how candidates might perform and interact within the organization.

Peer Interaction Assessments: Observing candidates during less formal interactions with potential peers and colleagues can offer valuable insights into their cultural fit. These interactions might occur during lunch meetings, group discussions, or informal meet-and-greets. Such settings allow candidates to demonstrate their social skills and adaptability in a more relaxed environment, providing a fuller picture of their compatibility with the team and the organization.

Cultural Fit Surveys: Conducting surveys that include questions about workplace preferences, values, and expectations can help assess a candidate's cultural fit. These surveys can be standardized or tailored to the specific cultural attributes of the organization. The results provide a quantitative measure of how well a candidate's attitudes and behaviors align with the company's cultural norms.

Long-Term Fit Evaluation: Assessing a candidate's potential for long-term cultural fit involves considering how their career goals and aspirations align with the organization's vision and growth plans. This evaluation helps determine whether the candidate will remain motivated and engaged over time, contributing to the organization's long-term success.

Feedback Integration: Gathering and integrating feedback from various stakeholders involved in the hiring process, including managers, team members, and HR professionals, is crucial for a comprehensive cultural fit evaluation. This collective input ensures a balanced and well-rounded assessment of the candidate's potential fit within the organization.

Cultural Onboarding Programs: Implementing cultural onboarding programs for new hires can further assess and reinforce cultural fit. These programs introduce new employees to the organization's values, practices, and expectations, helping them integrate more smoothly and confirming their alignment with the company culture early in their tenure.

Alignment with Mission and Vision: Evaluating how well a candidate's personal mission and vision align with those of the organization is essential for ensuring cultural fit. This alignment ensures that the candidate not only fits in with the current culture but also contributes to advancing the organization's long-term goals and strategic objectives.

Example Cultural Fit Questions

- What aspects of our company culture appeal to you?
- How do you handle feedback and criticism?
- Describe a work environment where you feel most productive and engaged.

The Long-Term Benefits of Comprehensive Hiring Practices

Implementing comprehensive hiring practices yields significant long-term benefits for organizations. These benefits include improved employee satisfaction, reduced turnover, and enhanced organizational performance, all of which contribute to the overall health and success of the business.

Improved Employee Satisfaction: Ensuring that employees are well-matched to their roles and the organizational culture greatly enhances job satisfaction. When employees feel that their skills and values align with their job requirements and the company ethos, they are more likely to be engaged and motivated. This alignment fosters a sense of belonging and purpose, which are critical for sustained job satisfaction. Engaged employees are not only more productive but also exhibit higher levels of creativity and commitment to their work. They are more likely to take initiative, contribute innovative ideas, and work collaboratively toward common goals. Overall, a satisfied workforce is a more resilient and adaptive one, capable of navigating challenges and seizing opportunities.

Reduced Turnover: High turnover rates can be extremely costly and disruptive for organizations. Turnover involves direct costs such as recruiting, hiring, and training new employees, as well as indirect costs like lost productivity, decreased morale, and the potential loss of institutional knowledge. Comprehensive hiring practices help mitigate these costs by ensuring a better fit between the employee and the organization from the outset. When employees feel that they are in the right role and that their personal values align with the company's culture, they are more likely to stay with the organization long-term. This stability allows the organization to benefit from the cumulative expertise and experience of its workforce, leading to more efficient and effective operations.

Enhanced Organizational Performance: Employees who are well-suited to their roles and the organizational culture are more likely to perform at high levels. They can meet and exceed performance expectations, contribute meaningfully to team objectives, and drive the organization toward its strategic goals. High-performing employees are essential for maintaining a competitive edge in the market, as they bring innovation, efficiency, and quality to their work. Over time, this enhanced performance translates into improved organizational outcomes, such as increased revenue, higher customer satisfaction, and a stronger market presence. Additionally, a workforce that is well-aligned with the organization's mission and values is better equipped to adapt to changes in the business environment, ensuring long-term resilience and success.

Strategic Alignment and Goal Achievement: Comprehensive hiring practices ensure that new hires not only fit the current needs of the organization but also align with its long-term strategic goals. Employees who understand and buy into the organization's mission are more likely to work toward achieving these goals, contributing to a unified and coherent effort across the company. This alignment helps streamline decision-making processes, as employees are clear on the organization's priorities and objectives. Moreover, a strategic alignment fosters a culture of accountability and performance, where employees are motivated to achieve both personal and organizational milestones.

Enhanced Team Dynamics: A well-executed hiring process considers the team dynamics and the specific contributions each new hire will make. By selecting individuals who complement the existing team's strengths and address its weaknesses, organizations can build more cohesive and effective teams. Improved team dynamics lead to better communication, collaboration, and problem-solving capabilities. Teams that work well together are more likely to innovate and achieve higher levels of productivity, driving overall organizational performance.

Better Adaptability and Innovation: Organizations that prioritize comprehensive hiring practices are better positioned to adapt to changes in the market and industry. By hiring individuals who are not only skilled but also adaptable and open to continuous learning, companies can ensure that their workforce remains relevant and capable of responding to new challenges and opportunities. This adaptability is crucial for fostering a culture of innovation, where employees are encouraged to think creatively and pursue new ideas that can drive the organization forward.

Stronger Employer Brand and Talent Attraction: Implementing robust hiring practices enhances the organization's reputation as an employer of choice. Companies known for their thorough and thoughtful hiring processes are more likely to attract top talent, as prospective employees recognize the organization's commitment to finding the right fit. A strong employer brand not only makes it easier to attract high-quality candidates but also improves employee morale and retention, as current employees feel proud to be associated with a reputable and respected company.

Sustainable Growth and Profitability: Ultimately, the long-term benefits of comprehensive hiring practices contribute to sustainable growth and profitability for the organization. By investing in the right talent and ensuring a strong fit between employees and the company, organizations can achieve a more stable and productive workforce. This stability and productivity drive operational efficiencies, reduce costs associated with turnover and recruitment, and enhance overall business performance. Over time, these factors contribute to a stronger bottom line and a more competitive position in the market.

Implement Comprehensive Hiring Practices

Comprehensive hiring practices ensure new hires align with their roles and organizational culture.. *By focusing on detailed job descriptions, robust screening processes, behavioral interviews, skills assessments, and cultural fit evaluations, organizations can improve productivity, job satisfaction, and retention. Through strategic action and continuous improvement, organizations can build a strong, aligned workforce that drives success.*

Invest in Training and Development

Investing in training and development is essential for helping employees build the skills needed to align with their roles and contribute to the organization's success. Ongoing training and career development opportunities not only enhance employees' capabilities but also boost their engagement and retention. This chapter explores the importance of training and development, effective strategies for implementing training programs, and actionable steps to create a culture of continuous learning in your organization.

Importance of Training and Development: Training and development are fundamental components of an effective workforce strategy. By investing in these areas, organizations not only enhance the skills of their employees but also drive productivity, engagement, and retention. Here's a detailed exploration of why training and development are critical, focusing on skill enhancement, increased productivity, employee engagement, and retention.

Skill Enhancement: Skill enhancement is one of the primary benefits of training and development programs. It ensures that employees have the necessary skills to perform their current roles effectively and are prepared for future challenges.

- **Building Core Competencies:** Training programs help employees develop the essential skills required for their specific roles. For example, a sales training program might focus on negotiation techniques, customer relationship management, and product knowledge.

- **Staying Current:** In fast-evolving industries, continuous training ensures that employees stay up-to-date with the latest technologies, methodologies, and industry trends. This is particularly important in fields such as IT, healthcare, and finance.

- **Advanced Skills:** Training and development also facilitate the acquisition of advanced skills that can lead to career progression. For instance, leadership training prepares employees for management roles, while specialized technical training can qualify them for more complex tasks.

Increased Productivity: Well-trained employees are generally more productive and efficient. Training programs equip employees with the knowledge and skills they need to perform their tasks effectively, reducing the likelihood of errors and increasing overall productivity.

- **Efficiency Gains:** Employees who have received comprehensive training are more proficient in their tasks, which leads to faster and more efficient work processes. For example, training on new software tools can dramatically improve productivity by streamlining workflows.

- **Quality Improvement:** Training programs that focus on quality control and best practices ensure that employees produce high-quality work. This reduces the need for rework and enhances the overall output quality.

- **Adaptability:** Training also makes employees more adaptable to changes. Whether it's new technology, updated procedures, or changes in market conditions, well-trained employees can quickly adapt and maintain productivity.

Employee Engagement: Opportunities for growth and development are key drivers of employee engagement and satisfaction. When employees feel that their employer is investing in their personal and professional growth, they are more likely to be engaged and motivated.

- **Career Growth:** Training and development programs provide clear pathways for career advancement. Employees who see a future within the company are more likely to be engaged and committed to their work.

- **Job Satisfaction:** Employees who continuously learn and develop new skills are generally more satisfied with their jobs. This satisfaction comes from the sense of accomplishment and the ability to take on new challenges.

- **Recognition and Value:** Providing training opportunities shows employees that the organization values their contributions and is willing to invest in their future. This recognition fosters a positive work environment and increases employee morale.

Retention: Investing in employees' development is a powerful retention strategy. When employees feel valued and see opportunities for advancement, they are more likely to stay with the company long-term.

- **Reducing Turnover:** High turnover rates can be costly for organizations. Training and development programs help reduce turnover by addressing one of the main reasons employees leave – the lack of growth opportunities.

- **Loyalty:** Employees who receive continuous training are more likely to feel loyal to their employer. This loyalty stems from the understanding that the company is invested in their success and career progression.

- **Competitive Advantage:** Offering robust training and development programs can also be a competitive advantage in attracting top talent. Prospective employees are often drawn to companies that provide clear paths for growth and development.

Strategies for Implementing Training Programs

To effectively implement training and development programs, organizations should consider a variety of strategies:

1. **Needs Assessment**
2. **Tailored Training Programs**
3. **Blended Learning Approaches**
4. **Continuous Learning Culture**

1. **Needs Assessment: A needs assessment identifies specific training requirements, ensuring relevant and effective program development..** Here are key components involved in a needs assessment:

Key Components of Needs Assessment

Skills Gap Analysis: Skills gap analysis involves identifying the disparity between the current skills of employees and the skills required to perform their job roles effectively. This process includes comparing current skill levels with desired competencies, often through performance reviews, observations, and benchmark comparisons. The outcome highlights areas needing development to enhance workforce competency.

Employee Surveys: Employee surveys gather direct feedback from employees regarding their training needs and preferences. By developing and distributing surveys or questionnaires, organizations can understand employees' self-perceived skill deficiencies, desired training topics, and preferred learning methods. This feedback informs the design of targeted training programs.

Performance Data: Performance data analysis involves reviewing key performance indicators (KPIs), productivity reports, and performance appraisals to identify areas where employees or departments are underperforming. This data-driven approach helps pinpoint specific weaknesses that can be addressed through focused training initiatives.

Interviews and Focus Groups: Interviews and focus groups provide qualitative insights into the training needs and challenges faced by employees. Through structured discussions, these methods uncover nuanced issues that might not be captured through surveys or data analysis, offering a deeper understanding of employees' perspectives on their training requirements.

Job Analysis: Job analysis aims to understand the specific tasks, responsibilities, and required skills for each role within the organization. This detailed breakdown helps in designing targeted training programs that align with job requirements, ensuring employees possess the necessary competencies for their roles.

Training Evaluations: Training evaluations measure the effectiveness of existing training programs to determine their impact and identify areas for improvement. This process includes pre- and post-training assessments, feedback collection, and analysis of performance metrics, facilitating continuous refinement of training efforts.

Competency Mapping: Competency mapping identifies the core competencies required for different roles within the organization and evaluates employees' proficiency in these areas. By defining key competencies, using assessment tools, and comparing current levels with desired standards, organizations can design training programs focused on building necessary competencies.

Example Needs Assessment Steps

- **Conduct Surveys:** Gather comprehensive employee feedback on perceived training needs and preferred learning methods.
- **Analyze Performance Reviews:** Examine performance appraisals to identify common skill gaps and areas for improvement.
- **Hold Focus Groups:** Engage employees in discussions to gain deeper insights into their training needs and preferences.

2. **Tailored Training Programs: Tailored training programs address specific needs identified during assessment, ensuring relevance and effectiveness through customization.**

Key Components of Tailored Training Programs

Role-Specific Training: Role-specific training focuses on providing training that is directly applicable to the specific tasks and responsibilities of a job role. It involves developing training modules focused on the technical and functional skills required for particular roles, ensuring employees gain the necessary expertise to perform their job effectively.

Soft Skills Training: Soft skills training enhances interpersonal skills that are crucial for effective teamwork, communication, and leadership. This involves offering workshops, seminars, and interactive sessions that focus on skills like communication, leadership, conflict resolution, and emotional intelligence. Such training aims to improve employees' ability to interact effectively and harmoniously with others.

While soft skills training can enhance existing abilities, it's important to recognize that these skills are often inherent. Focus on leveraging and developing employees' natural strengths rather than attempting to fundamentally change their soft skills

Hard Skills Training: Hard skills training develops the technical abilities and knowledge necessary for job-specific tasks. It provides training in technical competencies, such as programming, data analysis, or financial modeling, relevant to the employees' roles. This type of training ensures employees have the practical skills needed to perform their duties proficiently.

Onboarding Training: Onboarding training introduces new employees to the organization's culture, policies, and procedures. It includes orientation sessions, company overviews, and initial training on job-specific tasks to help new hires acclimate quickly and effectively.

Leadership Development Programs: Leadership development programs aim to cultivate the skills needed for effective leadership and management. These programs include training on strategic thinking, decision-making, team management, and other leadership competencies, preparing employees for current or future leadership roles.

Continuous Learning Opportunities: Continuous learning opportunities encourage ongoing skill development and professional growth. These programs provide employees with access to ongoing training resources, such as online courses, certification programs, and professional development workshops, to keep their skills up-to-date and relevant.

Customized Learning Paths: Customized learning paths are tailored to individual employee's career goals and learning preferences. These paths provide personalized training plans that align with employees' specific needs and aspirations, fostering targeted skill development and career advancement.

Example Training Programs

- **Role-Specific Training:** Advanced programming courses for software developers tailored to their specific languages and tools.

- **Soft Skills Training:** Communication workshops for customer service representatives to improve client interactions and problem-solving skills.

- **Hard Skills Training:** Data analysis training for marketing analysts to enhance their ability to interpret and use data effectively.

3. **Blended Learning Approaches:** Blended learning combines various training methods to cater to different learning styles, thereby maximizing the effectiveness of training programs.

Key Components of Blended Learning Approaches

Online Training: Online training offers flexibility and convenience, allowing employees to learn at their own pace. It includes providing e-learning modules, webinars, and online courses on relevant topics, making it accessible anytime and anywhere.

In-Person Training: In-person training facilitates interactive and hands-on learning experiences. It involves conducting workshops, seminars, and face-to-face training sessions that encourage participation and engagement, fostering a more immersive learning environment.

On-the-Job Training: On-the-job training allows employees to learn in a real-world context under the guidance of experienced mentors. This approach pairs new hires with experienced employees for mentoring, shadowing, and practical hands-on training, providing immediate application of skills and knowledge.

Self-Paced Learning: Self-paced learning enables employees to manage their learning schedules according to their personal and professional commitments. It includes access to online resources, recorded webinars, and training materials that they can study at their convenience, promoting autonomy in the learning process.

Collaborative Learning: Collaborative learning encourages teamwork and knowledge sharing among employees. This approach involves group projects, discussion forums, and collaborative exercises that allow employees to learn from each other's experiences and insights, enhancing collective skill development.

Simulation-Based Training: Simulation-based training provides realistic scenarios where employees can practice and hone their skills in a controlled environment. It includes using virtual simulations, role-playing activities, and interactive exercises to replicate job-related challenges and scenarios, enhancing problem-solving abilities.

Mobile Learning: Mobile learning supports training on-the-go through mobile-friendly platforms and apps. This component allows employees to access learning materials, complete courses, and participate in training activities using their smartphones or tablets, ensuring continuous learning regardless of location.

Formal Assessments and Feedback: Formal assessments and feedback ensure that employees' learning progress is monitored and evaluated. This involves quizzes, tests, performance evaluations, and feedback sessions that provide insights into learning outcomes and areas for improvement, guiding ongoing development.

Example Blended Learning Approach

- **Develop E-Learning Modules:** Create online courses on key topics that employees can access anytime.
- **Schedule In-Person Workshops:** Organize interactive workshops for skill development and knowledge sharing.

- **On-the-Job Training:** Pair new hires with mentors for hands-on training and practical experience.

4. **Continuous Learning Culture:** Fostering a culture of continuous learning encourages employees to pursue ongoing development and enhances organizational agility and innovation.

Key Components of Continuous Learning Culture

Encouraging Self-Directed Learning: Encouraging self-directed learning empowers employees to take charge of their own learning and development. This involves providing access to online learning platforms, books, and other resources that employees can use for self-study, fostering a sense of ownership over their professional growth.

Offering Learning Incentives: Offering learning incentives motivates employees to participate in training programs and pursue further education. This includes providing financial incentives, such as bonuses or tuition reimbursement, for completing training programs and earning certifications, thereby encouraging continuous development.

Recognizing and Rewarding Learning: Recognizing and rewarding learning reinforces the value of continuous learning and acknowledges employees' efforts. This can be achieved by publicly recognizing and rewarding employees who actively engage in learning and development, through company newsletters or award ceremonies, highlighting their commitment and achievements.

Creating a Learning Environment: Creating a learning environment entails fostering a workplace culture that values and supports continuous education. This involves promoting open communication, encouraging knowledge sharing, and ensuring that employees have the time and resources needed to pursue learning activities.

Implementing Development Plans: Implementing development plans involves setting clear learning and career progression goals for employees. This includes creating personalized development plans that outline specific learning objectives and the steps needed to achieve them, ensuring structured and goal-oriented growth.

Facilitating Mentorship Programs: Facilitating mentorship programs pairs employees with experienced mentors who can provide guidance and support. This component encourages knowledge transfer, skill development, and professional growth through one-on-one mentoring relationships.

Utilizing Technology for Learning: Utilizing technology for learning involves leveraging digital tools and platforms to enhance the learning experience. This includes using learning management systems, mobile apps, and virtual training environments to provide flexible and accessible learning options.

Example Continuous Learning Initiatives

- **Access to Online Learning Platforms:** Provide subscriptions to platforms like Coursera or Udemy for employees to pursue courses of interest.
- **Offer Financial Incentives:** Implement a program that offers bonuses or tuition reimbursement for employees who complete training programs.
- **Recognize Learning Achievements:** Feature employees' learning achievements in company newsletters or during team meetings.

The Long-Term Benefits of Investing in Training and Development

Investing in training and development is crucial for organizations aiming to achieve sustained success and growth. Comprehensive training programs not only enhance the skills and capabilities of employees but also contribute significantly to the overall health and performance of the organization. By prioritizing training and development, companies can improve employee satisfaction, increase productivity, and foster a culture of continuous improvement.

Skill Enhancement

Up-to-Date Skills: Continuous training ensures that employees stay current with industry trends, technologies, and best practices. This relevance is crucial in a fast-paced, ever-evolving market.

Versatility and Adaptability: Training programs that cover a range of skills make employees more versatile and adaptable. This flexibility allows them to handle various tasks and challenges effectively.

Specialized Expertise: Targeted training helps employees develop specialized skills needed for specific roles or projects. This expertise contributes to higher-quality work and innovative solutions.

Innovation and Creativity: Well-trained employees are more likely to contribute innovative ideas and creative solutions. Training stimulates critical thinking and problem-solving skills, driving organizational growth and competitiveness.

Increased Productivity

Efficiency: Well-trained employees perform their tasks more efficiently, leading to increased productivity. They are better equipped to use tools, technologies, and methodologies relevant to their roles.

Error Reduction: Training reduces the likelihood of mistakes and errors. Employees who understand their roles thoroughly are less likely to make costly errors, improving overall work quality.

Optimized Processes: Continuous improvement in skills leads to optimized workflows and processes. Employees can identify and implement more efficient ways to complete tasks, boosting overall productivity.

Team Synergy: Training programs that include team-building exercises enhance collaboration and communication within teams. A well-coordinated team works more efficiently and effectively, contributing to higher productivity.

Employee Engagement

Career Development: Opportunities for growth and development increase employee engagement and satisfaction. When employees see a clear path for advancement, they are more motivated to excel in their roles.

Job Satisfaction: Employees who feel that their employer invests in their development are more satisfied with their jobs. This satisfaction translates into higher morale and a positive work environment.

Empowerment: Training empowers employees by equipping them with the skills and knowledge needed to perform their roles effectively. Empowered employees are more confident and proactive in their work.

Commitment: Investing in training demonstrates that the organization values its employees, fostering loyalty and commitment. Engaged employees are more likely to stay with the company long-term.

Retention

Employee Loyalty: Investing in employees' development fosters loyalty and reduces turnover. Employees are more likely to stay with a company that prioritizes their growth and career progression.

Cost Savings: Reducing turnover saves on the costs associated with recruiting, hiring, and training new employees. Retaining skilled employees also ensures continuity and stability within the organization.

Positive Reputation: A strong commitment to training and development enhances the company's reputation as an employer of choice. This reputation attracts top talent and retains existing employees.

Career Growth: Providing clear pathways for career growth encourages employees to stay and advance within the company. Employees are less likely to seek opportunities elsewhere if they see potential for advancement within their current organization.

Training and development investments help employees align with their roles and contribute to organizational success. *By conducting needs assessments, developing tailored training programs, implementing blended learning approaches, promoting continuous learning, and regularly evaluating and adjusting training programs, organizations can enhance productivity, engagement, and retention. A strong focus on training and development ensures that employees are continuously developing their skills and contributing to the organization's growth and success.*

Encourage Role Flexibility and Mobility

Encouraging role flexibility and mobility within an organization allows employees to transition to roles that better suit their skills and interests. This not only enhances job satisfaction and engagement but also ensures that the organization can adapt to changing needs and opportunities. This chapter explores the importance of role flexibility and mobility, strategies for promoting it, and actionable steps to create a flexible and dynamic work environment.

But the key to this encouragement, is to be able to re-align the employee if the newly assigned role is not a fit. Please refer back to the chapter on "Good People in Bad Roles" if needed. Employees will quickly realize the dangers of taking on a new role in your organization if others get managed out if the role is not a fit for them.

Importance of Role Flexibility and Mobility: Role flexibility and mobility within an organization are critical elements that contribute to both employee satisfaction and organizational effectiveness. By allowing employees to move fluidly within the organization, taking on different roles and responsibilities as needed, companies can maximize the potential of their workforce while also fostering a more engaged and dynamic work environment. Here, we delve into the key reasons why role flexibility and mobility are important, including optimized talent utilization, increased job satisfaction, adaptability, and career development.

Optimized Talent Utilization: Optimized talent utilization involves leveraging the diverse skills and abilities of employees to meet the organization's needs effectively. Role flexibility and mobility are instrumental in ensuring that the right people are in the right roles at the right times.

- **Maximizing Skills and Competencies:** When employees can move between roles, their diverse skills and competencies can be better utilized. For example, an employee with strong analytical skills might contribute significantly to both the finance and operations departments at different times, depending on where the greatest need lies.

- **Addressing Skill Gaps:** Flexibility in roles allows organizations to quickly address skill gaps as they arise. If a particular team lacks expertise in a certain area, an employee with the necessary skills can be temporarily reassigned to fill that gap, ensuring that projects continue to move forward smoothly.

- **Enhancing Efficiency:** By optimizing talent utilization, organizations can enhance efficiency and productivity. Employees working in roles that best match their skills are likely to perform tasks more efficiently and with higher quality, leading to overall better performance and outcomes for the organization.

Increased Job Satisfaction: Job satisfaction is a crucial factor in employee retention and productivity. Role flexibility and mobility significantly contribute to job satisfaction by allowing employees to find roles that best match their interests and strengths.

- **Alignment with Interests and Strengths:** Employees are more likely to be satisfied when they can move to roles that align with their personal interests and strengths. This alignment not only makes their work more enjoyable but also enables them to perform at their best.

- **Variety and Challenge:** Role flexibility introduces variety and challenge into employees' careers. Rather than being confined to a single role for an extended period, employees can experience new challenges and learning opportunities, which keeps their work experience fresh and engaging.

- **Reduced Burnout:** Flexibility in roles can help reduce burnout by allowing employees to switch roles before they become too stressed or disengaged. Moving to a new role can reinvigorate an employee's enthusiasm and commitment to the organization.

Adaptability: In today's fast-paced and ever-changing business environment, adaptability is essential for organizational success. Role flexibility and mobility enhance an organization's ability to adapt to changing needs and opportunities.

- **Responding to Market Changes:** When market conditions change or new opportunities arise, organizations need to be agile. Role flexibility allows the organization to quickly reallocate resources and talent to where they are most needed, ensuring that the company can respond effectively to external changes.

- **Cross-Functional Collaboration:** Flexibility in roles promotes cross-functional collaboration. Employees who have experience in multiple departments or roles can bridge gaps between teams, fostering a more integrated and cooperative work environment.

- **Innovation and Creativity:** Adaptability is closely linked to innovation and creativity. Employees who move between roles bring fresh perspectives and ideas, which can lead to innovative solutions and improvements in processes and products.

Career Development: Career development opportunities are a significant factor in employee engagement and retention. Role flexibility and mobility provide employees with numerous opportunities for growth and development.

- **Skill Enhancement:** Moving between roles allows employees to develop a broad set of skills. Each new role provides different challenges and learning opportunities, contributing to a more versatile and capable workforce.

- **Career Progression:** Flexible roles can pave the way for career progression within the organization. Employees can gain the experience and qualifications needed for higher-level positions by rotating through various roles and departments.

- **Mentorship and Networking:** Role mobility can also enhance mentorship and networking opportunities. Employees working in different roles have the chance to connect with a wider range of colleagues and leaders, gaining valuable insights and building a robust professional network.

Strategies for Promoting Role Flexibility and Mobility: To effectively promote role flexibility and mobility, organizations should consider a variety of strategies:

1. **Internal Job Postings**
2. **Cross-Training Programs**
3. **Job Rotation**
4. **Career Pathing**

1. **Internal Job Postings: Internal job postings enable employees to find roles that match their skills and interests, promoting mobility and improving satisfaction and retention**

Key Components of Internal Job Postings

Transparent Communication: Transparent communication ensures that all employees are aware of available opportunities within the organization. This involves utilizing multiple communication channels, such as the company intranet, email newsletters, and staff meetings, to announce job openings. Enhancing awareness and encouraging employees to consider internal roles fosters a culture of growth and opportunity.

Fair Selection Process: A fair selection process maintains a transparent and equitable method for evaluating internal candidates. This involves developing standardized criteria for assessing candidates, including qualifications, performance history, and potential for growth. Building trust in the internal hiring process ensures that the best candidates are selected for each role, promoting fairness and equity.

Support for Transitions: Support for transitions facilitates smooth movements for employees moving into new roles. This involves providing resources such as orientation sessions, training programs, and mentorship opportunities to help employees adjust to their new positions. Increasing the likelihood of successful transitions enhances employee confidence and performance in new roles.

Career Development Pathways: Career development pathways outline clear advancement opportunities within the organization. This involves mapping out potential career trajectories and providing guidance on the steps needed to achieve them. Clarifying career pathways motivates employees to pursue internal opportunities and fosters long-term commitment.

Feedback Mechanisms: Feedback mechanisms ensure continuous improvement in the internal hiring process. This involves gathering feedback from employees and hiring managers about their experiences with the internal hiring system. Using this feedback to refine and enhance the process helps maintain a transparent and effective internal mobility program.

Internal Job Boards: Internal job boards provide a centralized location for posting internal job opportunities. This involves regularly updating job listings and ensuring that all employees have access to the information. Promoting internal job boards enhances visibility of available positions and encourages internal applications.

Recognition of Internal Talent: Recognition of internal talent highlights the achievements and potential of current employees. This involves acknowledging and rewarding employees who have successfully transitioned into new roles. Recognizing internal talent reinforces the value of internal mobility and encourages others to pursue similar opportunities.

Ongoing Training and Development: Ongoing training and development support continuous learning and skill enhancement for all employees. This involves offering regular training sessions, workshops, and professional development programs tailored to the needs of the workforce. Committing to continuous development prepares employees for future internal opportunities.

Internal Networking Opportunities: Internal networking opportunities facilitate connections between employees across different departments and roles. This involves organizing events, workshops, and informal gatherings that promote networking and collaboration. Encouraging internal networking helps employees explore new roles and build relationships that support career growth.

Example Internal Job Posting Steps

- **Post Job Openings:** Regularly update the company intranet with new job postings and send email alerts to employees.

- **Communicate Opportunities:** Highlight job openings during team meetings and in company newsletters.

- **Support Applicants:** Offer workshops on resume writing and interview skills for employees interested in applying for internal roles.

2. **Cross-Training Programs:** Cross-training programs enable employees to acquire skills from different roles within the organization, enhancing their versatility and preparedness for various tasks.

Key Components of Cross-Training Programs

Identify Key Skills: Identifying key skills involves determining the essential skills required for different roles within the organization. This process includes conducting a skills inventory and consulting with department heads to pinpoint critical competencies. Focusing training on relevant skills ensures that both employees and the organization benefit from the cross-training program.

Develop Training Modules: Developing training modules entails creating structured learning materials that cover the identified skills. Collaborating with subject matter experts to design comprehensive training materials and interactive workshops is crucial. Providing high-quality, targeted training enhances employees' capabilities and confidence, contributing to their overall professional growth.

Schedule Cross-Training Sessions: Scheduling cross-training sessions involves organizing regular training opportunities to ensure continuous learning and skill development. This includes developing a training calendar and allocating time for employees to participate in cross-training without disrupting their regular duties. Promoting ongoing skill enhancement fosters a culture of continuous improvement and adaptability within the organization.

Monitor and Evaluate Progress: Monitoring and evaluating progress involves tracking employees' development and the effectiveness of the cross-training program. Implementing regular assessments and feedback mechanisms helps gauge the success of the training and identify areas for improvement. Ensuring that training objectives are met maintains the program's relevance and effectiveness.

Encourage Participation: Encouraging participation involves motivating employees to engage in cross-training opportunities. This can be achieved by highlighting the benefits of cross-training, such as skill diversification and career advancement. Promoting a positive attitude toward cross-training enhances employee involvement and commitment to the program.

Facilitate Knowledge Sharing: Facilitating knowledge sharing encourages employees to share their expertise and experiences with their peers. Creating platforms for knowledge exchange, such as peer mentoring and collaborative projects, fosters a supportive learning environment. Encouraging knowledge sharing enhances team cohesion and collective problem-solving abilities.

Align with Organizational Goals: Aligning cross-training with organizational goals ensures that the program supports the broader strategic objectives of the company. This involves integrating cross-training initiatives with the organization's long-term vision and performance metrics. Ensuring alignment with organizational goals maximizes the program's impact on overall business success.

Support from Leadership: Support from leadership involves securing commitment and advocacy from senior management for the cross-training program. Leaders play a crucial role in championing cross-training and allocating necessary resources. Gaining leadership support underscores the importance of the program and drives organizational buy-in.

Incorporate Technology: Incorporating technology involves utilizing digital tools and platforms to enhance the cross-training experience. Leveraging e-learning modules, virtual simulations, and online collaboration tools makes training more accessible and flexible.

Encourage Role Flexibility and Mobility

Integrating technology into cross-training programs modernizes the learning process and accommodates diverse learning preferences.

Track and Report Outcomes: Tracking and reporting outcomes involves measuring the impact of cross-training on employee performance and organizational effectiveness. Establishing metrics and reporting systems helps quantify the benefits of the program. Documenting outcomes provides insights into the program's success and areas for future development.

Example Cross-Training Program Steps

- **Identify Skills:** List critical skills for various roles and create training objectives.
- **Develop Modules:** Create detailed training guides, hands-on activities, and assessment tools.
- **Schedule Sessions:** Plan regular cross-training sessions and encourage employees to participate.

3. **Job Rotation: Job rotation moves employees between roles, offering diverse experiences and skill development opportunities.**

Key Components of Job Rotation

Identify Roles and Departments: Identifying roles and departments involves selecting positions and areas within the organization that are suitable for rotation. This process includes analyzing organizational needs and consulting with department managers to pinpoint appropriate rotation opportunities. Strategically planning job rotations ensures they meet both organizational goals and employee development needs.

Develop a Rotation Schedule: Developing a rotation schedule entails creating a structured timeline for moving employees between roles. This includes defining the duration of each rotation, establishing criteria for participation, and sequencing the roles. A well-organized rotation schedule provides clear expectations and ensures the program runs smoothly and effectively.

Provide Support and Feedback: Providing support and feedback involves offering continuous guidance and constructive feedback to employees during their rotations. This includes assigning mentors or supervisors to guide employees, conducting regular check-ins, and providing performance evaluations. Continuous support enhances learning experiences and helps employees integrate new skills effectively.

Set Clear Objectives: Setting clear objectives involves defining specific goals and outcomes for each rotation period. This includes outlining what skills and knowledge employees should gain during their rotations. Clear objectives ensure that both employees and supervisors understand the purpose and expectations of the rotation, leading to more focused and productive learning experiences.

Facilitate Knowledge Transfer: Facilitating knowledge transfer involves ensuring that employees share and document their learning and experiences. This can include creating knowledge-sharing sessions, maintaining detailed records, and encouraging collaborative projects. Effective knowledge transfer maximizes the benefits of job rotation by spreading valuable insights and best practices across the organization.

Evaluate and Adjust the Program: Evaluating and adjusting the program involves regularly assessing the effectiveness of the job rotation initiative and making necessary improvements. This includes gathering feedback from participants, analyzing performance data, and revising the rotation schedule as needed. Continuous evaluation ensures the program remains relevant and aligned with organizational and employee development goals.

Ensure Alignment with Career Development Plans: Ensuring alignment with career development plans involves integrating job rotations with employees' long-term career goals. This includes discussing career aspirations with employees and tailoring rotation assignments to support their professional growth. Aligning rotations with career development plans enhances employee motivation and commitment to the program.

Communicate Benefits and Expectations: Communicating benefits and expectations involves clearly explaining the advantages of job rotation and setting realistic expectations. This includes highlighting opportunities for skill development, career advancement, and organizational impact. Transparent communication helps employees understand the value of participation and what is expected of them during rotations.

Monitor Employee Well-being: Monitoring employee well-being involves ensuring that employees maintain a healthy work-life balance during rotations. This includes checking in on their stress levels, workload, and overall satisfaction. Prioritizing employee well-being helps prevent burnout and ensures that rotations are a positive and enriching experience.

Recognize and Reward Participation: Recognizing and rewarding participation involves acknowledging employees' efforts and achievements during job rotations. This can include formal recognition programs, performance bonuses, or opportunities for further career advancement. Recognition and rewards motivate employees to engage fully in the program and strive for excellence in their new roles.

Example Job Rotation Program Steps

- **Identify Roles:** Determine key roles and departments for rotation.
- **Develop Schedule:** Create a rotation timeline and outline participation criteria.
- **Support and Feedback:** Assign mentors, conduct regular check-ins, and provide feedback.

4. **Career Pathing:** Career pathing involves creating clear pathways for career progression within the organization, helping employees understand potential career moves and the skills needed for advancement.

Key Components of Career Pathing

Define Career Paths: Defining career paths involves establishing clear career trajectories for different roles within the organization. This process includes mapping out potential career paths and detailing the steps required for advancement. Providing clear career paths helps employees understand how they can progress within the organization and plan their professional growth accordingly.

Identify Skills and Experiences: Identifying skills and experiences involves outlining the specific competencies and experiences necessary for each step along the career path. This process requires collaboration with HR and department leaders to specify what is needed for career advancement. Clearly identifying these requirements guides employees in their professional development and prepares them for future roles.

Provide Resources and Support: Providing resources and support involves offering the necessary tools and assistance to help employees pursue their career paths. This includes access to training programs, mentoring, and career development workshops. Offering these resources encourages continuous growth and helps employees achieve their career goals, fostering a culture of development and progression.

Create Clear Advancement Criteria: Creating clear advancement criteria involves establishing specific benchmarks and milestones that employees need to achieve to move to the next level. This includes performance metrics, project completion, and skill acquisition. Clear criteria ensure that employees know exactly what is expected for promotion, which can drive motivation and effort.

Facilitate Regular Career Development Discussions: Facilitating regular career development discussions involves setting up periodic meetings between employees and their managers to discuss career aspirations and progress. These discussions help employees stay focused on their career goals and allow managers to provide guidance and support. Regular conversations about career development keep career paths dynamic and aligned with employees' evolving interests and the organization's needs.

Monitor and Evaluate Progress: Monitoring and evaluating progress involves tracking employees' advancements and achievements along their career paths. This includes regular performance reviews and assessments to ensure that employees are on track with their development plans. Continuous monitoring and evaluation help identify any barriers to progression and provide opportunities for timely intervention and support.

Align Career Paths with Organizational Goals: Aligning career paths with organizational goals involves ensuring that individual career progression supports the broader objectives of the company. This includes integrating career development initiatives with strategic business goals and ensuring that as employees advance, they contribute to the organization's success. Alignment with organizational goals ensures that career paths are relevant and beneficial to both employees and the company.

Encourage Cross-Functional Experiences: Encouraging cross-functional experiences involves providing opportunities for employees to gain exposure to different roles and departments. This includes job rotations, project assignments, and collaborative initiatives. Cross-functional experiences enhance employees' skills and knowledge, making them more versatile and better prepared for leadership roles.

Recognize and Reward Milestones: Recognizing and rewarding milestones involves acknowledging and celebrating employees' achievements as they progress along their career paths. This includes formal recognition programs, promotions, and performance bonuses. Recognizing milestones motivates employees to continue their development efforts and reinforces the value of career progression within the organization.

Promote a Culture of Continuous Learning: Promoting a culture of continuous learning involves fostering an environment where ongoing education and skill development are valued and encouraged. This includes offering continuous learning opportunities, such as workshops, certifications, and educational resources. A culture of continuous learning supports career pathing by ensuring that employees are always developing new skills and staying current with industry trends.

Example Career Pathing Steps

- **Define Paths:** Map out career paths for various roles.
- **Identify Skills:** Detail the skills and experiences needed for each career step.
- **Provide Support:** Offer training, mentoring, and development resources.

The Long-Term Benefits of Encouraging Role Flexibility and Mobility

Encouraging role flexibility and mobility within an organization is vital for fostering a dynamic and adaptable workforce. This strategic approach enables the company to optimize talent utilization, enhance job satisfaction, improve adaptability, and support career development. By promoting flexibility and mobility, organizations can ensure that employees are placed in roles where they can maximize their potential and contribute to the organization's long-term success.

Optimized Talent Utilization

Maximizing Skills: Allowing employees to move between roles ensures that their skills are utilized where they are most needed. This optimization leads to better performance and productivity across the organization.

Dynamic Workforce: Role flexibility creates a dynamic workforce capable of adapting to changing needs and priorities. Employees who can shift roles based on organizational requirements enhance operational efficiency.

Resource Allocation: Effective talent utilization ensures that resources are allocated appropriately, minimizing skill gaps and redundancies. This strategic alignment supports better decision-making and execution.

Innovation and Problem-Solving: Employees in flexible roles are exposed to various functions and challenges, fostering a culture of innovation and improved problem-solving capabilities.

Increased Job Satisfaction

Alignment with Interests: Employees are more satisfied when they can move to roles that align with their interests and strengths. This alignment increases engagement and motivation, leading to higher productivity.

Variety and Challenge: Role flexibility offers employees variety and new challenges, reducing monotony and burnout. Engaged employees are more likely to stay with the organization long-term.

Personal Growth: Opportunities for role mobility encourage personal growth and development. Employees who can explore different roles gain new skills and experiences, enhancing their overall job satisfaction.

Work-Life Balance: Flexible roles can accommodate employees' personal needs and circumstances, contributing to better work-life balance and overall well-being.

Adaptability

Responding to Change: A flexible workforce is better equipped to respond to changes in the market or industry. Employees who can adapt to new roles quickly help the organization remain competitive and resilient.

Continuous Improvement: Role flexibility encourages continuous improvement and learning. Employees who regularly take on new challenges and responsibilities stay updated with the latest industry trends and best practices.

Cross-Functional Collaboration: Mobility across roles promotes cross-functional collaboration and understanding. This broad perspective enhances teamwork and the ability to achieve organizational goals.

Crisis Management: In times of crisis or rapid change, a flexible workforce can pivot quickly to address urgent needs, maintaining operational stability and performance.

Career Development

Clear Pathways: Role flexibility provides employees with clear pathways for career advancement. Knowing that there are opportunities for growth within the organization encourages employees to invest in their professional development.

Skill Development: Mobility between roles allows employees to develop a broad range of skills and competencies. This diverse skill set makes them more valuable to the organization and enhances their career prospects.

Mentorship and Guidance: Employees in flexible roles often receive mentorship and guidance from various leaders within the organization. This exposure to different management styles and philosophies supports their career growth.

Employee Retention: Providing opportunities for role mobility demonstrates the organization's commitment to employee development, fostering loyalty and reducing turnover rates.

Encouraging role flexibility and mobility within an organization allows employees to transition to roles that better suit their skills and interests, enhancing job satisfaction and organizational adaptability. By communicating internal opportunities, developing cross-training programs, implementing job rotation programs, creating clear career paths, and supporting employee transitions, organizations can promote a flexible and dynamic work environment. A strong focus on role flexibility and mobility ensures that employees are continuously aligned with their roles and contributing to the organization's growth and success.

Foster a Positive Work Environment

Fostering a positive work environment is crucial for ensuring that employees are happy, engaged, and aligned with their roles. A positive work environment promotes productivity, reduces turnover, and enhances overall job satisfaction. This chapter explores the importance of a positive work environment, key elements that contribute to it, and examples to help create and maintain a positive work environment in your organization.

Importance of a Positive Work Environment: A positive work environment is crucial for the overall success and well-being of an organization. Creating and maintaining a positive work environment can have profound impacts on various aspects of the workplace. Here, we explore the importance of a positive work environment in greater detail, highlighting key benefits and the reasons why organizations should prioritize it.

Increased Productivity: One of the most significant benefits of a positive work environment is the increase in employee productivity. When employees are happy, engaged, and motivated, they tend to perform better and contribute more effectively to organizational goals.

- **Motivation and Engagement:** A positive work environment fosters a sense of motivation and engagement among employees. When employees feel valued and appreciated, they are more likely to take ownership of their tasks and put in extra effort to achieve their objectives. This heightened level of engagement directly translates into higher productivity levels.

- **Reduced Absenteeism:** Employees who enjoy their work environment are less likely to take unnecessary sick days or be absent without cause. A positive atmosphere can lead to better physical and mental health, reducing absenteeism and ensuring that employees are present and productive.

- **Enhanced Focus and Efficiency:** A supportive and positive workplace helps employees maintain focus and work more efficiently. When stress levels are low and morale is high, employees can concentrate better on their tasks, leading to quicker completion times and higher quality of work.

Reduced Turnover: High employee turnover can be costly and disruptive to any organization. A positive work environment plays a critical role in reducing turnover rates and fostering employee loyalty.

- **Employee Retention:** A positive work environment makes employees feel valued and respected, which encourages them to stay with the organization longer. Lower turnover rates mean that organizations can retain their top talent and reduce the costs associated with hiring and training new employees.

- **Loyalty and Commitment:** When employees feel a strong connection to their workplace, they are more likely to develop loyalty and commitment to the organization. This loyalty can result in employees going above and beyond their job requirements, contributing to the organization's long-term success.

- **Positive Reputation:** Organizations known for their positive work environments attract high-quality candidates. A good reputation as an employer of choice can lead to an influx of talented applicants, making it easier to fill positions with skilled and dedicated individuals.

Enhanced Job Satisfaction: Job satisfaction is a key driver of employee performance and organizational success. A positive work environment significantly enhances employees' job satisfaction, leading to numerous benefits for both individuals and the organization.

- **Work-Life Balance:** A positive work environment often includes policies and practices that support a healthy work-life balance. When employees can balance their work and personal lives effectively, they experience higher levels of job satisfaction.

- **Recognition and Appreciation:** Regular recognition and appreciation of employees' efforts contribute to a positive work environment. When employees feel that their hard work is acknowledged, they are more likely to feel satisfied and motivated.

- **Opportunities for Growth:** Providing employees with opportunities for professional development and career growth is a hallmark of a positive work environment. When employees see a clear path for advancement, they are more likely to be satisfied with their jobs and remain with the organization.

Improved Collaboration: Collaboration and teamwork are essential for achieving organizational goals and driving innovation. A positive work environment fosters a culture of collaboration, leading to better team dynamics and improved outcomes.

- **Open Communication:** A positive work environment encourages open communication and transparency. When employees feel comfortable sharing ideas and feedback, it enhances collaboration and fosters a culture of innovation.

- **Trust and Respect:** Trust and respect are foundational elements of a positive work environment. When employees trust and respect each other, they are more likely to work together effectively and resolve conflicts amicably.

- **Team Cohesion:** A supportive work environment promotes team cohesion and a sense of camaraderie among employees. Strong team bonds can lead to more effective collaboration, as team members are more willing to help each other and work toward common goals.

Strategies for promoting a Positive Work Environment: To create a positive work environment, organizations should focus on several key elements:

1. Open Communication
2. Recognition and Rewards
3. Work-Life Balance
4. Supportive Leadership
5. Healthy Workplace Culture

1. **Open Communication:** Open communication involves creating an environment where employees feel comfortable sharing their ideas, feedback, and concerns. It is the cornerstone of a healthy organizational culture, fostering trust, transparency, and collaboration. When employees know that their voices are heard and valued, they are more likely to engage actively, contribute innovative ideas, and commit to the organization's goals. To achieve this, organizations must implement several key practices that facilitate open communication.

Key Components of Open Communication

Regular Meetings: Holding regular team meetings and one-on-one check-ins. Regular meetings ensure that communication lines remain open and that both managers and employees have the opportunity to discuss progress, challenges, and opportunities in a structured setting.

Feedback Channels: Providing channels for anonymous feedback and suggestions. Anonymous feedback mechanisms allow employees to share their thoughts without fear of retribution, leading to more honest and constructive feedback.

Transparent Communication: Ensuring transparency in organizational decisions and changes. Transparent communication involves keeping employees informed about significant organizational decisions, changes, and the rationale behind them, which helps in building trust and reducing uncertainty.

Example Open Communication Practices

1. **Hold Weekly Team Meetings to Discuss Progress and Challenges**: Weekly team meetings provide a consistent platform for employees to share updates on their work, discuss any challenges they are facing, and collaborate on solutions. These meetings foster a sense of community and ensure that everyone is on the same page regarding team goals and progress.

2. **Provide an Anonymous Suggestion Box for Employee Feedback**: An anonymous suggestion box, whether physical or digital, allows employees to voice their ideas, concerns, and suggestions without fear of identification. This practice encourages more candid feedback and can reveal issues or ideas that might not surface through regular channels.

3. **Communicate Organizational Changes and Decisions Transparently**: When making significant decisions or changes within the organization, it's crucial to communicate these transparently. This includes explaining the reasons behind the decisions, how they will impact the team, and what steps will be taken moving forward. Transparency helps build trust and ensures that employees feel involved in the process.

2. **Recognition and Rewards:** Recognizing and rewarding employees' achievements and contributions is essential for maintaining a positive work environment. When employees feel appreciated and valued, they are more likely to be motivated, engaged, and committed to their work. Recognition and reward programs can significantly enhance morale, increase productivity, and reduce turnover. Effective recognition can be both formal and informal, ensuring that employees receive acknowledgment for their efforts in various meaningful ways.

Key Components of Recognition and Rewards

Formal Recognition Programs: Implementing programs to formally recognize and reward employees. Formal recognition programs provide structured and consistent ways to celebrate employee achievements. These programs are often tied to specific criteria and offer tangible rewards that reinforce desired behaviors and outcomes.

Informal Recognition: Providing informal recognition through praise and appreciation. Informal recognition can be just as powerful as formal programs. Simple gestures like a thank-you note, verbal praise, or a shout-out during a meeting can make employees feel valued and appreciated.

Incentives and Rewards: Offering incentives and rewards for outstanding performance. Incentives and rewards can take many forms, including financial bonuses, extra time off, gift cards, and other perks. These rewards motivate employees to maintain high performance and strive for excellence.

Example Recognition and Reward Programs

1. **Employee of the Month Program with Rewards and Recognition**: Establish an Employee of the Month program to highlight exceptional performance. This program can include

public recognition during company meetings, a dedicated spot on a recognition board, and tangible rewards such as a gift card, a reserved parking spot, or a special lunch with executives.

2. **Regularly Praising Employees for Their Hard Work and Achievements:** Make it a habit to regularly praise employees for their efforts and successes. This can be done during team meetings, through emails, or with personal notes. Consistent, sincere appreciation helps build a positive workplace culture where employees feel recognized for their contributions.

3. **Offering Bonuses or Additional Time Off for Exceptional Performance:** Provide financial incentives or additional time off for employees who go above and beyond. This could include performance-based bonuses, extra vacation days, or special perks such as tickets to events or a wellness package. These rewards can be tailored to individual preferences to maximize their impact.

3. **Work-Life Balance:** Promoting work-life balance helps employees manage their professional and personal lives effectively, leading to higher job satisfaction, reduced stress, and improved overall well-being. When organizations prioritize work-life balance, they create an environment where employees feel valued and supported, which in turn enhances productivity and retention. Here are key components and example initiatives to foster a healthy work-life balance:

Key Components of Work-Life Balance

Flexible Work Arrangements: Offering flexible work hours and remote work options gives employees the autonomy to structure their workday in a way that best suits their personal and professional responsibilities. This flexibility can lead to increased job satisfaction and better work performance. Key aspects include:

- **Flexible Hours:** Allow employees to choose their start and end times within a given range to accommodate personal schedules, reducing stress and improving focus.

- **Remote Work:** Provide options for employees to work from home or other remote locations, which can increase productivity and job satisfaction by eliminating commutes and offering a more comfortable work environment.

Paid Time Off: Providing adequate paid time off for vacation and personal needs allows employees to rest, recharge, and attend to personal matters without the stress of lost income. This time away from work is crucial for maintaining mental and physical health. Key aspects include:

- **Vacation Days:** Ensure that employees have enough vacation days to take meaningful breaks from work, promoting relaxation and reducing burnout.

- **Personal Days:** Offer personal days for employees to manage personal affairs, medical appointments, or emergencies, supporting their overall well-being.

- **Sick Leave:** Provide sufficient sick leave to ensure that employees can recover from illness without the pressure to work, which helps prevent the spread of sickness in the workplace.

Wellness Programs: Offering wellness programs and resources to support employees' physical and mental health demonstrates a company's commitment to the holistic well-being of its employees. Key aspects include:

- **Fitness Programs:** Provide access to gym memberships, fitness classes, or on-site exercise facilities to encourage physical activity and healthy living.

- **Mental Health Support:** Offer mental health resources, such as counseling services, stress management workshops, and mindfulness training, to support emotional well-being.
- **Healthy Lifestyle Initiatives:** Implement programs that promote healthy eating, smoking cessation, and other healthy lifestyle choices, contributing to overall employee health.

Example Work-Life Balance Initiatives

Implement Flexible Work Hours and Remote Work Options: By allowing employees to choose their work hours and offering remote work options, companies can accommodate diverse personal schedules and reduce commute-related stress. This flexibility can lead to higher productivity and job satisfaction. Specific actions include:

- **Flexible Scheduling Policies:** Create policies that outline the flexibility available to employees, including core hours during which all employees must be available.
- **Remote Work Infrastructure:** Invest in technology and tools that facilitate remote work, such as video conferencing software, collaboration platforms, and secure access to company networks.

Provide Generous Paid Time Off Policies: Ensuring that employees have sufficient paid time off for vacations, personal days, and sick leave is essential. Encouraging the use of this time off helps employees maintain a healthy balance between work and personal life, preventing burnout and promoting overall well-being. Specific actions include:

- **Transparent PTO Policies:** Clearly communicate paid time off policies to all employees, ensuring they understand their entitlements and how to request time off.

- **Encouragement from Leadership:** Encourage managers and leaders to model taking time off and to support their teams in doing the same, reinforcing the importance of work-life balance.

Offer Wellness Programs: Providing access to wellness programs, such as gym memberships, mental health resources, and wellness workshops, supports employees in maintaining their health. These programs can include yoga classes, meditation sessions, nutritional counseling, and more, addressing both physical and mental health needs. Specific actions include:

- **Fitness Benefits:** Partner with local gyms or fitness centers to offer discounted memberships or on-site fitness classes.
- **Mental Health Initiatives:** Provide access to confidential counseling services and host regular stress management and mindfulness workshops.
- **Health Challenges:** Organize company-wide health challenges, such as step competitions or healthy eating contests, to promote wellness and team building.

4. **Supportive Leadership:** Promoting work-life balance helps employees manage their professional and personal lives effectively, leading to higher job satisfaction, reduced stress, and improved overall well-being. When organizations prioritize work-life balance, they create an environment where employees feel valued and supported, which in turn enhances productivity and retention. Here are key components and example initiatives to foster a healthy work-life balance:

Key Components of Supportive Leadership

Flexible Work Arrangements: Offering flexible work hours and remote work options. Flexible work arrangements give employees the autonomy to structure their workday in a way that best suits their personal and professional responsibilities. This flexibility can lead to increased job satisfaction and better work performance.

Paid Time Off: Providing adequate paid time off for vacation and personal needs. Generous paid time off policies allow employees to rest, recharge, and attend to personal matters without the stress of lost income. This time away from work is crucial for maintaining mental and physical health.

Wellness Programs: Offering wellness programs and resources to support employees' physical and mental health. Wellness programs can include a variety of resources, such as gym memberships, mental health counseling, stress management workshops, and healthy lifestyle initiatives. These programs demonstrate a company's commitment to the holistic well-being of its employees.

Example Work-Life Balance Initiatives

1. **Implement Flexible Work Hours and Remote Work Options**: By allowing employees to choose their work hours and offering remote work options, companies can accommodate diverse personal schedules and reduce commute-related stress. This flexibility can lead to higher productivity and job satisfaction.

2. **Provide Generous Paid Time Off Policies**: Ensuring that employees have sufficient paid time off for vacations, personal days, and sick leave is essential. Encouraging the use of this time off helps employees maintain a healthy balance between work and personal life, preventing burnout and promoting overall well-being.

3. **Offer Wellness Programs**: Providing access to wellness programs, such as gym memberships, mental health resources, and wellness workshops, supports employees in maintaining their health. These programs can include yoga classes, meditation sessions, nutritional

counseling, and more, addressing both physical and mental health needs.

5. **Healthy Workplace Culture:** A healthy workplace culture promotes positive behaviors, values, and attitudes within the organization, fostering an environment where employees can thrive. This culture is crucial for enhancing employee satisfaction, productivity, and retention. To cultivate a healthy workplace culture, organizations must focus on several key areas:

Key Components of Healthy Workplace Culture

Values and Ethics: Promoting values and ethical behavior throughout the organization. Core values and ethical standards guide how employees interact with each other, make decisions, and approach their work. Emphasizing these principles helps create a cohesive and trustworthy environment.

Team Building Activities: Organizing activities to build teamwork and camaraderie. Team-building activities encourage collaboration, strengthen relationships, and create a sense of community among employees. These activities can range from casual team outings to structured retreats and workshops.

Inclusive Environment: Creating an inclusive environment where all employees feel valued and respected. Inclusivity ensures that diverse perspectives are heard and appreciated, fostering a sense of belonging and encouraging innovation.

Example Healthy Workplace Culture Initiatives

1. **Promote Core Values and Ethical Behavior in All Interactions**: Ensure that the organization's core values and ethical standards are clearly communicated and integrated into everyday practices. This

can be achieved through regular training sessions, leadership examples, and clear policies that reinforce ethical behavior.

2. **Organize Team-Building Activities, Such as Team Outings and Retreats**: Plan regular team-building events to enhance collaboration and camaraderie. Activities such as team outings, retreats, workshops, and social events help employees connect on a personal level and build stronger working relationships.

3. **Foster an Inclusive Environment with Diversity and Inclusion Initiatives**: Implement diversity and inclusion programs that promote equality and respect for all employees. This can include diversity training, employee resource groups, mentorship programs, and inclusive hiring practices.

The Long-Term Benefits of Fostering a Positive Work Environment

Fostering a positive work environment is essential for the overall health and success of an organization. It involves creating a culture where employees feel valued, supported, and motivated. A positive work environment contributes to increased productivity, reduced turnover, enhanced job satisfaction, and improved collaboration. By focusing on building and maintaining a supportive and engaging workplace, organizations can achieve sustained success and growth.

Increased Productivity

A motivated workforce performs better when employees feel valued and supported. This leads to fewer sick days, enhanced focus, and continuous improvement, as employees are more willing to contribute new ideas in a positive atmosphere.

Reduced Turnover

A positive environment promotes employee retention, reducing the costs associated with recruitment and training. A stable workforce also improves team dynamics and enhances employer branding, making the organization more attractive to top talent.

Enhanced Job Satisfaction

When employee well-being, work-life balance, and career development are prioritized, job satisfaction increases. Regular recognition and appreciation keep employees motivated and engaged.

Improved Collaboration

Positive work environments strengthen team cohesion, foster open communication, and build trust. Inclusive cultures encourage diverse perspectives, which boosts creativity and problem-solving.

A positive work environment ensures employee happiness, engagement, and role alignment. *By encouraging open communication, implementing recognition and reward programs, promoting work-life balance, providing supportive leadership, and cultivating a healthy workplace culture, organizations can create a positive work environment that enhances productivity, reduces turnover, and improves overall job satisfaction. A strong focus on a positive work environment ensures that employees are continuously aligned with their roles and contributing to the organization's growth and success.*

Monitor and Evaluate Alignment

Monitoring and evaluating alignment between employees and their roles is crucial for ensuring continuous alignment and making necessary adjustments. Regular monitoring and evaluation help identify misalignments early and take corrective actions to maintain productivity and engagement. This chapter explores the importance of monitoring and evaluating alignment, effective strategies for doing so, and examples to help implement a continuous alignment process in your organization.

Importance of Monitoring and Evaluating Alignment: Monitoring and evaluating the alignment between employees' roles and organizational goals is crucial for maintaining a productive, engaged, and effective workforce. Here's an in-depth look at why this process is so important:

1. **Early Identification of Misalignments:** One of the primary benefits of monitoring and evaluating alignment is the ability to identify misalignments early. Catching these issues promptly allows for timely interventions, preventing small problems from escalating into significant issues.

    - **Proactive Problem Solving:** Early detection of misalignments enables managers to address and rectify issues before they affect productivity and morale. This proactive approach can prevent the frustration and disengagement that often result from prolonged misalignment.

- **Minimizing Disruptions:** By identifying and addressing misalignments early, organizations can minimize disruptions to workflows and team dynamics. This ensures that teams remain cohesive and projects stay on track.

- **Tailored Interventions:** Early identification allows for more tailored interventions, such as additional training, role adjustments, or changes in responsibilities, which can help realign employees with their roles effectively.

2. **Continuous Improvement:** Regularly monitoring and evaluating alignment fosters a culture of continuous improvement. It ensures that both employees and the organization are consistently striving to enhance their performance and achieve better alignment with organizational goals.

    - **Feedback Loop:** Establishing a regular feedback loop allows employees to voice their concerns and suggestions, leading to ongoing adjustments and improvements. This feedback can provide valuable insights into areas where alignment can be strengthened.

    - **Adaptive Strategies:** Continuous evaluation helps organizations adapt their strategies in response to changing circumstances, such as market shifts, technological advancements, or internal changes. This adaptability is crucial for maintaining alignment over time.

    - **Goal Refinement:** Regular monitoring and evaluation allow for the refinement of goals and expectations, ensuring that they remain relevant and attainable. This ongoing process helps maintain a clear and achievable path for employees and the organization.

3. **Enhanced Productivity:** When employees' roles are well-aligned with their skills, interests, and organizational goals, productivity is significantly enhanced. Monitoring and evaluating alignment ensures that employees are in the right roles and are equipped to perform at their best.

    - **Optimal Resource Utilization:** Proper alignment ensures that employees' talents and skills are utilized effectively, maximizing their contributions to the organization. This optimal use of resources leads to higher efficiency and output.

    - **Reduced Errors:** Employees who are well-aligned with their roles are less likely to make errors or require extensive supervision. This reduction in mistakes improves overall productivity and quality of work.

    - **Focus and Clarity:** Clear alignment provides employees with a better understanding of their responsibilities and how their work contributes to organizational goals. This clarity helps them focus their efforts on high-impact tasks, boosting productivity.

4. **Increased Engagement:** Employee engagement is closely tied to how well their roles match their skills, interests, and career aspirations. Monitoring and evaluating alignment helps maintain high levels of engagement by ensuring that employees are in roles that suit them best.

    - **Job Satisfaction:** Employees who feel that their roles align with their strengths and interests are more likely to experience job satisfaction. This satisfaction translates into higher engagement and motivation.

    - **Retention:** High levels of engagement lead to lower turnover rates, as employees are more likely to stay with an organization that values their contributions and provides fulfilling work.

Monitoring alignment helps identify and address factors that might lead to disengagement or turnover.

- **Commitment:** Engaged employees are more committed to their organization's success. They are willing to go the extra mile, contribute innovative ideas, and collaborate effectively with their colleagues.

Strategies for Monitoring and Evaluating Alignment: To effectively monitor and evaluate alignment, organizations should consider a variety of strategies:

1. **Regular Check-Ins**
2. **Performance Metrics and Analytics**
3. **Employee Feedback Surveys**
4. **Role and Skills Assessments**

1. **Regular Check-Ins:** Regular check-ins involve frequent one-on-one meetings between employees and their managers to discuss alignment, progress, and challenges. These meetings are essential for maintaining open lines of communication, fostering a strong relationship between managers and employees, and ensuring that everyone is working toward common goals. By implementing regular check-ins, organizations can proactively address issues, provide timely feedback, and support continuous development.

Key Components of Effective Regular Check-Ins

Weekly or Biweekly Meetings: Scheduling regular meetings to discuss alignment and performance. Frequent check-ins, whether weekly or biweekly, allow managers and employees to stay aligned on priorities, discuss ongoing projects, and address any immediate concerns. These meetings help in maintaining momentum and ensuring that employees feel supported and valued.

Goal Setting and Review: Setting and reviewing goals to ensure alignment with roles. During check-ins, managers and employees should collaboratively set short-term and long-term goals. Regularly reviewing these goals helps in tracking progress, making necessary adjustments, and ensuring that the employee's work remains aligned with organizational objectives.

Feedback and Coaching: Providing feedback and coaching to address misalignments. Constructive feedback and coaching during check-ins are crucial for employee development. Managers can offer guidance, identify areas for improvement, and recognize accomplishments. This ongoing support helps employees improve their performance and grow in their roles.

Example Regular Check-In Practices

1. **Schedule Weekly One-on-One Meetings with Each Team Member**: Establishing a routine of weekly one-on-one meetings ensures that managers and employees have dedicated time to discuss any issues, updates, and progress. This consistency helps build trust and fosters a culture of open communication.

2. **Set and Review Individual Goals Regularly**: During check-ins, managers and employees should set clear, achievable goals. Regularly reviewing these goals helps track progress and make any necessary adjustments. This practice ensures that employees remain focused and aligned with the organization's objectives.

3. **Provide Constructive Feedback and Coaching During Check-Ins**: Use check-ins as an opportunity to provide constructive feedback and coaching. Managers should highlight areas where employees excel and offer suggestions for improvement. This

balanced approach helps employees feel recognized for their achievements while also understanding how they can continue to grow.

2. **Performance Metrics and Analytics: Performance metrics and analytics track and evaluate employee-role alignment.** Data-driven insights ensure proper role matching, identify improvement areas, and enhance productivity and job satisfaction. This approach enables a more objective and comprehensive understanding of how well employees are performing and how effectively they are aligned with organizational goals.

Key Components of Metrics and Analytics

Key Performance Indicators (KPIs): Defining KPIs that align with roles and tracking performance. KPIs are specific, measurable, and relevant metrics that help quantify an employee's performance and contributions to the organization. By establishing clear KPIs for each role, organizations can monitor performance consistently and ensure that employees are meeting their expected standards.

Data Analysis: Analyzing performance data to identify trends and areas for improvement. Through regular analysis of performance data, organizations can uncover patterns and trends that indicate whether employees are effectively aligned with their roles. This analysis helps in pinpointing specific areas where performance may be lacking and provides insights into potential causes and solutions.

Dashboard Tools: Using dashboard tools to visualize performance and alignment metrics. Dashboard tools offer a visual representation of performance data, making it easier to track and interpret key metrics. These tools can display real-time data and trends, providing a clear and concise overview of how well employees are performing and how aligned they are with their roles.

Example Performance Metrics and Analytics Practices

1. **Define KPIs for Each Role and Track Performance Regularly**: Establishing specific KPIs for each role ensures that performance expectations are clear and measurable. Regularly tracking these KPIs helps managers and employees stay focused on key objectives and provides a basis for performance evaluations.

2. **Analyze Performance Data to Identify Trends and Misalignments**: Regular data analysis allows organizations to identify trends and patterns in employee performance. By examining this data, managers can detect misalignments between employees and their roles, such as skills gaps, lack of engagement, or areas where additional training may be needed.

3. **Use Dashboard Tools to Visualize Performance and Alignment Metrics**: Implementing dashboard tools enables organizations to visualize performance data in an easily interpretable format. Dashboards can display a range of metrics, from individual KPIs to overall team performance, helping managers quickly identify issues and track progress toward alignment goals.

3. **Employee Feedback Surveys:** Conducting employee feedback surveys helps gather insights into alignment and identify areas for improvement. These surveys are instrumental in understanding the real-time perceptions, challenges, and suggestions of employees, enabling organizations to make data-driven decisions that enhance workplace culture and productivity. By actively seeking employee feedback, organizations can uncover hidden issues, recognize trends, and develop targeted strategies to foster a more engaged and effective workforce.

Key Components of Employee Surveys

Anonymous Surveys: Conducting anonymous surveys to gather honest feedback. When employees feel secure that their responses cannot be traced back to them, they are more likely to provide candid feedback. This honesty is crucial for obtaining a true picture of the workplace environment and identifying genuine areas of concern.

Regular Surveys: Scheduling surveys regularly to track changes in alignment. By conducting surveys on a consistent basis, such as quarterly or biannually, organizations can monitor the impact of implemented changes over time and adapt strategies accordingly. Regular surveys help in maintaining a continuous dialogue with employees and keeping the pulse on organizational health.

Actionable Insights: Analyzing survey results to identify actionable insights and areas for improvement. It is essential not just to collect data but to thoroughly analyze it to pinpoint specific issues and opportunities. These insights should be translated into concrete action plans aimed at addressing the identified gaps and enhancing overall employee satisfaction and performance.

Example Employee Feedback Survey Practices

1. **Conduct Anonymous Surveys Every Quarter**: Gathering feedback quarterly ensures that the organization maintains a regular check-in with employees, fostering an environment where continuous improvement is prioritized. This frequency helps in identifying and addressing issues before they escalate.

2. **Use Survey Results to Identify Misalignments and Areas for Improvement**: Once the survey data is collected, it should be systematically analyzed to uncover any misalignments between employee roles, expectations, and actual experiences. This

analysis helps in formulating targeted interventions to improve alignment and address specific concerns.

3. **Share Survey Results and Action Plans with Employees:** Transparency is key to building trust and ensuring that employees feel heard. Sharing the survey results and the subsequent action plans with employees demonstrates a commitment to making meaningful changes based on their feedback. This practice not only enhances trust but also encourages further participation in future surveys.

4. **Role and Skills Assessments:** Regular role and skills assessments are crucial for ensuring that employees' skills align with their roles. These assessments help organizations identify gaps in skills, provide opportunities for development, and ensure that roles evolve to meet changing organizational needs. By conducting thorough and regular evaluations, businesses can foster a more competent and adaptable workforce, leading to enhanced productivity and employee satisfaction.

Key Components of Effective Role and Skills Assessments

Skills Assessments: Conducting skills assessments to identify gaps and areas for development. Skills assessments are tools used to evaluate an employee's current capabilities and identify any gaps that may exist. These assessments can include tests, simulations, peer reviews, and self-assessments, and they help in pinpointing specific areas where employees may need additional training or support.

Role Evaluations: Evaluating roles regularly to ensure they align with organizational needs. Regular role evaluations involve reviewing job descriptions, responsibilities, and required competencies to ensure that they align with the organization's evolving goals and needs. This process helps in identifying any mismatches between the role requirements and the employee's skill set, allowing for adjustments that enhance alignment.

Training and Development: Providing training and development opportunities to address skills gaps. Once skills gaps are identified through assessments, it is essential to offer targeted training and development programs. These programs can include workshops, online courses, mentoring, and on-the-job training, aimed at closing the gaps and enhancing employees' abilities to perform their roles effectively.

Example Role and Skills Assessment Practices

1. **Conduct Skills Assessments Annually to Identify Gaps**: Performing annual skills assessments helps organizations keep track of their employees' capabilities and development needs. This regular evaluation ensures that any skills gaps are promptly identified and addressed, preventing them from affecting overall performance.

2. **Evaluate Roles Regularly to Ensure Alignment with Organizational Needs**: Regular role evaluations involve reviewing and updating job descriptions and responsibilities to reflect the current needs of the organization. This practice ensures that roles remain relevant and that employees are equipped with the necessary skills to fulfill their duties effectively.

3. **Provide Training and Development to Address Skills Gaps**: Offering continuous training and development opportunities based on the results of skills assessments ensures that employees have the resources they need to improve their skills. This proactive approach helps maintain a skilled and adaptable workforce that meets the organization's demands.

When conducting assessments, focus on identifying and leveraging employees' existing soft skills and strengths, rather than attempting to fundamentally change them. This approach ensures that employees are guided towards tasks and roles that naturally align with their abilities.

The Long-Term Benefits of Monitoring and Evaluating Alignment

Monitoring and evaluating alignment within an organization is a critical practice that ensures employees' roles, responsibilities, and goals are in sync with the overall objectives of the company. Regularly assessing alignment helps maintain a coherent strategy, boosts productivity, increases employee satisfaction, and supports continuous improvement. Here's a detailed exploration of the long-term benefits of monitoring and evaluating alignment:

Early Identification of Misalignments

Proactive Corrections: Monitoring alignment allows organizations to identify misalignments early. By addressing these issues proactively, companies can make necessary adjustments before they escalate into significant problems, ensuring smooth operations and minimizing disruptions.

Resource Optimization: Early identification of misalignments ensures that resources are allocated effectively. By aligning roles and responsibilities with organizational goals, resources such as time, budget, and personnel are utilized optimally, avoiding wastage.

Maintained Focus: Regularly assessing alignment helps maintain focus on strategic objectives. When employees understand how their roles contribute to the bigger picture, they are more likely to stay on course and prioritize tasks that align with organizational goals.

Reduced Errors: Identifying and correcting misalignments early reduces errors and inconsistencies in work processes. This leads to higher quality output and a more reliable performance across the organization.

Continuous Improvement

Ongoing Development: Continuous monitoring fosters a culture of ongoing development. Employees receive regular feedback on their performance and alignment with goals, encouraging them to constantly improve and adapt their skills and behaviors to meet organizational standards.

Enhanced Adaptability: Organizations that regularly evaluate alignment are better positioned to adapt to changes in the market or industry. This agility allows companies to pivot strategies and realign roles as needed, ensuring sustained competitiveness.

Innovation Encouragement: Continuous improvement initiatives often lead to innovation. As employees strive to align better with organizational goals, they are likely to propose new ideas and solutions that drive the company forward.

Benchmarking Progress: Regular evaluations provide benchmarks for progress. By tracking alignment over time, organizations can measure improvements and identify trends, facilitating more informed decision-making and strategic planning.

Enhanced Productivity

Efficient Operations: Aligning roles and responsibilities with organizational goals enhances overall efficiency. Employees who understand their contributions to the company's objectives are more motivated and focused, leading to improved productivity.

Goal Achievement: Regular alignment assessments ensure that employees' goals are in sync with the organization's strategic objectives. This coherence facilitates the achievement of both individual and company-wide goals, driving overall success.

Streamlined Processes: Evaluating alignment helps identify redundant or misaligned tasks, allowing organizations to streamline processes. This streamlining reduces unnecessary work, enabling employees to focus on high-impact activities.

Motivated Workforce: A workforce that understands its role in achieving organizational goals is more motivated. This motivation translates into higher productivity as employees are driven to contribute meaningfully to the company's success.

Increased Engagement

Clear Direction: Regularly communicating and reviewing alignment ensures that employees have a clear understanding of their roles and how they contribute to the organization's success. This clarity enhanced engagement, as employees feel their work is meaningful and impactful.

Feedback and Recognition: Monitoring alignment provides opportunities for regular feedback and recognition. Acknowledging employees' efforts and aligning their performance with organizational goals boosts morale and fosters a positive work environment.

Personal Growth: Regular assessments identify areas where employees can grow and develop. By aligning personal career aspirations with organizational objectives, companies can create personal and professional growth pathways, enhancing overall engagement.

Inclusive Culture: Continuous alignment evaluations promote an inclusive culture where everyone understands their role and feels valued.

This inclusivity strengthens team cohesion and collaboration, leading to a more engaged and committed workforce.

Alignment with Organizational Goals

Strategic Coherence: Regularly evaluating alignment ensures that all employees are working toward the same strategic goals. This coherence minimizes conflicting priorities and maximizes the organization's ability to achieve its objectives.

Performance Tracking: Alignment assessments provide a framework for tracking performance against strategic goals. By regularly reviewing progress, organizations can adjust strategies and ensure that efforts are consistently directed toward achieving the desired outcomes.

Resource Allocation: Ensuring alignment with organizational goals allows for better resource allocation. Companies can direct resources to areas that are most aligned with their strategic objectives, maximizing the impact of their investments.

Long-Term Success: Consistent alignment with organizational goals contributes to long-term success. By keeping all parts of the organization focused on shared objectives, companies build a strong foundation for sustained growth and achievement.

Monitoring and evaluating alignment between employees and their roles is crucial for ensuring continuous alignment and making necessary adjustments. By scheduling regular check-ins, defining and tracking performance metrics, conducting employee feedback surveys, performing role and skills assessments, and continuously adjusting and improving, organizations can maintain alignment, enhance productivity, and increase engagement. A strong focus on monitoring and evaluating alignment ensures that employees are continuously aligned with their roles and contributing to the organization's growth and success.

Aligning Roles with Organizational Goals

Aligning roles with organizational goals ensures that every employee's contributions are aligned with the broader objectives of the organization. This alignment promotes a cohesive and focused effort toward achieving the organization's goals. This chapter explores the importance of aligning roles with organizational goals, effective strategies for doing so, and actionable steps to ensure that employees' roles contribute to the organization's overall success.

Aligning roles with organizational goals is a fundamental aspect of effective organizational management and strategy. It ensures that every employee contributes meaningfully to the company's overall mission and objectives. This alignment is crucial for fostering a cohesive and productive work environment, enhancing employee engagement, and ultimately achieving the organization's goals.

Here's an expanded look at the importance of aligning roles with organizational goals:

1. **Cohesive Effort:** Cohesive Effort refers to the synchronized and unified actions of all employees working toward a common purpose. When roles are aligned with organizational goals, it ensures that all departments and individuals are moving in the same direction, contributing to a cohesive effort.

    - **Synergy:** When roles are aligned, the collective efforts of the team can create a synergistic effect, where the combined output is greater than the sum of individual efforts. This synergy enhances efficiency and effectiveness in achieving organizational goals.

- **Collaboration:** Alignment fosters better collaboration among departments and teams, as everyone understands how their work interconnects with others. This cooperation is crucial for executing complex projects that require input from various functions.

2. **Enhanced Productivity:** Aligning roles with organizational goals directly impacts productivity by ensuring that employees' work is relevant and focused on achieving key objectives.

    - **Focused Efforts:** Employees who understand how their tasks contribute to broader company goals are more likely to prioritize their work effectively. This focus reduces wasted effort and enhances overall efficiency.

    - **Efficient Resource Utilization:** Proper alignment ensures that resources, including time, skills, and technology, are allocated efficiently. This optimal use of resources minimizes waste and maximizes output, leading to better organizational performance.

    - **Reduced Redundancy:** When roles are clearly defined and aligned with organizational goals, it reduces redundancy and overlap in tasks. This clarity prevents employees from duplicating efforts, allowing them to concentrate on value-added activities.

3. **Increased Engagement:** Aligning roles with organizational goals plays a significant role in increasing employee engagement by providing a clear sense of purpose and direction.

    - **Purpose and Meaning:** Employees who see a clear connection between their work and the organization's mission are more likely to feel that their contributions matter. This sense of purpose is a powerful motivator and enhances job satisfaction.

- **Motivation and Morale:** When employees understand how their work impacts the organization's success, it boosts their motivation and morale. They feel valued and recognized, which leads to higher levels of engagement and commitment.

- **Professional Growth:** Alignment often involves setting personal and professional development goals that align with organizational objectives. This alignment provides employees opportunities for growth and advancement, further enhancing engagement.

4. **Achieving Organizational Goals:** Aligning roles with organizational goals is essential for effectively achieving the company's strategic objectives. It ensures that all efforts are directed toward common targets, facilitating the accomplishment of key goals.

- **Strategic Execution:** Clear alignment allows for the strategic execution of plans and initiatives. It ensures that all employees are aware of their responsibilities and how they contribute to achieving the organization's goals, leading to more coordinated and effective execution.

- **Measurable Outcomes:** By aligning roles with specific goals, organizations can set measurable outcomes and track progress more accurately. This clarity helps in assessing performance and making necessary adjustments to stay on track.

- **Adaptability and Agility:** When roles are aligned with organizational goals, it becomes easier for the organization to adapt to changes in the market or industry. Employees can quickly understand new directions and adjust their work accordingly, maintaining agility and responsiveness.

Additional Considerations

- **Leadership and Vision:** Strong leadership is crucial in aligning roles with organizational goals. Leaders must communicate the company's vision effectively and inspire employees to align their work with this vision. This leadership fosters a culture of alignment and ensures that everyone is working toward the same objectives.

- **Feedback and Communication:** Continuous feedback and open communication are vital for maintaining alignment. Regular check-ins, performance reviews, and goal alignment meetings help keep everyone on the same page and address any misalignments promptly.

- **Cultural Fit:** Aligning roles with organizational goals also involves ensuring that employees fit well with the company culture. A good cultural fit enhances engagement and reduces turnover, as employees are more likely to feel connected to the organization's values and mission.

Strategies for Aligning Roles with Organizational Goals: To effectively align roles with organizational goals, organizations should consider a variety of strategies:

1. Clear Communication of Goals
2. Role Clarity and Definition
3. Goal Alignment Meetings
4. Performance Management Systems

1. **Clear Communication of Goals:** Clear communication of organizational goals ensures that all employees understand the broader objectives of the organization. When goals are communicated effectively, employees can see how their individual roles contribute to

the success of the organization, fostering a sense of purpose and alignment. Clear communication involves several key components:

Key Components of Clear Communication of Goals

Goal Setting Sessions: Goal setting sessions are critical for establishing and communicating the organization's objectives. These sessions can take various forms, such as workshops, retreats, or structured meetings, and should involve employees at different levels to ensure a comprehensive understanding of the goals.

- **Inclusive Participation:** Involve key stakeholders, including executives, managers, and team leaders, in the goal-setting process to ensure diverse perspectives and buy-in from different departments.

- **Clear Objectives:** Clearly define both short-term and long-term goals. Ensure these goals are Specific, Measurable, Achievable, Relevant, and Time-bound (SMART).

- **Documentation:** Document the goals and distribute them to all employees. This ensures everyone has a reference and understands what is expected.

- **Feedback Mechanism:** Provide a platform for employees to ask questions and give feedback during and after goal-setting sessions. This can help identify any areas of confusion and promote engagement.

Regular Updates: Providing regular updates on progress toward organizational goals keeps employees informed and engaged. Regular communication can take many forms, including:

- **Monthly Newsletters:** Send out newsletters that highlight progress toward goals, celebrate milestones, and outline any changes or new objectives.

- **Team Meetings:** Use weekly or bi-weekly team meetings to discuss progress, address challenges, and realign efforts as necessary.
- **Digital Platforms:** Utilize digital platforms such as intranet dashboards, emails, or collaboration tools to keep everyone updated in real-time. This can include progress bars, charts, and other visual aids to illustrate progress.

Transparent Communication: Ensuring transparent communication means being open about how individual roles and departments contribute to achieving organizational goals. Transparency fosters trust and helps employees see the value of their work.

- **Role Mapping:** Develop and share a role map that shows how each department and individual role contributes to the overall goals. This can be a visual representation that makes it easy to understand the interdependencies.
- **Regular Briefings:** Hold regular briefings where leaders explain how the work of different teams and individuals is aligned with the organizational goals.
- **Open Dialogue:** Encourage open dialogue where employees feel comfortable discussing their contributions and asking questions about how their work fits into the bigger picture.

Example Clear Communication Practices

Hold Annual Goal-Setting Sessions:

- **Structure:** Organize annual goal-setting sessions where leadership and key stakeholders collaborate to define and communicate the organization's objectives for the year. These sessions should be well-structured, with a clear agenda and defined outcomes.

- **Engagement:** Engage employees from various departments to ensure diverse input and broader buy-in. Use these sessions to explain the rationale behind the goals and how they align with the company's mission and vision.

Provide Regular Updates on Progress toward Goals:

- **Monthly Newsletters:** Create and distribute monthly newsletters that highlight key achievements, upcoming milestones, and any changes to the goals. Include stories or case studies of teams or individuals who have made significant contributions.

- **Team Meetings:** Use regular team meetings to provide updates on goal progress. These meetings can include presentations, progress reports, and Q&A sessions to ensure everyone is on the same page.

Clearly Articulate How Each Role Contributes to the Organization's Goals:

- **Role Descriptions:** Ensure that job descriptions explicitly state how each role contributes to the organizational goals. This can help employees understand the importance of their work and how it fits into the larger strategy.

- **Performance Reviews:** Incorporate discussions about goal alignment into regular performance reviews. Use these reviews to reinforce how individual performance impacts the achievement of organizational goals.

2. **Role Clarity and Definition:** Ensuring role clarity and definition is essential for helping employees understand their responsibilities and how they contribute to organizational goals. Clear roles and well-defined responsibilities provide a framework within which employees can operate effectively, reducing confusion, enhancing

performance, and ensuring alignment with the organization's objectives.

Key Components of Role Clarity and Definition

Clear Job Descriptions: Clear job descriptions are the foundation of role clarity. They provide a comprehensive overview of what each role entails and set clear expectations for employees. Here are the key components of an effective job description:

- **Job Title:** The official title of the position.

- **Role Overview:** A brief summary of the role and its importance within the organization.

- **Key Responsibilities:** A detailed list of the primary tasks and responsibilities associated with the role.

- **Required Skills and Qualifications:** A clear outline of the necessary skills, experience, and qualifications for the role.

- **Performance Expectations:** Specific metrics or goals that the employee is expected to achieve.

- **Reporting Structure:** Information on who the employee reports to and, if applicable, who reports to them.

- **Work Environment:** Details about the work environment, including any physical requirements or special conditions.

Defined Roles and Responsibilities: Defined roles and responsibilities go beyond job descriptions to provide detailed information on what each employee is accountable for. This clarity helps prevent overlap, confusion, and gaps in job functions.

Alignment with Goals: Ensuring that each role is aligned with the organization's goals is crucial for overall success. This alignment ensures that every employee's work contributes to the broader objectives of the organization.

Example Role Clarity and Definition Practices: Implementing practices to ensure role clarity and definition involves several actionable steps:

Develop Detailed Job Descriptions for Each Role:

- **Collaborative Creation:** Involve managers and current role holders in the creation and review of job descriptions to ensure accuracy and completeness.
- **Regular Updates:** Regularly update job descriptions to reflect any changes in responsibilities or organizational goals.
- **Accessibility:** Make job descriptions easily accessible to all employees, possibly through an internal HR portal.

Clearly Define Roles and Responsibilities for Each Employee:

- **Role Mapping:** Create role maps that visually depict the responsibilities and interconnections between different roles within the organization.
- **Onboarding Programs:** Use onboarding programs to ensure new hires understand their roles and responsibilities from the outset.
- **Ongoing Communication:** Regularly communicate any changes in roles and responsibilities through team meetings and individual check-ins.

Ensure that Job Descriptions and Roles are Aligned with Organizational Goals:

- **Goal Setting:** During annual goal-setting sessions, ensure that each role's responsibilities are aligned with the organizational goals.

- **Performance Reviews:** Use performance reviews to reinforce how individual roles contribute to organizational goals.

- **Role Adaptation:** Be willing to adapt and evolve roles as the organization's goals change to maintain alignment.

3. **Goal Alignment Meetings:** Goal alignment meetings are an essential strategy for ensuring that individual employee goals are in harmony with the overarching objectives of the organization. These meetings foster a clear understanding of how each team member's contributions support the larger mission, driving coherence and coordinated effort across the company.

Key Components of Goal Alignment Meetings

Regular Alignment Meetings: Scheduling regular alignment meetings is crucial for maintaining a continuous dialogue about goals and expectations between managers and employees. These sessions are not just a formality but a strategic touchpoint that keeps everyone focused and aligned with the company's priorities.

Setting Individual Goals: Setting individual goals that align with organizational objectives is fundamental to goal alignment meetings. Each employee should have clear, specific, and measurable goals that contribute to the broader company targets.

Reviewing Progress: Regularly reviewing progress toward individual and organizational goals is vital for ensuring that efforts are on track and making the necessary impact. These reviews provide an opportunity to celebrate successes, identify areas for improvement, and make necessary adjustments.

Example Goal Alignment Meeting Practices

Schedule Quarterly Goal Alignment Meetings:

- **Planning:** Schedule quarterly meetings well in advance to ensure availability and preparedness.

- **Consistency:** Maintain consistency in scheduling to establish a routine and expectation for these meetings.

Set Individual Goals Aligned with Organizational Goals:

- **Goal Mapping:** Map out how individual goals contribute to organizational goals during the meetings.

- **Clarity:** Ensure each employee understands how their specific goals support the company's broader objectives.

Review Progress toward Individual and Organizational Goals in Regular Check-Ins:

- **Monthly Check-Ins:** Conduct shorter, monthly check-ins to monitor ongoing progress and address any issues promptly.

- **Documentation:** Keep detailed notes on progress and discussions during these check-ins to track performance over time.

4. **Performance Management Systems:** Performance management systems align employee performance with organizational goals, ensuring improvement and productivity through structured evaluations, feedback, and development plans. Here's an in-depth exploration of the key components and benefits of effective performance management systems:

Key Components of Performance Management Systems

Scheduled Assessments: Regularly scheduled performance reviews are crucial for continuously evaluating employee performance.

These assessments help identify strengths, weaknesses, and areas for improvement, ensuring that employees remain aligned with organizational objectives.

Setting and Tracking Goals: Implementing goal tracking systems is essential for ensuring employee goals align with organizational objectives. These systems help in setting clear, measurable goals and tracking progress toward achieving them.

Constructive Feedback: Providing constructive feedback is a critical component of performance management systems. Regular feedback helps employees understand their performance, recognize their achievements, and identify areas for improvement.

Development Plans: Creating development plans based on performance reviews and feedback is essential for employee growth. These plans outline specific actions and resources needed to address skill gaps and enhance competencies.

Example Performance Management System Practices

Implementing effective performance management systems involves several practical steps and best practices:

Conduct Annual Performance Reviews:

Planning: Schedule annual performance reviews well in advance to ensure availability and preparedness. **Consistency:** Maintain consistency in conducting these reviews to establish a routine and expectation for performance evaluation.

Implement Goal Tracking Systems:

SMART Criteria: Ensure that all goals meet the SMART criteria. **Monitoring Tools:** Use goal tracking tools to monitor progress and adjust goals as needed.

Provide Constructive Feedback:

Regular Feedback Sessions: Conduct regular feedback sessions to provide specific, balanced, and actionable feedback. **Recognition Programs:** Implement recognition programs to acknowledge and reward employee achievements.

Develop and Review Development Plans:

Personalized Development Goals: Set personalized development goals that align with organizational needs. **Training Resources:** Provide access to relevant training programs and resources. **Regular Updates:** Regularly review and update development plans to ensure continuous growth and relevance.

The Long-Term Benefits of Aligning Roles with Organizational Goals

Aligning roles with organizational goals is a strategic practice that ensures every employee's efforts contribute directly to the broader objectives of the company. This alignment fosters a cohesive, productive, and motivated workforce, driving the organization toward sustained success. Here's an in-depth exploration of the long-term benefits of aligning roles with organizational goals:

Cohesive Effort

Unified Direction: When roles are aligned with organizational goals, all employees work toward common objectives. This unity fosters a sense of purpose and direction, ensuring that everyone is on the same page and moving toward the same targets.

Synergistic Collaboration: Aligning roles enhances collaboration across teams. Employees understand how their responsibilities intersect with those of their colleagues, promoting teamwork and cooperative problem-solving.

Minimized Conflicts: Clear alignment reduces the likelihood of conflicts arising from misaligned priorities. When everyone understands their role in achieving organizational goals, it reduces friction and promotes a harmonious work environment.

Enhanced Coordination: A cohesive effort ensures better coordination of activities and resources. This alignment streamlines processes and reduces redundancy, leading to more efficient operations.

Enhanced Productivity

Focused Efforts: Aligning roles with organizational goals ensures that employees focus their efforts on tasks that directly contribute to the company's success. This focus maximizes productivity by eliminating distractions and non-essential activities.

Efficient Resource Use: Alignment ensures that human resources, time, and budget are used efficiently. By directing efforts toward strategic priorities, organizations can optimize resource allocation and achieve better outcomes.

Clear Performance Metrics: With aligned roles, performance metrics are clearly linked to organizational goals. Employees understand how their performance is measured and how it impacts the company's success, driving them to perform at their best.

Streamlined Processes: Aligning roles helps streamline work processes by eliminating unnecessary steps and ensuring that every action taken supports the organization's objectives. This streamlining leads to faster and more efficient workflows.

Increased Engagement

Meaningful Work: Employees who understand how their roles contribute to organizational goals find their work more meaningful. This sense of purpose enhances engagement, as employees see the value of their contributions.

Ownership and Accountability: Alignment fosters a sense of ownership and accountability. Employees feel responsible for achieving goals and are more committed to their roles, leading to higher levels of engagement and motivation.

Career Development: When roles are aligned with organizational goals, employees can see a clear path for career development. They understand how advancing their skills and responsibilities can contribute to both their personal growth and the company's success.

Recognition and Reward: Aligned roles make it easier to recognize and reward employees for their contributions to organizational goals. This recognition boosts morale and encourages continued high performance.

Achieving Goals

Strategic Execution: Aligning roles with organizational goals ensures that strategic plans are executed effectively. Employees' daily tasks and responsibilities directly support the broader objectives, driving the company toward its targets.

Improved Decision-Making: When roles are clearly aligned with goals, employees are better equipped to make decisions that support the organization's strategy. This alignment enhances decision-making at all levels, ensuring consistency and coherence.

Goal Achievement: Clear alignment helps track progress toward organizational goals. Employees and managers can easily monitor achievements and make necessary adjustments to stay on course, increasing the likelihood of meeting targets.

Long-Term Vision: Aligning roles with organizational goals supports the company's long-term vision. It ensures that daily operations are not only focused on immediate outcomes but also contribute to sustainable growth and future success.

Aligning roles with organizational goals ensures that every employee's contributions are aligned with the broader objectives of the organization. By communicating organizational goals clearly, ensuring role clarity and definition, scheduling goal alignment meetings, implementing performance management systems, and continuously monitoring and adjusting, organizations can promote a cohesive and focused effort toward achieving their goals. A strong focus on aligning roles with organizational goals ensures that employees are continuously aligned with their roles and contributing to the organization's growth and success.

The Future of Role Alignment

As we've explored in previous chapters, effective role alignment is crucial for organizational success. However, the rapidly evolving workplace demands that we look beyond current practices and prepare for future challenges and opportunities. This chapter builds upon the strategies we've discussed, examining how emerging trends and technologies will reshape role alignment in the coming years.

The concepts of clear communication, performance management, and employee engagement that we've covered will remain fundamental, but their implementation will evolve. Technological advancements, particularly in AI, will transform how we approach hiring, performance reviews, and skill development. The rise of remote and hybrid work models will necessitate new approaches to maintaining alignment across distributed teams. Additionally, the increasing focus on employee well-being will require us to rethink how we define and measure successful role alignment.

By understanding these future trends, we can begin adapting our current practices to ensure continued effectiveness in an ever-changing work environment.

Key Trends Shaping the Future of Role Alignment

Several key trends are shaping the future of role alignment:

1. **Technological Advancements**
2. **Remote and Hybrid Work Models**
3. **Focus on Employee Well-being**

1. **Technological Advancements:** Technological advancements are rapidly transforming the workplace. The evolution of artificial intelligence (AI) is one such advancement that is driving significant changes in how businesses operate . Here's an expanded look at how AI will help shape the modern workplace:

   The Role of AI in Future Role Alignment

   Artificial Intelligence (AI) will revolutionize various aspects of business operations, including the alignment of roles within organizations. AI technologies will offer powerful tools for enhancing hiring processes, conducting performance reviews, and implementing effective role alignment strategies. This section explores how AI will be leveraged to optimize role alignment, ensuring that employees are well-matched to their roles and contributing effectively to organizational goals.

   AI in Future Hiring Practices

   Enhanced Candidate Screening: AI-driven tools will significantly improve the efficiency and effectiveness of candidate screening processes. By leveraging machine learning algorithms (systems that improve their performance based on data patterns, making predictions or decisions without being explicitly programmed for each task)., these tools will analyze large volumes of resumes and application forms quickly, identifying the most suitable candidates based on predefined criteria.

   - **Automated Resume Parsing:** AI will extract relevant information from resumes, such as skills, experience, and education, and match these against job requirements. This will reduce the manual effort involved in initial screenings and help identify the best-fit candidates more quickly.

     Example: A tech company implements an AI tool that screens 10,000 applications in hours instead of weeks, highlighting top candidates for further review.

- **Predictive Analytics:** AI will use historical hiring data to predict the likelihood of a candidate's success in a role. By analyzing patterns from previous successful hires, AI will help identify traits and qualifications that correlate with high performance, improving the quality of hires.

  Example: A finance firm uses AI to predict which candidates will thrive based on traits observed in their top performers, leading to a 30% increase in retention rates.

Bias Reduction: One of the significant advantages of AI in hiring will be its potential to reduce unconscious bias. AI algorithms will be designed to focus solely on objective criteria, such as skills and experience, rather than subjective factors that can lead to biased hiring decisions.

- **Blind Hiring Practices:** AI will anonymize candidate information during the initial screening process, ensuring that decisions are based on qualifications rather than demographic factors like gender, age, or ethnicity.

  Example: A multinational corporation uses an AI system to hide candidate names and photos during the first review stage, leading to a more diverse set of interviewees.

- **Diverse Talent Pools:** AI tools will help identify and source candidates from diverse backgrounds by using broader and more inclusive search parameters, enhancing the diversity of the workforce.

  Example: A software company employs AI to target job postings to a wider range of platforms and demographics, increasing the diversity of their applicant pool by 40%.

AI in Future Performance Reviews

Continuous Performance Monitoring: AI-powered tools will enable continuous performance monitoring, providing real-time insights into employee performance. This will allow for more timely and accurate evaluations compared to traditional annual performance reviews.

- **Real-Time Feedback:** AI systems will analyze data from various sources, such as project management tools, communication platforms, and productivity software, to provide continuous feedback on employee performance. This will help managers and employees address issues promptly and make necessary adjustments.

  Example: An AI platform integrates with project management software to send real-time performance insights to managers, allowing for immediate feedback and support.

- **Performance Metrics Analysis:** AI will track and analyze key performance indicators (KPIs) to assess employee performance objectively. By identifying trends and patterns, AI will help managers understand areas where employees excel and where they may need additional support or development.

  Example: A retail chain uses AI to analyze sales data, employee interactions, and customer feedback, providing a holistic view of performance and areas for improvement.

Personalized Development Plans: AI will assist in creating personalized development plans for employees based on their performance data and career aspirations. These plans will include targeted training programs, mentorship opportunities, and skill development initiatives.

- **Skill Gap Analysis:** AI will identify gaps in an employee's skill set by comparing their current abilities with the requirements of their role and the organization's strategic goals. This analysis will help in designing tailored development programs to address these gaps.

    Example: A healthcare provider uses AI to assess clinical staff skills against new regulatory standards, creating customized training plans to bridge identified gaps.

- **Career Pathing:** AI will suggest potential career paths for employees based on their skills, interests, and performance history. This will help employees visualize their growth within the organization and motivate them to achieve their professional goals.

    Example: An AI career advisor tool suggests potential roles and progression paths within a tech company, helping employees plan their careers and stay motivated.

AI in Future Role Alignment Strategies and Implementation

Dynamic Role Matching: AI will dynamically match employees to roles that best fit their skills, experience, and career aspirations, ensuring optimal alignment with organizational goals.

- **Skills Mapping:** AI tools will create comprehensive skills maps for employees, allowing managers to understand the strengths and weaknesses of their teams. This will facilitate better role assignments and project allocations.

    Example: A consultancy firm uses AI to map consultants' skills and automatically assign them to projects where their expertise will have the most impact.

- **Adaptive Role Assignment:** AI will continuously analyze employee performance and organizational needs, suggesting role adjustments in real-time to maintain optimal alignment. This will ensure that employees are always in positions where they can contribute most effectively.

  Example: An AI system at a manufacturing company reallocates tasks among workers based on real-time analysis of their performance and operational needs, improving overall efficiency.

Predictive Workforce Planning: AI will play a crucial role in predictive workforce planning by forecasting future talent needs based on business trends and organizational goals.

- **Demand Forecasting:** AI will analyze market trends, business growth projections, and internal data to predict future talent needs. This will enable organizations to plan for hiring, training, and development well in advance.

  Example: An AI tool helps an e-commerce company predict seasonal hiring needs based on past sales data, ensuring they have enough staff during peak times.

- **Succession Planning:** AI will identify potential successors for key positions by analyzing employee performance and career trajectories. This will ensure a smooth transition and continuity in leadership roles.

  Example: A financial services firm uses AI to identify high-potential employees and prepare them for leadership roles, reducing the risk of gaps when key executives retire.

Enhanced Employee Engagement: AI will enhance employee engagement by providing personalized experiences and development opportunities.

- **Engagement Analytics:** AI will monitor employee engagement levels through surveys, performance data, and social interactions, providing insights into factors affecting morale and motivation. This will help managers take proactive measures to improve engagement.

  Example: A tech startup uses AI to analyze employee engagement survey data, identifying key areas for improvement and implementing targeted initiatives to boost morale.

- **Personalized Learning and Development:** AI will recommend personalized learning paths and development programs for employees based on their career goals and performance data. This will ensure continuous growth and development, keeping employees motivated and aligned with organizational objectives.

  Example: An AI learning platform at a pharmaceutical company suggests courses and training modules tailored to each employee's career goals, increasing participation and satisfaction.

Outcomes and Benefits

The implementation of AI-driven solutions will lead to significant improvements in role alignment, hiring processes, and performance management. Key benefits will include:

- **Enhanced Productivity:** Employees will be better matched to roles that suit their skills and career aspirations, leading to increased productivity and job satisfaction.

- **Reduced Bias:** AI-driven hiring processes will significantly reduce unconscious bias, resulting in a more diverse and inclusive workforce.

- **Continuous Improvement:** Real-time performance monitoring and personalized development plans will foster a culture of continuous improvement and professional growth.

- **Strategic Alignment:** Predictive workforce planning and dynamic role matching will ensure that the workforce remains aligned with organizational goals, supporting long-term success.

By leveraging AI technologies, companies will optimize role alignment, enhancing overall organizational performance and employee engagement. This case study illustrates the transformative potential of AI in shaping the future of role alignment in modern organizations.

2. **Remote Work Options:** We now live in the post covid world and "back to the office" strategies are being deployed by some organizations. There is a bit of employee vs employer tension currently in play. Because of the challenges with our economy at the moment, the labor market pendulum has swung in favor of the employer, which is driving the return to the office momentum. However, as history has shown us, these economic headwinds will pass and the pendulum will swing back to a tighter labor market and remote work options will give a competitive edge to those who implement it. This flexibility has several benefits for both employees and employers:

    - **Employee Satisfaction:** Remote work provides employees with the flexibility to balance their personal and professional lives more effectively. This can lead to higher job satisfaction and lower turnover rates. According to a study by Owl Labs, remote workers report being happier and staying in their jobs longer compared to on-site workers.

- **Access to a Wider Talent Pool:** By offering remote work options, companies can tap into a global talent pool, attracting skilled professionals regardless of their geographic location. This is particularly beneficial for roles that are difficult to fill locally.

- **Cost Savings:** Remote work can reduce overhead costs associated with maintaining a physical office space, such as rent, utilities, and office supplies. These savings can be reinvested into other areas of the business.

Hybrid Work Models: Hybrid work models combine remote and in-office work arrangements, offering a balanced approach that caters to diverse employee preferences and job requirements. This model typically involves employees splitting their time between working from home and working in the office.

- **Flexibility and Structure:** Hybrid work models provide employees with the flexibility to work remotely while also maintaining the structure and social interaction of an office environment. This balance can enhance productivity and job satisfaction.

- **Enhanced Collaboration:** While remote work offers many benefits, some tasks are better suited to in-person collaboration. Hybrid models allow teams to come together for meetings, brainstorming sessions, and collaborative projects while still enjoying the flexibility of remote work for individual tasks.

- **Reduced Commuting:** Hybrid work models can significantly reduce the time and stress associated with daily commuting, contributing to better work-life balance and overall well-being.

Flexible Work Policies: Implementing flexible work policies is essential to support diverse work models and meet the evolving needs of the workforce. These policies can encompass various aspects of work arrangements, including hours, location, and job sharing.

- **Flexible Scheduling:** Allowing employees to set their own working hours can accommodate different lifestyles and peak productivity times. This flexibility can be particularly beneficial for employees with caregiving responsibilities or those pursuing further education.

- **Job Sharing:** Job sharing involves two employees sharing the responsibilities of one full-time position. This arrangement can provide greater work-life balance and is particularly useful for roles that do not require a full-time presence.

- **Compressed Workweeks:** Some organizations offer compressed workweeks, where employees work longer hours over fewer days (e.g., four 10-hour days instead of five 8-hour days). This model can provide extended weekends and improve overall job satisfaction.

Challenges and Solutions: While remote and hybrid work models offer numerous benefits, they also present certain challenges that organizations need to address:

- **Communication Barriers:** Ensuring effective communication between remote and in-office employees can be challenging. Solutions include adopting unified communication platforms, setting clear communication protocols, and encouraging regular virtual meetings.

- **Maintaining Company Culture:** Preserving a strong company culture in a remote or hybrid setting requires intentional efforts. Organizations can focus on virtual team-building activities, regular all-hands meetings, and creating opportunities for informal interactions.

- **Performance Management:** Monitoring and evaluating employee performance can be more complex in remote and hybrid work environments. Implementing clear performance metrics, regular check-ins, and continuous feedback mechanisms can help maintain accountability and productivity.

3. **Focus on Employee Well-being:** Employee well-being is increasingly reshaping role alignment and workplace practices, emphasizing the need for a supportive and healthy work environment..** This holistic approach to well-being encompasses mental health support, work-life balance, and comprehensive well-being programs, all of which contribute to a more engaged, productive, and satisfied workforce. Here's an expanded look at these elements and how they are being integrated into modern workplace practices:

Mental Health Support: The recognition of mental health as a critical component of overall well-being has led organizations to implement various support systems for their employees. Providing mental health support is not only beneficial for employees' personal lives but also enhances their productivity and job satisfaction.

- **Counseling Services:** Many companies now offer access to professional counseling services either in-house or through external providers. This support can include one-on-one therapy sessions, mental health hotlines, and online counseling platforms.

- **Employee Assistance Programs (EAPs):** EAPs provide a range of services designed to help employees manage personal and work-related issues. These programs often include mental health counseling, stress management resources, and referrals to specialized services.

- **Mental Health Awareness Training:** Training programs aimed at raising awareness about mental health issues can equip employees and managers with the knowledge to recognize signs of distress and provide appropriate support. This training can also reduce stigma and encourage employees to seek help when needed.

Work-Life Balance: Promoting work-life balance is essential for maintaining employee well-being. Flexible work arrangements allow employees to manage their professional responsibilities alongside personal commitments, reducing stress and burnout.

- **Flexible Work Hours:** Allowing employees to set their own work hours can help them better manage their time and reduce conflicts between work and personal life. Flexible schedules can accommodate various needs, such as childcare, education, or personal interests.

- **Remote Work Options:** Offering remote work opportunities provides employees with the flexibility to work from different locations, reducing the time and stress associated with commuting. Remote work can also support a better work-life balance by allowing employees to create a more comfortable and personalized work environment.

- **Paid Time Off and Leave Policies:** Generous paid time off (PTO) policies and leave options, such as parental leave, sabbaticals, and mental health days, are crucial for helping employees recharge and manage life events without sacrificing their job security or financial stability.

Well-being Programs: Implementing comprehensive well-being programs is an effective way to support employees' physical, mental, and emotional health. These programs can take various forms, from fitness initiatives to mindfulness workshops.

- **Physical Health Programs:** Encouraging physical activity through initiatives like on-site fitness centers, gym memberships, or organized sports activities can improve employees' physical health and overall well-being. Regular physical activity is linked to reduced stress and increased energy levels.

- **Mental Health Programs:** Mindfulness and meditation programs, stress management workshops, and resilience training can help employees develop coping strategies to manage stress and enhance their mental well-being. These programs can be offered in-person or through virtual platforms.

- **Nutritional Support:** Providing access to healthy food options in the workplace, nutrition counseling, and educational sessions on healthy eating can promote better dietary habits among employees, contributing to their overall health.

- Example Focus on Employee Well-being Practices

Challenges and Solutions: While focusing on employee well-being offers numerous benefits, organizations may encounter challenges in implementing these practices effectively:

- **Resource Allocation:** Providing comprehensive well-being programs can require significant investment. Solutions include starting with small, scalable initiatives and gradually expanding based on employee feedback and engagement.

- **Employee Engagement:** Ensuring that employees actively participate in well-being programs can be challenging. Solutions involve promoting the benefits of these programs, integrating them into the company culture, and seeking continuous feedback to improve participation rates.

- **Measuring Impact:** Quantifying the impact of well-being initiatives on productivity and satisfaction can be difficult. Solutions include using surveys, health metrics, and productivity data to assess the effectiveness of programs and make necessary adjustments.

As we move into the future, role alignment will be significantly influenced by emerging trends and technologies, reshaping the workplace and how organizations operate. Staying ahead of these changes is crucial for organizations to ensure continuous alignment between employees and their roles. This chapter has delved into key trends shaping the future of role alignment, innovative strategies to navigate these changes, and actionable steps to prepare for an evolving work environment.

Technological Advancements are set to revolutionize the workplace, particularly through the integration of artificial intelligence (AI). AI will play a pivotal role in enhancing hiring processes, conducting performance reviews, and implementing effective role alignment strategies. By leveraging AI, organizations can optimize role alignment, ensuring that employees are well-matched to their roles and contributing effectively to organizational goals. This includes AI-driven tools for enhanced candidate screening, predictive analytics to improve hiring quality, and continuous performance monitoring to provide real-time insights and personalized development plans.

The Remote and Hybrid Work Models will continue to evolve, providing flexibility that benefits both employees and employers. These models enhance job satisfaction, access to a wider talent pool, and cost savings. However, they also pose challenges such as maintaining effective communication and company culture, which organizations must address through clear communication protocols and regular virtual interactions.

Focus on Employee Well-being is becoming increasingly important, with organizations recognizing the need to support mental health, work-life balance, and overall well-being. This holistic approach includes offering counseling services, flexible work hours, generous paid time off, and comprehensive well-being programs. While implementing these initiatives may present challenges, such as resource allocation and measuring impact, the benefits in terms of enhanced employee engagement and productivity are substantial.

By embracing these trends and technologies, organizations can ensure that they are well-positioned for future success. The integration of AI, the flexibility of remote and hybrid work models, and a strong focus on employee well-being will collectively drive the future of role alignment. By staying proactive and adaptive, organizations can maintain a productive, engaged, and satisfied workforce, ultimately contributing to long-term organizational growth and success.

The Final Climb

Throughout this book, we've journeyed through the complexities of role alignment, delving into the intrinsic nature of soft skills and the myriad psychological, organizational, and cultural factors that shape personal and professional growth. We've shared transformative stories of individuals like Luis, Tony, and Susan, who evolved from underperformers to exceptional contributors once placed in roles that leveraged their true strengths.

In this final chapter, aptly titled "The Final Climb," we will explore the broader implications of role alignment and the critical importance of nurturing each individual's unique talents. This chapter serves as a comprehensive conclusion, weaving together the insights and lessons from previous chapters and providing a blueprint for creating an environment where everyone can thrive.

As with the title of this book, imagine a scenario where two fish are evaluated by their ability to climb a tree. This absurd expectation not only sets the fish up for failure but also disregards their true capabilities. This parable illustrates the folly of misalignment in evaluating talent. In the workplace context, it underscores the necessity of recognizing and valuing each individual's unique strengths and aligning roles accordingly. Role misalignment goes beyond mere job dissatisfaction. It represents a fundamental mismatch between an employee's skills, interests, and the demands of their position. This misalignment can trigger a cascade of negative effects that ultimately undermine the overall health and performance of an organization. Misalignment can quietly undermine workplace productivity and morale, often remaining unnoticed until its impact becomes significant.

When employees are assigned responsibilities that do not align with their skills, they struggle to perform effectively. This struggle not only leads to decreased productivity but also significantly increases stress levels. The constant frustration of failing to meet expectations can result in burnout and a decline in mental health. Misalignment frequently results in high turnover rates. Employees who feel undervalued or incapable of succeeding in their roles are more likely to leave the organization. This turnover is costly, both financially and in terms of lost knowledge and continuity. A workforce that is not engaged or satisfied with their roles can negatively impact the overall morale of the organization. This dissatisfaction can spread, affecting team dynamics and the organizational culture.

The stories of Luis, Tony, and Susan highlight the critical importance of recognizing and leveraging individual strengths. Each of these individuals possessed unique capabilities that were initially overlooked due to misalignment. Once placed in roles that suited their strengths, they excelled and significantly contributed to their organizations' success.

Luis' transformation from an underperformer to a top executive underscores the pivotal role of proper role alignment. Initially struggling in a detail-oriented position, Luis' natural talent for building relationships and managing client accounts was eventually recognized. This shift revitalized his career and led to substantial revenue growth for the company. Luis' story teaches us the importance of understanding individual strengths, maintaining flexibility in role assignments, and providing supportive leadership.

Tony's story serves as a powerful reminder of the dangers of stretching employees beyond their core strengths. Initially a top performer in a role that matched his skills, Tony was moved to a position that did not leverage his abilities. This misstep led to decreased performance and ultimately his exit from the company. However, once Tony found a role that aligned with his strengths at a new organization, he thrived again. Tony's experience highlights the need to recognize the limits of versatility, provide adequate support, and regularly reassess role assignments.

Susan's story exemplifies the positive impact of role realignment. Initially in a leadership position that did not suit her evolving strengths, Susan struggled. Once reassigned to a role that leveraged her attention to detail and work ethic, she flourished. Susan's success story emphasizes the importance of ongoing development and assessment, encouraging self-awareness, and creating a supportive environment.

Achieving effective role alignment requires a multifaceted approach that involves understanding individual strengths, providing continuous support, and fostering a flexible and supportive organizational culture. The foundation of role alignment begins with the hiring process. Ensuring that new hires are well-suited for their roles from the outset can prevent many issues associated with misalignment. Detailed job descriptions, thorough candidate assessments, and effective onboarding programs are crucial elements of this process. Role alignment is an ongoing process that requires regular monitoring and support. Implementing regular performance reviews, offering continuous training and development opportunities, and establishing mentorship programs are essential strategies.

To implement effective role alignment strategies, organizations should follow these actionable steps:

1. Conduct a comprehensive skills assessment: Use tools like personality tests, skills inventories, and performance data to identify each employee's strengths and weaknesses.

2. Develop detailed role profiles: Create clear, comprehensive descriptions for each role, outlining required skills, responsibilities, and how they contribute to organizational goals.

3. Implement regular check-ins: Schedule monthly or quarterly meetings between employees and managers to discuss role fit, challenges, and opportunities for growth.
4. Establish a feedback system: Create anonymous channels for employees to provide feedback on their role alignment and suggestions for improvement.
5. Offer role rotation programs: Allow employees to temporarily work in different roles to explore their strengths and interests.
6. Provide targeted training: Develop training programs that focus on enhancing employees' existing strengths rather than trying to correct weaknesses.
7. Create a role alignment task force: Form a dedicated team responsible for monitoring and improving role alignment across the organization.

By following these steps, organizations can create a structured approach to role alignment, ensuring that it becomes an integral part of their operational strategy.

Organizations must be flexible and willing to reassess and adjust role assignments based on performance and alignment. Encouraging lateral moves, creating open feedback mechanisms, and supporting leadership that is receptive to change are key components. A supportive organizational culture is vital for effective role alignment. This involves creating an environment where employees feel valued and supported. Organizations should recognize and value each employee's unique contributions, fostering a sense of belonging and appreciation. Implementing recognition programs and promoting an inclusive culture are essential strategies. Open communication is key to understanding and addressing employees' needs. Transparent leadership and encouraging employee feedback are fundamental to this process. Organizations should provide opportunities for continuous growth and development, helping employees reach their full potential. Offering professional development programs and clear pathways for career advancement are crucial elements.

Technology is poised to revolutionize the way organizations achieve effective role alignment. Advanced tools and systems, particularly those powered by artificial intelligence (AI), will be integral in transforming key processes such as hiring, performance reviews, and the implementation of role alignment strategies. AI's capabilities in data analysis, predictive modeling, and personalized insights will underpin the evolution of these practices, enabling organizations to optimize their workforce alignment with unprecedented precision and efficiency. As the workplace continues to evolve, the importance of role alignment will only grow. Organizations must be proactive in adopting new strategies and technologies to ensure that their workforce remains aligned and engaged. Organizations must embrace change and be willing to adapt to new challenges and opportunities. Developing an agile workforce and fostering a culture of continuous improvement are essential strategies.

As we conclude this book, it's essential to recognize that achieving effective role alignment is an ongoing process that requires dedication, flexibility, and continuous improvement. Organizations must remain committed to understanding and leveraging the unique strengths of their employees, fostering a supportive and inclusive culture, and embracing new strategies and technologies to ensure long-term success. By adopting the principles and strategies outlined in this book, organizations can unlock the full potential of their workforce, leading to increased productivity, higher employee satisfaction, and greater overall success. Just as the fish should not be judged by their ability to climb a tree, employees should be placed in roles that allow them to thrive and excel.

Remember, the key to a thriving organization lies in recognizing and nurturing the unique talents of each individual. By doing so, we can create a workplace where everyone has the opportunity to climb their own trees and achieve their fullest potential.

References

Chapter 1:

1. **Harvard University, the Carnegie Foundation,** and Stanford Research Center study on job success attributed to soft skills.

2. **LinkedIn 2016 survey** on the importance of soft skills compared to hard skills.

3. **National Soft Skills Association** research highlighting the importance of soft skills.

4. **2019 LinkedIn report** on the role of soft skills in hiring decisions and job retention.

5. **2020 Society for Human Resource Management** (SHRM) survey on soft skills and promotion to leadership positions.

6. **National Association of Colleges and Employers** (NACE) study identifying top attributes employers seek in new hires.

7. **World Economic Forum** report on future workforce skills.

Chapter 2:

1. **Merrill, D. W., & Reid, R. H.** (1981). Personal Styles and Effective Performance: Make Your Style Work for You. CRC Press.

2. **Goleman, D.** (1995). Emotional Intelligence: Why It Can Matter More Than IQ. Bantam Books.

3. **Covey, S. R.** (1989). The 7 Habits of Highly Effective People: Powerful Lessons in Personal Change. Free Press.

4. **Carnegie, D.** (1936). How to Win Friends and Influence People. Simon & Schuster.

5. **Robbins, S. P., & Judge, T. A.** (2018). Organizational Behavior. Pearson.

6. **Lencioni, P.** (2002). The Five Dysfunctions of a Team: A Leadership Fable. Jossey-Bass.

7. **Briggs Myers, I., & Myers, P. B.** (1995). Gifts Differing: Understanding Personality Type. Davies-Black Publishing.

Chapter 4:

1. Bradberry, T., & Greaves, J. (2009). **Emotional Intelligence 2.0**. TalentSmart.

2. Covey, S. R. (1989). **The 7 Habits of Highly Effective People: Powerful Lessons in Personal Change**. Free Press.

3. Gardner, H. (1983). **Frames of Mind: The Theory of Multiple Intelligences**. Basic Books.

4. Pink, D. H. (2009). **Drive: The Surprising Truth About What Motivates Us**. Riverhead Books.

5. Dweck, C. S. (2006). **Mindset: The New Psychology of Success**. Random House.

6. Merrill, D. W., & Reid, R. H. (1981). **Personal Styles and Effective Performance: Make Your Style Work for You**. CRC Press.

7. Carnegie, D. (1936). **How to Win Friends and Influence People**. Simon & Schuster.

8. Collins, J. (2001). **Good to Great: Why Some Companies Make the Leap…and Others Don't**. HarperBusiness.

9. Tannen, D. (1994). **Talking from 9 to 5: Women and Men at Work**. William Morrow and Company.

10. Kotter, J. P. (1996). **Leading Change**. Harvard Business Review Press.

11. Rogers, E. M. (2003). **Diffusion of Innovations (5th ed.)**. Free Press.

References

Chapter 5:

1. Sharma, R. (2010). The Leader Who Had No Title: A Modern Fable on Real Success in Business and in Life. Simon & Schuster.

2. Obesity Reviews. (2018). **The Effectiveness of Long-term Diet and Exercise Interventions for Weight Management: A Review**. [Journal article]

3. The American Journal of Clinical Nutrition. (2015). **Long-term Weight Loss Maintenance**. [Journal article]

4. Bandura, A. (1977). **Self-efficacy: Toward a Unifying Theory of Behavioral Change**. Psychological Review.

5. Prochaska, J. O., & DiClemente, C. C. (1983). **Stages and Processes of Self-Change of Smoking: Toward An Integrative Model of Change**. Journal of Consulting and Clinical Psychology.

6. Baumeister, R. F., & Tierney, J. (2011). **Willpower: Rediscovering the Greatest Human Strength**. Penguin Books.

7. Goleman, D. (1995). **Emotional Intelligence: Why It Can Matter More Than IQ**. Bantam Books.

8. Covey, S. R. (1989). **The 7 Habits of Highly Effective People: Powerful Lessons in Personal Change**. Free Press.

9. Dweck, C. S. (2006). **Mindset: The New Psychology of Success**. Random House.

10. Gardner, H. (1983). **Frames of Mind: The Theory of Multiple Intelligences**. Basic Books.

11. Heath, C., & Heath, D. (2010). **Switch: How to Change Things When Change Is Hard**. Crown Business.

12. Clear, J. (2018). **Atomic Habits: An Easy & Proven Way to Build Good Habits & Break Bad Ones**. Avery.

Chapter 6:

1. Baumeister, R. F., & Tierney, J. (2011). **Willpower: Rediscovering the Greatest Human Strength**. Penguin Books.
2. Covey, S. R. (1989). **The 7 Habits of Highly Effective People: Powerful Lessons in Personal Change**. Free Press.
3. Clear, J. (2018). **Atomic Habits: An Easy & Proven Way to Build Good Habits & Break Bad Ones**. Avery.
4. Dweck, C. S. (2006). **Mindset: The New Psychology of Success**. Random House.
5. Goleman, D. (1995). **Emotional Intelligence: Why It Can Matter More Than IQ**. Bantam Books.
6. Heath, C., & Heath, D. (2010). **Switch: How to Change Things When Change Is Hard**. Crown Business.
7. Prochaska, J. O., & DiClemente, C. C. (1983). **Stages and Processes of Self-Change of Smoking: Toward An Integrative Model of Change**. Journal of Consulting and Clinical Psychology.
8. Bandura, A. (1977). **Self-efficacy: Toward a Unifying Theory of Behavioral Change**. Psychological Review.
9. Obesity Reviews. (2018). **The Effectiveness of Long-term Diet and Exercise Interventions for Weight Management: A Review**. [Journal article]
10. The American Journal of Clinical Nutrition. (2015). **Long-term Weight Loss Maintenance**. [Journal article]
11. Sharma, R. (2010). **The Leader Who Had No Title: A Modern Fable on Real Success in Business and in Life**. Simon & Schuster.
12. Neuroscience Research. (2020). **Neuroplasticity and the Adult Brain: Mechanisms and Implications for Rehabilitation**. [Journal article]

13. Journal of Behavioral Neuroscience. (2019). **The Role of Dopamine in Motivation and Learning.** [Journal article]
14. The American Journal of Psychology. (2016). **Fear and the Status Quo Bias: Cognitive and Emotional Mechanisms.** [Journal article]

Chapter 7:

1. Bresciani Ludvik, M. J., & Martin, F. C. (2016). **The Neuroscience of Learning and Development: Enhancing Creativity, Compassion, Critical Thinking, and Peace in Higher Education.** Stylus Publishing, LLC.
2. Hodges, J., Lloyd, C., & Payne, J. (2015). **Soft Skills and Hard Values: A Systematic Review of "Soft" Interventions in the Workplace.** Human Resource Development International.
3. Dweck, C. S. (2006). **Mindset: The New Psychology of Success.** Random House.
4. LeDoux, J. E. (1996). **The Emotional Brain: The Mysterious Underpinnings of Emotional Life.** Simon & Schuster.
5. Kahneman, D. (2011). **Thinking, Fast and Slow.** Farrar, Straus and Giroux.
6. Fuster, J. M. (2015). **The Prefrontal Cortex: Executive and Cognitive Functions.** Academic Press.
7. Salovey, P., & Mayer, J. D. (1990). **The Science of Emotional Intelligence: Knowns and Unknowns.** Psychological Inquiry.
8. Wright, J. H., & Sudak, D. M. (2012). **Building a Better Brain: Neuroplasticity and Cognitive Behavioral Therapy.** Journal of Cognitive Psychotherapy.
9. Hölzel, B. K., Carmody, J., Vangel, M., Congleton, C., Desbordes, G., & Lazar, S. W. (2011). **The Impact of Mindfulness Training on Brain Plasticity: An Integrative Review.** NeuroImage.

10. Goleman, D. (2006). **Social Intelligence: The New Science of Human Relationships**. Bantam Books.

11. Schultz, W. (2007). **Dopamine, Learning, and Motivation**. Nature Reviews Neuroscience.

12. Fields, B. L., & Ziegler, R. F. (2017). **The Role of Myelination in Learning and Development**. Neuropsychology Review.

Chapter 8:

1. Bresciani Ludvik, M. J., & Martin, F. C. (2016). **The Neuroscience of Learning and Development: Enhancing Creativity, Compassion, Critical Thinking, and Peace in Higher Education**. Stylus Publishing, LLC.

2. Hodges, J., Lloyd, C., & Payne, J. (2015). **Soft Skills and Hard Values: A Systematic Review of "Soft" Interventions in the Workplace**. Human Resource Development International.

3. Dweck, C. S. (2006). **Mindset: The New Psychology of Success**. Random House.

4. LeDoux, J. E. (1996). **The Emotional Brain: The Mysterious Underpinnings of Emotional Life**. Simon & Schuster.

5. Kahneman, D. (2011). **Thinking, Fast and Slow**. Farrar, Straus and Giroux.

6. Fuster, J. M. (2015). **The Prefrontal Cortex: Executive and Cognitive Functions**. Academic Press.

7. Salovey, P., & Mayer, J. D. (1990). **The Science of Emotional Intelligence: Knowns and Unknowns**. Psychological Inquiry.

8. Wright, J. H., & Sudak, D. M. (2012). **Building a Better Brain: Neuroplasticity and Cognitive Behavioral Therapy**. Journal of Cognitive Psychotherapy.

References

9. Hölzel, B. K., Carmody, J., Vangel, M., Congleton, C., Desbordes, G., & Lazar, S. W. (2011). **The Impact of Mindfulness Training on Brain Plasticity: An Integrative Review.** NeuroImage.

10. Goleman, D. (2006). **Social Intelligence: The New Science of Human Relationships.** Bantam Books.

11. Schultz, W. (2007). **Dopamine, Learning, and Motivation.** Nature Reviews Neuroscience.

12. Fields, B. L., & Ziegler, R. F. (2017). **The Role of Myelination in Learning and Development.** Neuropsychology Review.

13. Obesity Reviews. (2018). **The High Failure Rate of Diets and Its Implications.** John Wiley & Sons, Ltd.

14. The American Journal of Clinical Nutrition. (2010). **Long-term Adherence to Weight Loss Diets and its Impact on Health.** American Society for Nutrition.

15. The Journal of Cognitive Psychology. (2015). **Mindfulness and Emotional Regulation.** Taylor & Francis.

16. The Harvard Business Review. (2013). **The Power of Feedback in Improving Performance.** Harvard Business Publishing.

Chapter 9:

1. Gallup, Inc. (2017). **State of the American Workplace.** Gallup Press.

2. Buckingham, M., & Clifton, D. O. (2001). **Now, Discover Your Strengths.** The Free Press.

3. Goleman, D. (2000). **Leadership That Gets Results.** Harvard Business Review.

4. Rath, T., & Conchie, B. (2008). **Strengths-Based Leadership: Great Leaders, Teams, and Why People Follow.** Gallup Press.

5. Buckingham, M. (2005). **The One Thing You Need to Know: About Great Managing, Great Leading, and Sustained Individual Success**. Free Press.

6. Clifton, D. O., & Harter, J. K. (2003). **Investing in Strengths**. In K. S. Cameron, J. E. Dutton, & R. E. Quinn (Eds.), **Positive Organizational Scholarship: Foundations of a New Discipline** (pp. 111-121). Berrett-Koehler Publishers.

7. Collins, J. (2001). **Good to Great: Why Some Companies Make the Leap... and Others Don't**. HarperBusiness.

8. Drucker, P. F. (1999). **Management Challenges for the 21st Century**. HarperBusiness.

9. Spreitzer, G., & Porath, C. (2012). **Creating Sustainable Performance**. Harvard Business Review.

10. Martin, J. (2006). **Cultures in Organizations: Three Perspectives**. Oxford University Press.

11. Schwartz, T. (2010). **The Way We're Working Isn't Working**. Free Press.

12. Grant, A. (2013). **Give and Take: Why Helping Others Drives Our Success**. Viking.

13. Amabile, T. M., & Kramer, S. J. (2011). **The Progress Principle: Using Small Wins to Ignite Joy, Engagement, and Creativity at Work**. Harvard Business Review Press.

14. Rock, D. (2009). **Your Brain at Work: Strategies for Overcoming Distraction, Regaining Focus, and Working Smarter All Day Long**. HarperBusiness.

15. Deci, E. L., & Ryan, R. M. (2000). **The "What" and "Why" of Goal Pursuits: Human Needs and the Self-Determination of Behavior**. Psychological Inquiry, 11(4), 227-268.

References

Chapter 10:

1. Gallup, Inc. (2017). **State of the Global Workplace Report**. Gallup Press.
2. American Institute of Stress. (n.d.). **Workplace Stress**. Retrieved from https://www.stress.org/workplace-stress
3. Society for Human Resource Management (SHRM). (2019). **The Cost of Turnover**. SHRM.
4. McKinsey & Company. (2020). **The Impact of Workforce Alignment on Organizational Performance**. McKinsey Global Institute.
5. Deloitte Insights. (2018). **The Financial Impact of Employee Engagement**. Deloitte.
6. Buckingham, M., & Clifton, D. O. (2001). **Now, Discover Your Strengths**. The Free Press.
7. Goleman, D. (2000). **Leadership That Gets Results**. Harvard Business Review.
8. Rath, T., & Conchie, B. (2008). **Strengths-Based Leadership: Great Leaders, Teams, and Why People Follow**. Gallup Press.
9. Collins, J. (2001). **Good to Great: Why Some Companies Make the Leap… and Others Don't**. HarperBusiness.
10. Drucker, P. F. (1999). **Management Challenges for the 21st Century**. HarperBusiness.
11. Spreitzer, G., & Porath, C. (2012). **Creating Sustainable Performance**. Harvard Business Review.
12. Martin, J. (2006). **Cultures in Organizations: Three Perspectives**. Oxford University Press.
13. Schwartz, T. (2010). **The Way We're Working Isn't Working**. Free Press.
14. Grant, A. (2013). **Give and Take: Why Helping Others Drives Our Success**. Viking.

15. Amabile, T. M., & Kramer, S. J. (2011). **The Progress Principle: Using Small Wins to Ignite Joy, Engagement, and Creativity at Work**. Harvard Business Review Press.

16. Rock, D. (2009). **Your Brain at Work: Strategies for Overcoming Distraction, Regaining Focus, and Working Smarter All Day Long**. HarperBusiness.

17. Deci, E. L., & Ryan, R. M. (2000). **The "What" and "Why" of Goal Pursuits: Human Needs and the Self-Determination of Behavior**. Psychological Inquiry, 11(4), 227-268.

Chapter 11:

1. Gallup, Inc. (2017). **State of the Global Workplace Report**. Gallup Press.

2. American Institute of Stress. (n.d.). **Workplace Stress**. Retrieved from https://www.stress.org/workplace-stress

3. Society for Human Resource Management (SHRM). (2019). **The Cost of Turnover**. SHRM.

4. McKinsey & Company. (2020). **The Impact of Workforce Alignment on Organizational Performance**. McKinsey Global Institute.

5. Deloitte Insights. (2018). **The Financial Impact of Employee Engagement**. Deloitte.

6. Buckingham, M., & Clifton, D. O. (2001). **Now, Discover Your Strengths**. The Free Press.

7. Goleman, D. (2000). **Leadership That Gets Results**. Harvard Business Review.

8. Rath, T., & Conchie, B. (2008). **Strengths-Based Leadership: Great Leaders, Teams, and Why People Follow**. Gallup Press.

9. Collins, J. (2001). **Good to Great: Why Some Companies Make the Leap… and Others Don't**. HarperBusiness.

References

10. Drucker, P. F. (1999). **Management Challenges for the 21st Century**. HarperBusiness.

11. Spreitzer, G., & Porath, C. (2012). **Creating Sustainable Performance**. Harvard Business Review.

12. Martin, J. (2006). **Cultures in Organizations: Three Perspectives**. Oxford University Press.

13. Schwartz, T. (2010). **The Way We're Working Isn't Working**. Free Press.

14. Grant, A. (2013). **Give and Take: Why Helping Others Drives Our Success**. Viking.

15. Amabile, T. M., & Kramer, S. J. (2011). **The Progress Principle: Using Small Wins to Ignite Joy, Engagement, and Creativity at Work**. Harvard Business Review Press.

16. Rock, D. (2009). **Your Brain at Work: Strategies for Overcoming Distraction, Regaining Focus, and Working Smarter All Day Long**. HarperBusiness.

17. Deci, E. L., & Ryan, R. M. (2000). **The "What" and "Why" of Goal Pursuits: Human Needs and the Self-Determination of Behavior**. Psychological Inquiry, 11(4), 227-268.

18. Merril, D., & Reid, R. (1981). **Personal Styles and Effective Performance**. CRC Press.

19. Robbins, S. P., & Judge, T. (2018). **Organizational Behavior** (18th ed.). Pearson.

20. Pinder, C. C. (2008). **Work Motivation in Organizational Behavior** (2nd ed.). Psychology Press.

21. Csikszentmihalyi, M. (1990). **Flow: The Psychology of Optimal Experience**. Harper & Row.

22. Johnson, S. (1998). **Who Moved My Cheese?** G.P. Putnam's Sons.

23. Covey, S. R. (1989). **The 7 Habits of Highly Effective People**. Free Press.

Chapter 13:

1. **Gallup, Inc.** (2017). State of the Global Workplace Report. Gallup Press.
2. **American Institute of Stress.** (n.d.). Workplace Stress. Retrieved from https://www.stress.org/workplace-stress
3. **Society for Human Resource Management (SHRM).** (2019). The Cost of Turnover. SHRM.
4. **McKinsey & Company.** (2020). The Impact of Workforce Alignment on Organizational Performance. McKinsey Global Institute.
5. **Deloitte Insights.** (2018). The Financial Impact of Employee Engagement. Deloitte.
6. **Buckingham, M., & Clifton, D. O.** (2001). Now, Discover Your Strengths. The Free Press.
7. **Goleman, D.** (2000). Leadership That Gets Results. Harvard Business Review.
8. **Rath, T., & Conchie, B.** (2008). Strengths-Based Leadership: Great Leaders, Teams, and Why People Follow. Gallup Press.
9. **Collins, J.** (2001). Good to Great: Why Some Companies Make the Leap… and Others Don't. HarperBusiness.
10. **Drucker, P. F.** (1999). Management Challenges for the 21st Century. HarperBusiness.
11. **Spreitzer, G., & Porath, C.** (2012). Creating Sustainable Performance. Harvard Business Review.
12. **Martin, J.** (2006). Cultures in Organizations: Three Perspectives. Oxford University Press.
13. **Schwartz, T.** (2010). The Way We're Working Isn't Working. Free Press.
14. **Grant, A.** (2013). Give and Take: Why Helping Others Drives Our Success. Viking.

References

15. **Amabile, T. M., & Kramer, S. J.** (2011). The Progress Principle: Using Small Wins to Ignite Joy, Engagement, and Creativity at Work. Harvard Business Review Press.

16. **Rock, D.** (2009). Your Brain at Work: Strategies for Overcoming Distraction, Regaining Focus, and Working Smarter All Day Long. HarperBusiness.

17. **Deci, E. L., & Ryan, R. M.** (2000). The "What" and "Why" of Goal Pursuits: Human Needs and the Self-Determination of Behavior. Psychological Inquiry, 11(4), 227-268.

18. **Merril, D., & Reid, R.** (1981). Personal Styles and Effective Performance. CRC Press.

19. **Robbins, S. P., & Judge, T.** (2018). Organizational Behavior (18th ed.). Pearson.

20. **Pinder, C. C.** (2008). Work Motivation in Organizational Behavior (2nd ed.). Psychology Press.

21. **Csikszentmihalyi, M.** (1990). Flow: The Psychology of Optimal Experience. Harper & Row.

22. **Johnson, S.** (1998). Who Moved My Cheese? G.P. Putnam's Sons.

23. **Covey, S. R.** (1989). The 7 Habits of Highly Effective People. Free Press.

24. **Clifton, D. O., & Harter, J. K.** (2003). Investing in Strengths. Gallup Press.

25. **Nohria, N., & Groysberg, B.** (2008). Employee Motivation: A Powerful New Model. Harvard Business Review.

26. **Heathfield, S. M.** (2020). The Importance of Role Clarity. The Balance Careers. Retrieved from https://www.thebalancecareers.com/the-importance-of-role-clarity-1918611

Chapter 14:

1. **Gallup, Inc.** (2017). State of the Global Workplace Report. Gallup Press.
2. **American Institute of Stress.** (n.d.). Workplace Stress. Retrieved from https://www.stress.org/workplace-stress
3. **Society for Human Resource Management (SHRM).** (2019). The Cost of Turnover. SHRM.
4. **McKinsey & Company.** (2020). The Impact of Workforce Alignment on Organizational Performance. McKinsey Global Institute.
5. **Deloitte Insights.** (2018). The Financial Impact of Employee Engagement. Deloitte.
6. **Buckingham, M., & Clifton, D. O.** (2001). Now, Discover Your Strengths. The Free Press.
7. **Goleman, D.** (2000). Leadership That Gets Results. Harvard Business Review.
8. **Rath, T., & Conchie, B.** (2008). Strengths-Based Leadership: Great Leaders, Teams, and Why People Follow. Gallup Press.
9. **Collins, J.** (2001). Good to Great: Why Some Companies Make the Leap… and Others Don't. HarperBusiness.
10. **Drucker, P. F.** (1999). Management Challenges for the 21st Century. HarperBusiness.
11. **Spreitzer, G., & Porath, C.** (2012). Creating Sustainable Performance. Harvard Business Review.
12. **Martin, J.** (2006). Cultures in Organizations: Three Perspectives. Oxford University Press.
13. **Schwartz, T.** (2010). The Way We're Working Isn't Working. Free Press.
14. **Grant, A.** (2013). Give and Take: Why Helping Others Drives Our Success. Viking.

References

15. **Amabile, T. M., & Kramer, S. J.** (2011). The Progress Principle: Using Small Wins to Ignite Joy, Engagement, and Creativity at Work. Harvard Business Review Press.

16. **Rock, D.** (2009). Your Brain at Work: Strategies for Overcoming Distraction, Regaining Focus, and Working Smarter All Day Long. HarperBusiness.

17. **Deci, E. L., & Ryan, R. M.** (2000). The "What" and "Why" of Goal Pursuits: Human Needs and the Self-Determination of Behavior. Psychological Inquiry, 11(4), 227-268.

18. **Merril, D., & Reid, R.** (1981). Personal Styles and Effective Performance. CRC Press.

19. **Robbins, S. P., & Judge, T.** (2018). Organizational Behavior (18th ed.). Pearson.

20. **Pinder, C. C.** (2008). Work Motivation in Organizational Behavior (2nd ed.). Psychology Press.

21. **Csikszentmihalyi, M.** (1990). Flow: The Psychology of Optimal Experience. Harper & Row.

22. **Johnson, S.** (1998). Who Moved My Cheese? G.P. Putnam's Sons.

23. **Covey, S. R.** (1989). The 7 Habits of Highly Effective People. Free Press.

24. **Clifton, D. O., & Harter, J. K.** (2003). Investing in Strengths. Gallup Press.

25. **Nohria, N., & Groysberg, B.** (2008). Employee Motivation: A Powerful New Model. Harvard Business Review.

26. **Heathfield, S. M.** (2020). The Importance of Role Clarity. The Balance Careers. Retrieved from https://www.thebalancecareers.com/the-importance-of-role-clarity-1918611

Chapter 15:

1. **American Institute of Stress.** (n.d.). Workplace Stress. Retrieved from https://www.stress.org/workplace-stress
2. **Society for Human Resource Management (SHRM).** (2019). The Cost of Turnover. SHRM.
3. **McKinsey & Company.** (2020). The Impact of Workforce Alignment on Organizational Performance. McKinsey Global Institute.
4. **Deloitte Insights.** (2018). The Financial Impact of Employee Engagement. Deloitte.
5. **Buckingham, M., & Clifton, D. O.** (2001). Now, Discover Your Strengths. The Free Press.
6. **Goleman, D.** (2000). Leadership That Gets Results. Harvard Business Review.
7. **Rath, T., & Conchie, B.** (2008). Strengths-Based Leadership: Great Leaders, Teams, and Why People Follow. Gallup Press.
8. **Collins, J.** (2001). Good to Great: Why Some Companies Make the Leap… and Others Don't. HarperBusiness.
9. **Drucker, P. F.** (1999). Management Challenges for the 21st Century. HarperBusiness.
10. **Spreitzer, G., & Porath, C.** (2012). Creating Sustainable Performance. Harvard Business Review.
11. **Martin, J.** (2006). Cultures in Organizations: Three Perspectives. Oxford University Press.
12. **Schwartz, T.** (2010). The Way We're Working Isn't Working. Free Press.
13. **Grant, A.** (2013). Give and Take: Why Helping Others Drives Our Success. Viking.

References

14. **Amabile, T. M., & Kramer, S. J.** (2011). The Progress Principle: Using Small Wins to Ignite Joy, Engagement, and Creativity at Work. Harvard Business Review Press.

15. **Rock, D.** (2009). Your Brain at Work: Strategies for Overcoming Distraction, Regaining Focus, and Working Smarter All Day Long. HarperBusiness.

16. **Deci, E. L., & Ryan, R. M.** (2000). The "What" and "Why" of Goal Pursuits: Human Needs and the Self-Determination of Behavior. Psychological Inquiry, 11(4), 227-268.

17. **Merril, D., & Reid, R.** (1981). Personal Styles and Effective Performance. CRC Press.

18. **Robbins, S. P., & Judge, T.** (2018). Organizational Behavior (18th ed.). Pearson.

19. **Pinder, C. C.** (2008). Work Motivation in Organizational Behavior (2nd ed.). Psychology Press.

20. **Csikszentmihalyi, M.** (1990). Flow: The Psychology of Optimal Experience. Harper & Row.

21. **Johnson, S.** (1998). Who Moved My Cheese? G.P. Putnam's Sons.

22. **Covey, S. R.** (1989). The 7 Habits of Highly Effective People. Free Press.

23. **Clifton, D. O., & Harter, J. K.** (2003). Investing in Strengths. Gallup Press.

24. **Nohria, N., & Groysberg, B.** (2008). Employee Motivation: A Powerful New Model. Harvard Business Review.

25. **Heathfield, S. M.** (2020). The Importance of Role Clarity. The Balance Careers. Retrieved from https://www.thebalancecareers.com/the-importance-of-role-clarity-1918611

Chapter 16:

1. **American Institute of Stress.** (n.d.). Workplace Stress. Retrieved from https://www.stress.org/workplace-stress
2. **Society for Human Resource Management (SHRM).** (2019). The Cost of Turnover. SHRM.
3. **McKinsey & Company.** (2020). The Impact of Workforce Alignment on Organizational Performance. McKinsey Global Institute.
4. **Deloitte Insights.** (2018). The Financial Impact of Employee Engagement. Deloitte.
5. **Buckingham, M., & Clifton, D. O.** (2001). Now, Discover Your Strengths. The Free Press.
6. **Goleman, D.** (2000). Leadership That Gets Results. Harvard Business Review.
7. **Rath, T., & Conchie, B.** (2008). Strengths-Based Leadership: Great Leaders, Teams, and Why People Follow. Gallup Press.
8. **Collins, J.** (2001). Good to Great: Why Some Companies Make the Leap... and Others Don't. HarperBusiness.
9. **Drucker, P. F.** (1999). Management Challenges for the 21st Century. HarperBusiness.
10. **Spreitzer, G., & Porath, C.** (2012). Creating Sustainable Performance. Harvard Business Review.
11. **Martin, J.** (2006). Cultures in Organizations: Three Perspectives. Oxford University Press.
12. **Schwartz, T.** (2010). The Way We're Working Isn't Working. Free Press.
13. **Grant, A.** (2013). Give and Take: Why Helping Others Drives Our Success. Viking.

References

14. **Amabile, T. M., & Kramer, S. J.** (2011). The Progress Principle: Using Small Wins to Ignite Joy, Engagement, and Creativity at Work. Harvard Business Review Press.

15. **Rock, D.** (2009). Your Brain at Work: Strategies for Overcoming Distraction, Regaining Focus, and Working Smarter All Day Long. HarperBusiness.

16. **Deci, E. L., & Ryan, R. M.** (2000). The "What" and "Why" of Goal Pursuits: Human Needs and the Self-Determination of Behavior. Psychological Inquiry, 11(4), 227-268.

17. **Merril, D., & Reid, R.** (1981). Personal Styles and Effective Performance. CRC Press.

18. **Robbins, S. P., & Judge, T.** (2018). Organizational Behavior (18th ed.). Pearson.

19. **Pinder, C. C.** (2008). Work Motivation in Organizational Behavior (2nd ed.). Psychology Press.

20. **Csikszentmihalyi, M.** (1990). Flow: The Psychology of Optimal Experience. Harper & Row.

21. **Johnson, S.** (1998). Who Moved My Cheese? G.P. Putnam's Sons.

22. **Covey, S. R.** (1989). The 7 Habits of Highly Effective People. Free Press.

23. **Clifton, D. O., & Harter, J. K.** (2003). Investing in Strengths. Gallup Press.

24. **Nohria, N., & Groysberg, B.** (2008). Employee Motivation: A Powerful New Model. Harvard Business Review.

25. **Heathfield, S. M.** (2020). The Importance of Role Clarity. The Balance Careers. Retrieved from https://www.thebalancecareers.com/the-importance-of-role-clarity-1918611

26. **ASTD.** (2012). The Value of Training: How Employee Training Benefits Your Business. American Society for Training and Development.

27. **Noe, R. A.** (2013). Employee Training and Development (6th ed.). McGraw-Hill Education.

28. **Garvin, D. A.** (1993). Building a Learning Organization. Harvard Business Review.

29. **Senge, P. M.** (2006). The Fifth Discipline: The Art and Practice of the Learning Organization. Currency/Doubleday.

30. **Kirkpatrick, D. L., & Kirkpatrick, J. D.** (2006). Evaluating Training Programs: The Four Levels (3rd ed.). Berrett-Koehler Publishers.

31. **Goldstein, I. L., & Ford, J. K.** (2002). Training in Organizations: Needs Assessment, Development, and Evaluation (4th ed.). Wadsworth.

32. **Brown, J.** (2002). Training Needs Assessment: A Must for Developing an Effective Training Program. Public Personnel Management, 31(4), 569-578.

33. **O'Leary, Z.** (2017). The Essential Guide to Doing Your Research Project (3rd ed.). SAGE Publications.

34. **Blanchard, P. N., & Thacker, J. W.** (2013). Effective Training: Systems, Strategies, and Practices (5th ed.). Pearson.

35. **Salas, E., Tannenbaum, S. I., Kraiger, K., & Smith-Jentsch, K. A.** (2012). The Science of Training and Development in Organizations: What Matters in Practice. Psychological Science in the Public Interest, 13(2), 74-101.

36. **Biech, E.** (2017). The Art and Science of Training. Association for Talent Development.

Chapter 17:

1. **Gallup, Inc.** (2017). State of the Global Workplace Report. Gallup Press.

2. **American Institute of Stress.** (n.d.). Workplace Stress. Retrieved from https://www.stress.org/workplace-stress

References

3. **Society for Human Resource Management (SHRM).** (2019). The Cost of Turnover. SHRM.
4. **McKinsey & Company.** (2020). The Impact of Workforce Alignment on Organizational Performance. McKinsey Global Institute.
5. **Deloitte Insights.** (2018). The Financial Impact of Employee Engagement. Deloitte.
6. **Buckingham, M., & Clifton, D. O.** (2001). Now, Discover Your Strengths. The Free Press.
7. **Goleman, D.** (2000). Leadership That Gets Results. Harvard Business Review.
8. **Rath, T., & Conchie, B.** (2008). Strengths-Based Leadership: Great Leaders, Teams, and Why People Follow. Gallup Press.
9. **Collins, J.** (2001). Good to Great: Why Some Companies Make the Leap… and Others Don't. HarperBusiness.
10. **Drucker, P. F.** (1999). Management Challenges for the 21st Century. HarperBusiness.
11. **Spreitzer, G., & Porath, C.** (2012). Creating Sustainable Performance. Harvard Business Review.
12. **Martin, J.** (2006). Cultures in Organizations: Three Perspectives. Oxford University Press.
13. **Schwartz, T.** (2010). The Way We're Working Isn't Working. Free Press.
14. **Grant, A.** (2013). Give and Take: Why Helping Others Drives Our Success. Viking.
15. **Amabile, T. M., & Kramer, S. J.** (2011). The Progress Principle: Using Small Wins to Ignite Joy, Engagement, and Creativity at Work. Harvard Business Review Press.

16. **Rock, D.** (2009). Your Brain at Work: Strategies for Overcoming Distraction, Regaining Focus, and Working Smarter All Day Long. HarperBusiness.

17. **Deci, E. L., & Ryan, R. M.** (2000). The "What" and "Why" of Goal Pursuits: Human Needs and the Self-Determination of Behavior. Psychological Inquiry, 11(4), 227-268.

18. **Merril, D., & Reid, R.** (1981). Personal Styles and Effective Performance. CRC Press.

19. **Robbins, S. P., & Judge, T.** (2018). Organizational Behavior (18th ed.). Pearson.

20. **Pinder, C. C.** (2008). Work Motivation in Organizational Behavior (2nd ed.). Psychology Press.

21. **Csikszentmihalyi, M.** (1990). Flow: The Psychology of Optimal Experience. Harper & Row.

22. **Johnson, S.** (1998). Who Moved My Cheese? G.P. Putnam's Sons.

23. **Covey, S. R.** (1989). The 7 Habits of Highly Effective People. Free Press.

24. **Clifton, D. O., & Harter, J. K.** (2003). Investing in Strengths. Gallup Press.

25. **Nohria, N., & Groysberg, B.** (2008). Employee Motivation: A Powerful New Model. Harvard Business Review.

26. **Heathfield, S. M.** (2020). The Importance of Role Clarity. The Balance Careers. Retrieved from https://www.thebalancecareers.com/the-importance-of-role-clarity-1918611

27. **ASTD.** (2012). The Value of Training: How Employee Training Benefits Your Business. American Society for Training and Development.

28. **Noe, R. A.** (2013). Employee Training and Development (6th ed.). McGraw-Hill Education.

References

29. **Garvin, D. A.** (1993). Building a Learning Organization. Harvard Business Review.

30. **Senge, P. M.** (2006). The Fifth Discipline: The Art and Practice of the Learning Organization. Currency/Doubleday.

31. **Kirkpatrick, D. L., & Kirkpatrick, J. D.** (2006). Evaluating Training Programs: The Four Levels (3rd ed.). Berrett-Koehler Publishers.

32. **Goldstein, I. L., & Ford, J. K.** (2002). Training in Organizations: Needs Assessment, Development, and Evaluation (4th ed.). Wadsworth.

33. **Brown, J.** (2002). Training Needs Assessment: A Must for Developing an Effective Training Program. Public Personnel Management, 31(4), 569-578.

34. **O'Leary, Z.** (2017). The Essential Guide to Doing Your Research Project (3rd ed.). SAGE Publications.

35. **Blanchard, P. N., & Thacker, J. W.** (2013). Effective Training: Systems, Strategies, and Practices (5th ed.). Pearson.

36. **Salas, E., Tannenbaum, S. I., Kraiger, K., & Smith-Jentsch, K. A.** (2012). The Science of Training and Development in Organizations: What Matters in Practice. Psychological Science in the Public Interest, 13(2), 74-101.

37. **Biech, E.** (2017). The Art and Science of Training. Association for Talent Development.

Chapter 18:

1. **Harter, J. K., Schmidt, F. L., & Keyes, C. L. M.** (2003). Well-being in the workplace and its relationship to business outcomes: A review of the Gallup studies. *Flourishing: Positive Psychology and the Life Well-Lived, 2,* 205-224.

2. **Locke, E. A., & Latham, G. P.** (2002). Building a practically useful theory of goal setting and task motivation: A 35-year odyssey. *American Psychologist, 57*(9), 705-717.

3. **Hackman, J. R., & Oldham, G. R.** (1976). Motivation through the design of work: Test of a theory. *Organizational Behavior and Human Performance, 16*(2), 250-279.

4. **Kahn, W. A.** (1990). Psychological conditions of personal engagement and disengagement at work. *Academy of Management Journal, 33*(4), 692-724.

5. **May, D. R., Gilson, R. L., & Harter, L. M.** (2004). The psychological conditions of meaningfulness, safety and availability and the engagement of the human spirit at work. *Journal of Occupational and Organizational Psychology, 77*(1), 11-37.

6. **Herzberg, F., Mausner, B., & Snyderman, B. B.** (1959). *The Motivation to Work.* John Wiley & Sons.

7. **Deci, E. L., & Ryan, R. M.** (1985). *Intrinsic Motivation and Self-Determination in Human Behavior.* Springer US.

8. **Katzenbach, J. R., & Smith, D. K.** (1993). *The Wisdom of Teams: Creating the High-Performance Organization.* Harvard Business School Press.

9. **Lencioni, P. (2002).** *The Five Dysfunctions of a Team: A Leadership Fable.* Jossey-Bass.

10. **Brown, S. P., & Leigh, T. W.** (1996). A new look at psychological climate and its relationship to job involvement, effort, and performance. *Journal of Applied Psychology, 81*(4), 358.

11. **Schein, E. H.** (2010). *Organizational Culture and Leadership.* John Wiley & Sons.

12. **Cameron, J., & Pierce, W. D.** (1994). Reinforcement, reward, and intrinsic motivation: A meta-analysis. *Review of Educational Research, 64*(3), 363-423.

13. **Deci, E. L., Koestner, R., & Ryan, R. M.** (1999). A meta-analytic review of experiments examining the effects of extrinsic rewards on intrinsic motivation. *Psychological Bulletin, 125*(6), 627-668.

References

14. **Greenhaus, J. H., & Beutell, N. J.** (1985). Sources of conflict between work and family roles. *Academy of Management Review, 10*(1), 76-88.

15. **Quick, J. C., & Cooper, C. L. (2003).** *Handbook of Occupational Health Psychology.* American Psychological Association.

16. **Yukl, G.** (2012). *Leadership in Organizations.* Pearson.

17. **Goleman, D.** (2000). Leadership that gets results. *Harvard Business Review, 78*(2), 78-90.

18. **Cameron, K. S., & Quinn, R. E.** (2011). *Diagnosing and Changing Organizational Culture: Based on the Competing Values Framework.* John Wiley & Sons.

19. **Collins, J.** (2001). *Good to Great: Why Some Companies Make the Leap... and Others Don't.* Harper Business.

20. **Drucker, P. F.** (1999). *Management Challenges for the 21st Century.* Harper Business.

21. **Luthans, F., Youssef, C. M., & Avolio, B. J.** (2007). *Psychological Capital: Developing the Human Competitive Edge.* Oxford University Press.

22. **Spreitzer, G. M., & Porath, C.** (2012). Creating sustainable performance. *Harvard Business Review, 90*(1), 92-99.

Chapter 19:

1. **Brown, S. P., & Leigh, T. W.** (1996). A new look at psychological climate and its relationship to job involvement, effort, and performance. *Journal of Applied Psychology, 81*(4), 358-368.

2. **Hackman, J. R., & Oldham, G. R.** (1976). Motivation through the design of work: Test of a theory. *Organizational Behavior and Human Performance, 16*(2), 250-279.

3. **Harter, J. K., Schmidt, F. L., & Keyes, C. L. M.** (2003). Well-being in the workplace and its relationship to business outcomes: A review of the Gallup studies. In C. L. M. Keyes & J. Haidt (Eds.), *Flourishing: Positive*

Psychology and the Life Well-Lived (pp. 205-224). American Psychological Association.

4. **Kahn, W. A. (1990).** Psychological conditions of personal engagement and disengagement at work. *Academy of Management Journal, 33*(4), 692-724.

5. **Kaplan, R. S., & Norton, D. P.** (1996). *The Balanced Scorecard: Translating Strategy into Action.* Harvard Business School Press.

6. **Locke, E. A., & Latham, G. P.** (2002). Building a practically useful theory of goal setting and task motivation: A 35-year odyssey. *American Psychologist, 57*(9), 705-717.

7. **May, D. R., Gilson, R. L., & Harter, L. M.** (2004). The psychological conditions of meaningfulness, safety and availability and the engagement of the human spirit at work. *Journal of Occupational and Organizational Psychology, 77*(1), 11-37.

8. **Quick, J. C., & Cooper, C. L. (2003).** *Handbook of Occupational Health Psychology.* American Psychological Association.

9. **Salas, E., Kosarzycki, M. P., Tannenbaum, S. I., & Carnegie, D.** (2005). Developing teamwork skills in a meaningful context: The use of team performance simulations. In W. J. Rothwell & A. Sullivan (Eds.), *Practicing Organization Development* (pp. 351-365). Pfeiffer.

Chapter 20:

1. **Brown, S. P., & Leigh, T. W.** (1996). A new look at psychological climate and its relationship to job involvement, effort, and performance. *Journal of Applied Psychology, 81*(4), 358.

2. **Katzenbach, J. R., & Smith, D. K.** (1993). *The Wisdom of Teams: Creating the High-Performance Organization.* Harvard Business School Press.

3. **Locke, E. A., & Latham, G. P.** (2002). Building a practically useful theory of goal setting and task motivation: A 35-year odyssey. *American Psychologist, 57*(9), 705-717.

4. **Hackman, J. R., & Oldham, G. R. (1976).** Motivation through the design of work: Test of a theory. *Organizational Behavior and Human Performance, 16*(2), 250-279.

5. **Kahn, W. A.** (1990). Psychological conditions of personal engagement and disengagement at work. *Academy of Management Journal, 33*(4), 692-724.

6. **May, D. R., Gilson, R. L., & Harter, L. M.** (2004). The psychological conditions of meaningfulness, safety and availability and the engagement of the human spirit at work. *Journal of Occupational and Organizational Psychology, 77*(1), 11-37.

7. **Kaplan, R. S., & Norton, D. P.** (1996). *The Balanced Scorecard: Translating Strategy into Action.* Harvard Business School Press.

8. **Collins, J. C., & Porras, J. I.** (1994). *Built to Last: Successful Habits of Visionary Companies.* Harper Business.

Chapter 21:

1. **Bessen, J. E.** (2019). AI and Jobs: The role of demand. NBER Working Paper No. 24235. National Bureau of Economic Research.

2. **Brynjolfsson, E., & McAfee, A.** (2014). *The Second Machine Age: Work, Progress, and Prosperity in a Time of Brilliant Technologies.* W.W. Norton & Company.

3. **Davenport, T. H., & Kirby, J.** (2016). Just How Smart Are Smart Machines? *MIT Sloan Management Review, 57*(3), 21-25.

4. **Manyika, J., Chui, M., Miremadi, M., Bughin, J., George, K., Willmott, P., & Dewhurst, M.** (2017). A future that works: Automation, employment, and productivity. *McKinsey Global Institute Report.*

5. **Bloom, N., Liang, J., Roberts, J., & Ying, Z. J.** (2015). Does working from home work? Evidence from a Chinese experiment. *The Quarterly Journal of Economics, 130*(1), 165-218.

6. **PwC. (2021).** It's Time to Reimagine Where and How Work Will Get Done. *PwC's US Remote Work Survey.*

7. **Harter, J. K., Schmidt, F. L., & Keyes, C. L. M.** (2003). Well-being in the workplace and its relationship to business outcomes: A review of the Gallup studies. *Flourishing: Positive Psychology and the Life Well-Lived, 2,* 205-224.

8. **Kelloway, E. K., & Day, A.** (2005). Building healthy workplaces: What we know so far. *Canadian Journal of Behavioural Science/Revue canadienne des sciences du comportement, 37*(4), 223-235.

9. **Quick, J. C., & Cooper, C. L.** (2003). *Handbook of Occupational Health Psychology.* American Psychological Association.

10. **Brynjolfsson, E., & McElheran, K.** (2016). Data in action: Data-driven decision making in US manufacturing. *MIT Sloan Management Review.*

11. **Provost, F., & Fawcett, T.** (2013). *Data Science for Business: What You Need to Know about Data Mining and Data-Analytic Thinking.* O'Reilly Media.

12. **Davenport, T. H., & Harris, J. G.** (2007). *Competing on Analytics: The New Science of Winning.* Harvard Business School Press.